MARGARET THATCHER

Other books by Penny Junor

Diana Princess of Wales
Babyware

MARGARET THATCHER
Wife · Mother · Politician

Penny Junor

SIDGWICK & JACKSON
LONDON

First published in Great Britain in 1983
by Sidgwick & Jackson Limited

Copyright © 1983 Penny Junor

ISBN 0–283–98969–6

Phototypeset by Falcon Graphic Art Ltd
Wallington, Surrey
Printed in Great Britain by
R.J. Acford, Industrial Estate, Chichester, Sussex
for Sidgwick & Jackson Limited
1 Tavistock Chambers, Bloomsbury Way
London WC1A 2SG

For J.J.

Contents

Acknowledgements

My sincere thanks to the many people who have helped me in the course of researching this book; people who have given their time – and trust – so generously to talk to me about their knowledge of and relationships with Margaret Thatcher. I couldn't have begun to write the book without them, and I am enormously grateful to each and every one.

My thanks also to Dr Jane Morgan for checking the manuscript so painstakingly, and to Deborah Pownall for her picture research. Special thanks also to Margaret Willes, my editor, who as always has been a joy to work with.

And once again I owe everything to James, Pam, Sam and Alex, for putting up with a workaholic in their midst.

Photographic
Acknowledgements

Between pages 54 and 55
Margaret and Muriel Roberts (*Camera Press*)
The grocer's shop in Grantham (*Express Newspapers*)
Class photograph, Kesteven and Grantham Girls School (*Madeline Hellaby*)
Dorothy Gillies, Margaret's headmistress (*Mrs Theo Golding*)
Miss Kay, Margaret's science mistress (*Mrs Theo Golding*)
The Roberts family, 1943 (*Camera Press*)
Somerville College, 1943 matriculation photograph (*Somerville College*)
Tory candidate for Dartford (*Fox Photos*)
Canvassing in Dartford (*Central Press*)
The marriage of Margaret and Denis Thatcher (*Sport & General*)
Margaret with her new-born twins (*Camera Press*)
Lady Hickman (*Associated Newspapers*)
The Thatcher family, 1959 (*Express Newspapers*)
Skiing in Switzerland (*Keystone Press*)
Home decorating (*Express Newspapers*)
Margaret with Carol and Mark, 1961 (*Associated Press*)
Margaret with Diana Powell (*Paddi Victor Smith*)
Arriving at the House of Commons, 1961 (*Express Newspapers*)

Between pages 86 and 87
Secretary of State for Education (*Daily Telegraph*)
With Edward Heath (*Press Association*)
Jon's cartoon of Grocer Heath (*Associated Newspapers*)
Margaret shopping (*Syndication International*)
Leaders of the Conservative Party (*Daily Telegraph*)
The new Leader of the Conservative Party, 1975 (*Central Press*)
Daily Mail Cartoon of Margaret Thatcher's rise to power (*Associated Newspapers*)
Margaret Thatcher with her Shadow Cabinet (*Central Press*)

Picture research by Deborah Pownall

I

The Slum End of Town

British prime ministers from Sir Robert Walpole to the present day have had just one thing in common: ultimate responsibility for every disaster that takes place during their term of office. Collective though the success or failure of a government might be in theory, in practice the buck stops at Number Ten Downing Street, at the feet of the current incumbent, whose unhappy lot it is to judge whether or not they made the right decision. It is a strain which has left most Prime Ministers coming to the end of a term in office looking ten years older than their true age – pale, puffy and thoroughly worn out.

Margaret Thatcher has proved the exception. She improved with office, she grew stronger, bolder and more radiant with every year that passed at Number Ten, and embarked upon a second term, after victory in the general election of 9 June 1983, with the certainty and confidence of a crusader who has glimpsed the holy grail.

Yet the life she has led since she became Britain's first woman Prime Minister in May 1979 has been gruelling enough to put strong men into basket chairs. She works a seven-day week and, regularly, a nineteen- or twenty-hour day. She has few friends, no hobbies and, with the possible exception of her family, no interest in anything outside politics. Right or wrong in her convictions about what is the remedy for Britain's ills, she has been utterly true to her own belief. She is no pragmatist; not given to compromise. She has a simplistic view of the world, a black and white picture of right and wrong, good and bad, with no room in it for grey. It is a picture coloured by a fundamental belief in Christianity, in which she sees the tide of Socialism as the biggest threat of the twentieth century.

In her early political career she was not driven by a desire to be Prime Minister. She had looked for someone else to save the country that she held so dear from the spoliation of Socialism. Finding no one amongst the leaders of the Conservative Party with the courage to lay their popularity on the line, in order to take the unpalatable steps necessary

1

to turn back the tide, she did it herself. 'I wouldn't be worth my salt,' she once said, 'if I weren't attracting some controversy and criticism. Everyone in the world who has done something in life has attracted criticism. If your main objective was, "please, I just want to be liked and have no criticism", you would end up by doing nothing in this world.'

Margaret wants to return to some of the values of Victorian Britain, to produce a society where people:

> Are self-reliant, self-respecting, if they always lend a hand to others, if they were always to improve themselves and work very hard to do it. If they reckon that they have got to be very good members of the community, not because anyone tells them to, but because that's the way we live. If they are prepared to take responsibility for their own actions, and responsibility for their own families, and respect other people's rights, it seems to me that you have the basis of an excellent society.

These were the very values with which Margaret Thatcher was herself brought up. Contempt of courting popularity was taught at her father's knee; and much of the character and attitudes with which she leads the country were cast in a lonely, and somewhat cheerless, youth in Grantham, under the influence of a forbidding and authoritarian father.

Margaret was the second daughter born to a self-made shopkeeper and his wife, both strict and devout Methodists, who owned a grocery business on a busy crossroads in the slum end of the Lincolnshire town. Everything they had was the result of grinding hard work, methodical saving, and careful budgeting. It was a worthy household, incorporating Margaret's maternal grandmother, Victorian in her strictness, whose life was governed by clichés extolling cleanliness and thorough work, which she imparted to her grandchildren at every opportunity. She lived with the family for the first ten years of Margaret's life, and she, too, played a significant part in the shaping of Margaret's values.

Her father, Alfred Roberts, was a very capable man whose ambitions had been thwarted by circumstance. As the eldest of seven children born to Benjamin Ebenezer Roberts, a shoemaker in Ringstead in Northamptonshire, he was forced to leave school at the age of thirteen and to go out to earn a living. Because of his poor eyesight, he didn't take up the family trade, but went instead into the grocery business. At the beginning of the century he moved from Ringstead to the market town of Grantham, some forty miles away, to take up a job as manager of a grocery store in the town. It was there that he met and married Beatrice Stephenson, a local seamstress, whose father worked as a cloakroom attendant on the railway which ran through Grantham.

Alfred had ambitions to improve himself, and he and Beatrice worked hard until, during the First World War, they were able to pool their savings and buy a small grocery shop of their own some distance from the centre of the town, in the less salubrious end, on North Parade. Beatrice gave up dressmaking in order to help work in the shop with her husband. In time they had two children, Muriel born in 1921, and Margaret Hilda, born four years later on 13 October 1925, in the small front room on the first floor above the shop.

Margaret was a pretty little girl, always clean and immaculately dressed in clothes made by her mother. But she had a serious childhood. The shop and the church dominated the family's life, and neither parent was blessed with much sense of humour. With the exception of the occasional game of bowls, which Alfred enjoyed with the local club, entertainment emanated from Finkin Street Methodist Church, or the Rotary Club, of which both Mr and Mrs Roberts were active members.

At home Alfred Roberts ruled the roost, and there was no question that what he said went. He was a tall man, almost 6ft 3in, with horn-rimmed glasses and a thick mop of blond hair, which in later years was to turn pure white. He improved his mind with the church and with books, reading anything he could lay his hands on, from biography to history and politics – but never novels. Fiction was for the little woman; and when Margaret was old enough, it used to be her task every Saturday to go to the library, about half a mile's walk away, and collect a new book for her father, and a novel for her mother.

Mrs Roberts lived very much under her husband's thumb. She was a quiet, plain-looking woman, with her hair in a bun, pulled severely back from her face. She dressed in neat, dull clothes, and was not given to displays of affection towards either her husband or her children. She was kind enough, but very proper, and never appeared to those who knew her as a woman who enjoyed life very much. She worked all the hours God sent, and was seldom seen about the town. She was certainly no match for her husband's intellect.

He ran a good business, which served the northern end of the town and some of the surrounding countryside. With prudent – some would say tight-fisted – management, his business prospered and grew, until in later years he was able to buy a second shop about a mile away at the other end of the town. With all his activity he became quite a well-known figure in the town, enhanced, when Margaret was two, by his election to the Grantham Borough Council as an Independent, Chamber of Trade nominee. He was to remain on the Council for twenty-five years.

He had begun life a Liberal by inclination, but he became a Conservative after the First World War. However, there were no Conservatives on borough councils in those days; they were run by Independent or Ratepayer councillors, and at that time were being newly challenged by the Socialists. Only later did the current three-party system move into local government.

Alfred Roberts employed two assistants to help run the shop, with a third to serve in the little sub-post office at one end of it. Unlike the corner shops of its kind today, which buy stock ready packeted from the local cash and carry, its provisions came in bulk: large sacks of flour and sugar, lentils, dried peas and pearl barley; barrels of treacle and jam; chests of tea; bags of coffee beans; tins of biscuits and dried fruit; and giant slabs of butter, margarine and lard. Everything had to be meticulously weighed, measured and decanted into smaller containers and brown paper bags – a job the children very often helped with in the warehouse at the back, where sides of bacon hung over the old ovens which had not been used since the shop had been a bakery in the previous century. A big slicing machine sat on the broad wooden counter at one end of the shop, next to a giant red coffee grinder. The main counter, which Alf Roberts would bend over closely to write out customers' orders, ran along the shop's length, with large open biscuit tins in front, and drawers and shelves on the walls behind, all neatly stocked. He made it a rule that either he or his wife should always be on duty in the shop during opening hours, which meant that the family could never take a day off together, with the exception of Sundays and bank holidays, and very seldom were able to sit down to a meal together. This lack of a real family life, while still being a closely-knit unit, is a pattern which Margaret came to repeat with her own family, when she too was a working wife and mother.

As a child, Bank Holidays became a treat to which Margaret looked forward for days. The family might travel by bus to Nottingham for the afternoon to see a Ginger Rogers and Fred Astaire film, or, at Christmas time, a pantomime. Summer holidays by the seaside at

Skegness were equally prized but, unlike the bank holidays, the shop was still open for business, so the parents had to take their break at different times. Margaret and Muriel went off for a week with their mother during the school holidays, staying in a boarding house in the town where they did their own catering; Alf, meanwhile, took his holiday later in the year to coincide with Bowls Week.

Mrs Roberts did all the cooking at home, too, and twice a week she regularly baked bread: on Thursday afternoons, which was early closing day, and on Sunday mornings – her only day off from the shop – when she would be up at the crack of dawn to get her baking done before church. She worked exceptionally long hours, and in addition to running the house and shop, doing the housework, as well as the family washing and ironing, not to mention making clothes for the two girls, she also put time into Rotary Ladies, and church activities.

Sunday was entirely given over to the church. Margaret and Muriel attended Finkin Street Methodist Church, a ten-minute walk away, four times most Sundays: Sunday school at 10.00, followed an hour later by morning service, where they joined their parents; home for lunch, then back again for another session of Sunday school at 2.30 p.m., at which Margaret sometimes played the piano; finally an evening service at 6.00.

No newspapers or entertainment of any sort were allowed in the house on Sundays; and there was no question of either girl being permitted to play with friends, or even to play so much as a game of cards or snakes and ladders with each other. Their grandmother, Phoebe Stephenson, wouldn't even let the girls sew or knit on a Sunday. It was a day for God, reserved for religious thought and discussion.

Alfred Roberts was a 'local preacher' (what in the Anglican church would be called a 'lay preacher'), and part of his Sunday would very often be spent visiting neighbouring villages. In the early days he would travel there by horse and trap; in later years the church provided him with a taxi, for he was one of the two most sought-after preachers in the district – a fine, but uninspired, orator with a rare ability to speak for long periods with scarcely a note – a gift which he passed on to his daughter.

The other local preacher of repute was George Hickinbotham, who worked as the dispenser in Boots the Chemists in the High Street, and who was one of Alfred Roberts' greatest friends. The Hickinbothams were very close to the Roberts – and one of the few families that were; for, although they were well known in the town, the Roberts kept themselves to themselves and didn't socialize outside the church.

Within the framework of the Finkin Street Church there was quite a range of activity, though all of a sober nature, such as recitals, oratorios and fund-raising socials. Mrs Roberts attended a sewing meeting on Wednesdays, where Margaret sometimes joined her after school; and she and Muriel occasionally went to youth guild evenings on Fridays, and participated in religious plays.

Knowing no other existence, Margaret initially took for granted this regime of work, church and culture. It was only when she went to school and was old enough to realize that other children had fun and freedom in their lives – visited one another, played games, rode bicycles, had picnics on Sundays – that she ever queried it with her father. 'Margaret' he is reputed to have replied, 'never do things or want to do things just because other people do them. Make up your own mind about what you are going to do and persuade people to go your way.' His words, like all his teachings, sunk in. When, years later, Margaret's own daughter wistfully compared the bustling family life of her friends with the Thatcher household, from which Mum was, perforce, so often absent, she was swiftly told much the same thing.

Alfred Roberts had ambitions for his daughters, particularly his younger in whom he recognized the spark of great potential, and no time was to be lost. He was determined that they should grow up with the advantages that he had never had as a child: with music with culture and with a good education – all the things that would enable them to get on in the world. And so, when Margaret went to elementary school at the age of five, she didn't go to the National School just round the corner, but to the school in Huntingtower Road, a good mile or more from her home. Huntingtower Road was in a better social area, and the school therefore was not populated with the lower-working-class children from the houses around North Parade, but with children from a wide range of backgrounds.

By this time Alf Roberts had his second shop in Grantham, which was just a stone's throw from the school. So, as he passed that way from time to time, he occasionally drove Margaret and a friend, from the dairy across the road in North Street, to or from school in his newly acquired delivery van. The alternative was a long walk, four times a day, coming home for lunch at noon.

Huntingtower Road Elementary School was a single-storey red-brick building overlooking Grantham railway station, with allotments to one side, and a football field and netball courts to the other. There were about forty children to a class, sitting at double-desks and learning by rote. Margaret shone as one of the brighter pupils in her year, and was very soon put up a form. But this was not surprising: Margaret wasn't allowed to go home and play childish games. A lot was expected of her. The words 'I can't' or 'it's too difficult' were not tolerated in the house.

The learning never stopped. The whole of life was a process of education, and a serious business. She was encouraged to read instructive books and discuss them, taken to lectures and concerts, and preached to by her father on a wide range of weighty topics for her young shoulders, including finance. She remembers him telling her how he apportioned the money he earned in his first job: out of fourteen shillings a week (in decimal, 70p), twelve went to his landlady, one was spent and one was saved. Margaret was encouraged to save her own pocket money; she took it to school every Monday morning with the milk money to buy savings stamps, which went towards buying savings certificates. And there was no question of the savings being withdrawn one day to buy some cherished toy or garment. 'We simply saved in order to have a little behind us, perhaps for when we went on to college or started work.' Any money she was given on her birthday also went straight into savings.

Margaret was never free to indulge in childish frivolity. There was no garden behind the shop for her to play in, no bicycle to ride. This was not because her father could ill afford gardens or bicycles. He became increasingly prosperous as Margaret grew up, with his two shops doing good business, but he was always extremely careful with his money, and not one penny was spent unless it was absolutely essential. The family had no running hot water in the house, for example, no bathroom, and no indoor lavatory. Baths were taken in the warehouse once a week by carrying hot water to the tub.

But for all his thrift at home, Mr Roberts and his wife both gave generously to others. Quite apart from the time put in to the Rotary Club, of which Alfred became president one year, Mrs Roberts gave away loaves of bread and cakes that she baked to folk who she knew were particularly needy, while the girls were directed to put any extra pennies they might have towards church missions.

As Margaret herself once recalled:

> We were always encouraged to think in terms of practical help, and to think very little of people who thought that their duty to

the less well-off started and finished by getting up and protesting in the market place. That was ducking it, passing off your responsibilities to someone else. The crucial thing was what you were prepared to do yourself out of your own slender income.

To outsiders it seemed that there was never much gaiety or laughter in the Roberts' household. There could be no television, of course, in those days, and until the family invested in a wireless, when Margaret was ten – a great event in her life – the only diversion was the piano, which sat prominently in the living room with a lace cloth draped over its top. From the age of five, Margaret was sent out to have piano lessons each week. Mrs Roberts was musical, and by all accounts Margaret had inherited her gift; some say she could have played professionally if she had continued. But Margaret had more important things to do with her time, and at the age of fifteen she gave up taking piano lessons to concentrate on her school work.

By this time Margaret had left Huntingtower Road, and was attending the local grammar school, the Kesteven and Grantham Girls School in Sandon Road, having passed the County Minor Scholarship in the summer of 1936, shortly before her eleventh birthday.

Kesteven was an imposing red-brick building, sitting on a hilltop overlooking the centre of the town, about a mile from North Parade, surrounded by grass tennis courts and, across the road, hockey fields. Muriel was already at the school when Margaret arrived, also on a scholarship, and their father had coincidentally just been made a governor, later to become chairman of the Board of Governors.

It was a grant-aided school (which meant that parents normally paid half the fees), although a large proportion of girls – about a quarter of the full complement of 350 – were on scholarships, providing a great assortment of backgrounds. There was also a sizeable number of boarders. In those days the school had a preparatory section known as the 'Kindo', but the majority of pupils arrived at the age of eleven and left after School Certificate at fifteen, although the school-leaving age at that time was only fourteen. A few girls went on to the VIth form to take Higher School Certificate at seventeen, and fewer still stayed on for a third year in the VIth form, which was the norm before going on to university at eighteen.

The classes were streamed into 'a' and 'b' divisions and scholarship entrants usually went into the 'a' class. Margaret, however, began in IIIb, with a class of about thirty other girls, who were divided into five houses: Brontë, Austen, Eliot, Rossetti and Browning. New girls' names were picked out of a hat by the house captains at the beginning of each new year, and, as chance had it, Margaret went into Brontë.

Surprisingly enough, she was never exceptionally clever in class. She nearly always came top of her form in exams, but this was not because of brilliance, but rather through sheer hard work. She was always rather quiet and withdrawn in class; but she was listening and would go away after school and study what she had been taught. The only subject that she was never any good at – and the one subject that cannot be swotted up – was art. Her marks in this tended to bring down her average somewhat but she was nevertheless put up into the 'a' stream after two years, and there she stayed, concentrating on science as she went up the school.

The day began at 8.45 with morning prayers in the oak-panelled hall, the focal point of the building, with a gallery above. The service comprised hymns, prayers and school notices, while the choir, of which Margaret was a member, sang an extra anthem. Lessons followed throughout the morning with a break for lunch at noon, and resumed again at 1.20 for the afternoon session until 4.15. Girls were then expected to go home and put in at least two hours' homework a night.

Margaret, like most of the girls who lived in the town, walked to school, walked home for lunch – only girls who lived in the country were allowed to take sandwiches – then back to school for the afternoon, and home again for tea: a total of about four miles each day, summer and winter, rain and shine.

School uniform, like everything else, was governed by strict rules: in winter, a saxe blue blouse with no tie, navy serge tunic, and thick long black stockings; in summer, blue cotton dresses. Hats had to be worn when walking to and from school, blue felt in winter, straw in summer, macs were forbidden unless it was actually raining, coats or blazers in summer were otherwise the order of the day. Cardigans and jumpers were outlawed at all times of the year. The most that would be tolerated for anyone weak enough to feel the cold was a blazer, but that was not encouraged.

Manners, discipline and correct English were expected from every girl, and the atmosphere was such, particularly amongst the scholarship girls, who were keenly aware of the opportunities that the school represented, that the girls did as they were told, and questioned the system far less than children do today. A few of them dallied with boys from the King's School on the way home – a forbidden delight – some turned their hats into more exotic shapes, some spun on the chemistry lab' stools or played up 'Daddy Brown', the music master, and Margaret's class once smuggled a dog into Miss Dutton's biology lesson. But it was all very mild stuff and Margaret remained very much on the fringe of it – always a bit of a goody-goody. Her friends felt that she was worried about possible repercussions from her father.

She never had any very close friends at the school, but tended to be one of a group, seldom seeing the others outside school hours. Her time then was always taken up with homework, work in the warehouse at the back of the shop, or church in one form or another. She never seemed quite to fit in with her peers, doubtless because she was always so serious, and gave the impression that she couldn't be bothered with giggly girls who had nothing to say for themselves. She tended to put a bit of a damper on their fun, to the extent that some of her classmates would walk a different route to school so as not to meet up with her on the way.

Margaret was further alienated from her classmates by a special privilege about going to the cinema, which they felt was afforded to her quite simply because her father was on the Board of Governors. There was a strict school rule that during term time girls could only go to the cinema on Fridays or Saturdays. So strict was the rule that mistresses and prefects used to be posted outside the cinema to make sure no one tried to sneak in on any other day. Fridays and Saturdays, however, were late nights at the shop for the Roberts, and the only day that they could go was on Thursday after early closing. (There were no Sunday cinemas in Grantham in those days, largely thanks to Alfred Roberts, with his seat on the Borough Council. Every time the question of Sunday opening for parks, swimming pools and cinemas came up, he stolidly voted against it.) Margaret Roberts was therefore given permission to accompany her father to the cinema on Thursdays and this rankled.

School games consisted of hockey and netball in the winter and tennis in the summer. Although Margaret has scarcely touched a ball or taken part in a game of any sort since, she was a very good hockey player, playing centre half in the school team for three years. The girls didn't change for hockey in those days; they simply took off their tunics and played in what they had on underneath: blouses, heavy black knickers and black stockings. To their intense embarrassment they were obliged to walk across the road to the hockey field in this state of semi-nakedness.

The only other period of relaxation in the school timetable was gardening, presided over by Miss Dutton, the biology teacher. Each girl shared a small plot with two or three others, where they grew vegetables and flowers, and kept the weeds at bay. Margaret was always the one who mysteriously seemed to come away at the end of the session with her hands and fingernails immaculately clean, while everyone else's would be engrained with mud. She was, and has remained ever since, very concerned about her appearance. She was quite a solid chubby teenager, with rich brown hair but an unremarkable face and no great presence at all. She was never a tomboy – not even at elementary school – never wore trousers, never indulged in anything wild or extravagant. She was the pefect little girl, always perfectly and neatly dressed, who turned into the perfect lady. She turned into that earlier than most. Muriel left home to train as a physiotherapist in Birmingham when Margaret was thirteen and, after discovering the delights of fashionable clothes and make-up that lay beyond the confines of North Parade, brought her sister a powder compact home for Christmas. Margaret thereafter carried the compact in her pocket and took to powdering her face at school, an act that shocked her friends rigid – almost as severely as another girl in the form who wore a roll-on under her tunic.

Margaret managed to set herself apart from the other children one way or another all the way up the school. When visiting speakers, who came to the school to lecture on anything from the history of costume to the state of the world, invited questions at the end, it would always be Margaret Roberts that got to her feet. At an age when her contemporaries were far too self-conscious to open their mouths in front of so many people, she would ask clear, well-formulated questions, while her friends just looked at each other and raised their eyes to heaven.

She was a member of the school debating club, where again she displayed great confidence in public speaking, much to the despair of those less earnest girls in the school who once a year were forced to sit on the hard floor of the hall and listen. Once she got going, Margaret Roberts could be relied upon to go on and on. She liked nothing more than a captive audience. But her schoolmates never saw brilliance, and few saw anything either exciting or likeable; they took Margaret for a 'swot'.

Margaret always spoke rather slowly, with the same well-modulated voice she has today, although several tones higher, and with a distinct

Lincolnshire tang. Several of the children took elocution lessons at the school as an extra subject. Margaret never did, although her father later organized private elocution lessons from a woman in the town shortly before she went up to Oxford.

After School Certificate, Margaret narrowed her subjects to science – chemistry, biology and maths – having been particularly inspired by the excellent teaching of the chemistry mistress at Kesteven, Miss Kay. But there were still subjects that everyone, no matter what their speciality, had to take in the VIth form such as scripture and civics, which was essentially current events.

This last was her forte. Margaret Roberts was always far more aware of what was going on in the world than anyone else in the school; and at an age when most of the other girls scarcely thought beyond Grantham. During the Second World War, a Jewish penfriend of Muriel's, who had lived in Vienna, came to stay with the Roberts to escape the Nazis. She brought with her tales of life under the Third Reich, which Margaret listened to with horror and fascination, thus becoming far more conscious than her contemporaries of what the war was all about.

Her father's personal ambitions stretched no further than the town, but he was passionately interested in what went on elsewhere, particularly in ideological terms. Being didactic by nature, he pressed these interests on his younger daughter, asking her opinions and spelling out his own. He was pleased, as she grew older, to enjoy the intellectual intercourse he had never been able to have in the same way with his wife.

Since Mr Roberts had sat on the Grantham Borough Council for as long as Margaret could remember, canvassing and electioneering had become second nature to her; just one of the things that happened every few years, until her father became an alderman in 1936 – the youngest in the borough's history – and was no longer subject to public re-election. He further gained the distinction of being chairman of the Council Finance Committee; he was Food Officer during the Second World War, chairman of the National Savings Committee, a JP, and in 1943 served a term as Mayor of Grantham.

Margaret thus lived and moved on the fringes of local politics throughout her childhood. She was taken to listen to any visiting politician who came to talk in Grantham, very often meeting them too. Her first taste of national politics, however, was in the 1935 election when, at the age of ten, she folded election addresses for the

Conservative candidate, Sir Victor Warrender. Along with other councillors' children, she also helped to run the numbers of those who had voted from the tellers at the polling station to the committee room so that they might be checked off.

She was involved again in 1942 when Sir Victor's elevation to the House of Lords caused a by-election in Grantham. But, despite her help in posting leaflets through people's doors in the town, the Conservative candidate, Sir Arthur Longmore, lost to the Independent, William Kendall.

The Second World War caused considerable disruptions to life. Quite apart from the shortages, rationing, black-outs and air-raids that everyone became accustomed to, Margaret's school day was curtailed. In October 1939 Camden High School for Girls was evacuated to Grantham from London, and shared the facilities at Kesteven. Kesteven girls had lessons in the morning, from 8.30 to 12.30, and Camden girls moved in in the afternoons, while the local children went home and did extra prep'. But this didn't last for long: the town soon proved too dangerous, and the pupils from Camden High were packed off to Uppingham.

For a relatively small country town, Grantham felt the war more than most. Being situated on both main-line road and rail routes, and with all its factories turned over to making munitions, the town became a prime target for air-raids; and at one stage had one of the highest ratios of bombs to fall, per head of the population, in Britain.

Two shelters were built in the grounds at Kesteven, but for anyone inside the building when there was an air-raid, the drill was to congregate in the cloakrooms with their wire reinforced windows. On one particularly memorable occasion a German plane flew low over the school dropping a succession of bombs which exploded one after another in a steady progression across the hockey field and stopped within feet of the main building.

With the war, coincidentally, came a change of headmistress. The much-loved, mild-mannered founder of the school, Miss Gladys Williams, retired and was succeeded by Dorothy Gillies, a rather short-tempered Scotswoman who managed to rub a number of the girls up the wrong way. She was a classics scholar, and immediately introduced Latin into the VIth form, a subject which previously had not been taught in the school at all. But, alas, because it clashed with her science timetable, Margaret was never taught by Miss Gillies when she reached the VIth form.

The war also put an end to the school trips, both in Britain and abroad, that had previously been one of the perks of the VIth form. Instead, the girls, usually on an inter-house basis, were put to potato-picking or gathering rose-hips and blackberries, and organizing activities for such events as War Weapons Week.

Prompted by her father, Margaret entered the Lower VIth in 1941 with every intention of trying for a scholarship to university. By this time she was locked into a science course but, by the beginning of her second year, having spent many a spare moment listening to the legal proceedings at Grantham Quarter Sessions, where Mr Roberts now sat as a JP on the Bench, she began to realize that the law represented a far more fascinating subject.

She confided her dilemma in the town's Recorder, Norman Winning KC, whom she would join with her father for lunch at the Angel and Royal Hotel. His advice provided much comfort for he too had been a scientist; he had read physics at Cambridge, but quite successfully changed to law afterwards. He recommended that she should stick with science, particularly as there were some areas, namely the Patent Bar, where both qualifications were necessary anyway.

For no very clear reason, Margaret had set her heart on Somerville College, Oxford, and determined to go there at the end of her second year in the VIth form, after Highers. This would be a year earlier than was the custom for girls to go to university at that time. She wanted to 'get on'; it was war-time, women were called up for National Service at twenty, and she thought that an extra year at school would be wasted. But the way ahead was fraught with obstacles, the most trying of which was Miss Gillies.

In the first instance, Margaret had learnt no Latin, and a Lower School Certificate in Latin was essential for entrance to either Oxford or Cambridge regardless of subject. In the second instance, Miss Gillies thought that Margaret was far too young to go to university at seventeen, and would benefit from another year at school. The headmistress was a stubborn, plain-speaking Scot, and so far as she was concerned, that was an end to the matter.

But Miss Gillies had met her match in Margaret Roberts. Margaret was furious, and it was many years before she forgave her old headmistress. 'You're thwarting my ambition,' she is reputed to have said; and promptly set about preparing for the entrance exam herself. She enlisted her father's support, and persuaded him to pay for private Latin tuition from Victor Waterhouse, the classics master at King's

School, of which Mr Roberts was also Governor. Alfred Roberts further sought the advice of all sorts of people who might be of some help, including Canon Goodrich, vicar at Corby Glen. His own daughter, Margaret, had recently gone up from Kesteven to Lady Margaret Hall, Oxford. The Canon lent Margaret Roberts books to read, and gave her a little extra coaching in preparation for the general paper. All that was left to be done was to put in her application, which had to go via the school. Mr Roberts wrote out a cheque to cover the examination fee and Margaret took it to Miss Gillies, as a *fait accompli*.

She had worked extremely hard and, in addition to the work that she was already doing for Higher School Certificate, she had successfully managed to cram a five-year Latin course into a matter of months. And so it was with some satisfaction that she went up to Somerville to sit the entrance exam, hopeful of a scholarship in chemistry.

She had chosen chemistry, as she has often said herself, because she had a marvellous chemistry teacher at school, namely Miss Kay. But it was also a shrewd choice; far fewer girls wanted a place at university to read chemistry than for almost any other subject. Had Margaret chosen an arts subject, such as English or history, the competition would have been far stiffer. Nevertheless, Margaret failed to get in, and her name was put on the waiting list.

It was a bitter disappointment; she was forced to swallow her pride and return to school for a third year in the VIth form, just as Miss Gillies had advised all along. In the meantime, however, Canon Goodrich, who by now had developed a keen interest in Margaret's progress, set about trying to secure a place for her at Nottingham, where he had some connections.

A unique situation arose at Kesteven that autumn term. Because of the war, the senior part of the school were to have three weeks off in October to go potato-picking on nearby farms. So, to compensate, they went back to school three weeks earlier than normal, on 30 August. There were only two girls in the third year VIth by then: Margaret Roberts and Madeline Edwards, and on the second day of term Miss Gillies appointed them joint head girls, the first time in the history of the school that the title had been shared.

But Margaret shared the title for only two weeks. Somerville College sent a telegram offering her a place in the coming year to begin in October. Someone had failed to take up their place, and Margaret Roberts was on her way.

II

The City of Dreams?

The sudden telegram from Somerville offering her a place in the coming Michaelmas term of 1943 gave Margaret Roberts less than three weeks to prepare for university, and threw the family into some turmoil.

Hitherto, Oxford had been a name; it hadn't really existed outside the realms of their dreams. Now it was a reality, and both Margaret and her father were uncertain about what lay ahead, and anxious that she should go well prepared.

Alf Roberts asked Wilfred Allen, the church organist at Finkin Street, to give Margaret a few lessons on the organ, just in case she might find it handy at university. He laid on some elocution lessons, to try to knock the edge off her country accent. And, through his connections in the town, he elicited the names of families with daughters at Oxford, so that they might be able to teach her the drill. Margaret was unsure about what she should take with her, and whether her clothes would be suitable, and generally she felt quite nervous about the whole expedition.

Oxford in October 1943 was a very different place from the Oxford of today, but it was still a world apart from the quiet country community of Grantham, and light years from the oppressive Methodist regime that had governed the Roberts household. But Margaret was not alone. There were many girls from sheltered country backgrounds who had been through grammar schools on scholarships, and who had never been away from home before. And she was not the only one to feel bitterly homesick, shut away in the solitude of her bedsitting room on the ground floor of Penrose, one of the less attractive halls of residence in Somerville.

When visiting his own Margaret one weekend in that first term, Canon Goodrich had suggested they go and take some crumpets round to Margaret Roberts' room to toast in front of her fire for tea, and had found her looking quite miserable. But those were early days, and she soon recovered.

Although older than Margaret Roberts, the arrangement of forms in the top of the school at Kesteven had been such that Margaret Goodrich had shared lessons with her, and regularly dissected dogfish and rabbits on the same lab' bench. They had thus come to know each other reasonably well, and where other girls rejected Margaret Roberts, Margaret Goodrich was magnanimous and befriended her namesake. And while they had, and have continued to have, little in common, Margaret Goodrich, now Margaret Wickstead, is one of the very few people with whom Margaret Thatcher has kept in touch.

Somerville in those days naturally fell into three quite distinct groups, symbolized by where a person sat at table in Hall. On the top three tables, nearest the high table where the Principal sat, was the more exotic element: the foreign students, of whom there were quite a high number in war-time. At the bottom three tables sat the public school intake, the Cheltenham Ladies College lot, the confident, the rich and the aristocratic. And in between, at the three middle tables, were to be found the grammar-school girls, with scholarships, good middle-class ethics and every accent from Yorkshire to Somerset.

Margaret gravitated to the middle tables, where she should have been in her element; but once again she was a misfit. She seemed unable to relax and chatter freely as the other girls did. She was always rather prim, and was mercilessly teased because of her naive and outspoken ambition to better herself. She told everyone quite openly that she had taken elocution lessons before coming to Oxford, and spoke somewhat like Eliza Doolittle taking tea with Mrs Higgins, with a clear grasp of the theory, but not yet enough practice to pull it off.

She spoke incessantly about 'Daddy' – Daddy the Mayor of Grantham, rather than Daddy the grocer of Grantham – repeated what Daddy thought of this and that, what Daddy said she should do and how she should behave, and the books that Daddy said she should read. The result, not surprisingly in the rather uncharitable atmosphere that groups propagate, was that Margaret Roberts very quickly became the subject of some ridicule. She never appeared to see that she was making a fool of herself until it was too late, and once teased would blush crimson from her neck to her hair roots.

In the chemistry labs, where she was away from the mob, and where the groups were generally more closely-knit than the students in other faculties as a result of the hours they spent in one another's company, Margaret remained aloof. They had fun: she didn't. She went through four years at the university with few friends, generating a feeling,

17

shared by many of her contemporaries, that she was only prepared to offer friendship to those people who might be of some use to her on her climb up the ladder. Those closest to her were fellow Methodists, and those she spent most of her time with were fellow Conservatives. Politics were her abiding interest, and she would talk about the heights she planned to achieve, without a hint of humility or uncertainty. It all seemed so highly improbable to those who knew her, that everyone dismissed it as ridiculous.

The Principal of Somerville during Margaret's latter years was Dame Janet Vaughan, a leading expert on bone structure and renowned for her research into blood disease and radiation effects. She was also well known for her left-wing politics, as was Margaret's principal tutor, Professor Dorothy Hodgkin, another extremely distinguished lady, a crystallographer who won the Nobel Prize for Chemistry in 1964 and the Order of Merit a year later. Somerville was a traditionally non-conformist college, which had always tended to attract political people. Other politicians educated at Somerville have included Mrs Indira Gandhi, Dr Edith Summerskill and Mrs Shirley Williams. The mood in the college during the early 1940s, in response to what was happening in Europe, was particularly left wing. Yet Margaret, to the astonishment of all around her, arrived at Oxford a convinced and unshakeable Conservative, and for this reason, and for this alone, made a very clear impression on many people in the college. Dame Janet Vaughan remembers no one either before or since with such strong political convictions of this sort, which Margaret apparently never questioned in four years.

She thus gravitated straight to the Oxford University Conservative Association, where she put in almost as much work as she did in the chemistry labs. The foremost breeding ground of politicians has always been the Oxford Union, whose former members have included an impressive number of prime ministers, such as Gladstone, Asquith, Lord Salisbury, Macmillan, Wilson and Heath. But in Margaret's time at the university, women were barred from membership of the Union, and she had no alternative but to join the only society open to her – OUCA. For many of the Association's members, OUCA was simply another interest, to be fitted into the myriad of clubs and societies to which they also belonged. To Margaret it was an obsession, into which she put more time and energy on the ground floor than any of her contemporaries. Her only distraction from politics and chemistry was the Bach Choir.

While her peers stayed out without passes until after 11.00 p.m., when the doors shut, and were reduced to climbing into Somerville via the Radcliffe Infirmary or over the bicycle shed, Margaret led a sober and rather serious existence. No essay crises overwhelmed her as they did her contemporaries. She put in long hours at the OUCA, but never to the detriment of her work. The light in her room would often be on until two or three o'clock in the morning, while Margaret sat up and wrote her essays. And she would be out of bed again at 6.30 or 7.00 for the day ahead, the next round of lectures, lab' work and tutorials, never seeming any the worse for so little sleep.

Most of the students did some form of war work in addition to their studies, and Margaret's was to dispense coffee and biscuits to servicemen at the local forces canteen. And in the summer of her second year at Oxford, she found six weeks' vacation work at the Grantham Central School for Boys, teaching chemistry, mathematics and general science. As a result she earned enough money to buy herself a bicycle – the first she had ever owned – as a means of getting about at university.

For part of her third year Margaret was living out of college, in digs at 12 Richmond Road with two other Somerville students, Pauline Cowan and Peggy Lapham. The three were friendly enough to one another – over breakfasts of mashed potatoes and hot pilchards in tomato sauce three times a week – but never close; Pauline was an active member of the Communist Party, and neither she nor Margaret were prepared to give an inch in their political convictions.

In her fourth year, Margaret was again living in digs, round the corner from Richmond Road, at 18 Walton Street, sharing with two post-graduate students, Mary Mallinson and Mary Foss. Life was considerably more cheerful here: although meat was still rationed, Mary Foss's father was a butcher and used to send up from Twickenham far better meat for their pooled coupons than they could ever have bought in Oxford. Margaret also found someone of her own size – Mary Mallinson – from whom she could borrow an evening dress to wear to a ball on one occasion. But neither of the Marys were close friends.

Margaret, moreover, was never very close to any of her female contemporaries. The three for whom she had the most time were two fellow Methodists, Mary Osbourne and Jean Southerst, and Canon Goodrich's daughter, Margaret. She clearly preferred, as she still does, the company of men, and those men she sought out were in the Conservative Association. Most of her friendships with them were entirely platonic; but she did fall in love for the first time at Oxford. In the summer of her second year she fell quite soundly for the son of an earl, who went on to become something of a luminary in the Tory Party. She made no secret of her feelings, and talked about him quite gushingly, unaware that by so doing she was laying herself open to more teasing from the other girls in Hall, who by this time were growing increasingly disillusioned by her blatant use of people. They felt that if she caught herself a lord, it would be the last straw. But Margaret failed to net her lord. The relationship came to an end soon after she had met his mother.

Margaret was painfully aware that her own background did not match up to those of the people with whom she was now mixing. Nevertheless, she quite bravely invited one subsequent boyfriend home to Grantham to meet her parents, and was filled with relief that he took the circumstances he found them in so well. That particular gentleman judged ladies by their morals more than by their circumstances, and Margaret was every bit the lady.

Her circumstances, however, had improved by this time. When Margaret was nineteen her parents had bought a sizeable semi-detached house in a row of Edwardian houses just across the road from the shop in North Parade. For the first time they had a garden – a tiny bit at the front, and a good stretch at the back – and the comforts of modern plumbing.

But Margaret very seldom invited friends home. Even in the vacations when she occasionally saw other people from Oxford who lived around Grantham, such as Mary Wallace, whose father was a dentist in the town, and Margaret Goodrich from Corby Glen, she would tend to go to their houses rather than entertain them in hers. Canon Goodrich was always very pleased to see Margaret – who would invariably arrive with a string bag full of groceries as a gift for the household. Having played some part in preparing her for university, he was interested to hear how she was getting on.

Romances came and went. One suitor, a boy from the Methodist church who caught her fancy for a while, presented her with a carnation, and Margaret was passionate that it should not die. She arrived at Corby Glen vicarage for Margaret Goodrich's twenty-first birthday party in the Christmas vacation, with the carnation clutched faithfully to her bosom, and began looking for means of keeping it alive. Mrs Goodrich suggested an aspirin, and so an aspirin it was; and when she left the following morning, the wretched flower went too.

But these relationships were all entirely wholesome. Pre-marital sex was quite unthinkable amongst her genre at Oxford in those days. Those people who sat on the middle tables were highly moral and would never have betrayed their solid middle-class upbringings; not to mention the teachings of the church.

Margaret was strongly religious, even at university, and was no more influenced by the atheist tendency among her fellow students than she was politically by their left-wing leanings. She never questioned either of her beliefs; never rebelled in any way against the strict mores of her father. She had an intense and, some have said, arrogant certainty that she was right; and was never shy about declaring herself. She never shared the frivolity of her contemporaries, nor the gossip, but was always very serious and worthy, and as often as not gave the impression that she disapproved of their way of life. Her very presence placed something of a damper on the conversation – in much the same way as it had at school.

Margaret's work in the chemistry faculty proved adequate, and her essays were always easy to read and a good account of the subject, but they always lacked the flair which would have turned her into a first-class chemist. Her heart was clearly not entirely in the subject, although no one could ever accuse her of skimping the work. And for this reason her tutors, who might have told other students to ease up on their extra-curricular activities because they were interfering with their Schools, never bothered to curb Margaret's OUCA involvement. It was their opinion that even had she devoted all of her time to chemistry, Margaret Roberts never had the intellect to get a first-class degree. So, all her spare time was put into the association and, as many of her contemporaries thought, to bettering herself. They are convinced that Margaret saw and used Oxford – including the people she cultivated there – as a stepping stone to the House of Commons, and for very little else.

This didn't bother Dorothy Hodgkin, although she never realized just how serious Margaret's political interests were. She was always quite relieved if her students had interests outside chemistry, firmly believing that there was more to university life than work. At that time, moreover, she herself was particularly absorbed in her own work, the isolation of crystalline penicillin, and admits that she didn't devote quite as much time to the students during Margaret's period at Oxford as she might have done.

There were very few science students at Somerville in Margaret's year – just two other chemists and a zoologist. This was predictable as, in war-time, many people had decided instead to read medicine. The first three years of the chemistry course involved practical and academic work: lectures every morning from 9.00 to 11.00, followed by compulsory lab' work, voluntary lab' work in the afternoons, plus a certain amount of reading and essays, and a weekly tutorial, which in the third year was quite often held in Dorothy Hodgkin's home, at 20 Bradwell Road, where the students helped to entertain two small children.

Margaret worked hard, and was methodical and neat; she was never late for lectures, never late with her essays, and always appeared to be interested in the subject. But she lacked that spark which sets one student above the rest. She did, nevertheless, win the Kirkauldy Essay Prize in her third year, which she shared with a fellow chemist at Somerville – and no accolade from that college is to be sniffed at.

At the end of that year there were final exams, or 'Schools' as they are called at Oxford, which Margaret sat in the summer of 1946. The approach of Schools is inevitably a nerve-racking time and the stories of people who have broken down before their finals are legion. Margaret Roberts was not unique; the strain did prove too much, and she wrote the first exam, the organic chemistry paper, from a bed in the sanatorium, affectionately known as the 'sicker'.

Having taken the plunge and begun, Margaret recovered her equilibrium and was able to write the second two papers in the Examination Schools, wearing her sub-fusc of black and white, complete with cap and gown, like everyone else. She came away at the end of the day with an adequate second-class degree, although she didn't know this for another year. The full chemistry degree involves a fourth year of research with a written thesis at the end of it, and the class of degree has always been concealed until the end of that fourth year, even though it is largely determined by the way in which the student fares in the third year 'Schools'.

This is a system peculiar to Oxford, devised by Professor Perkin, who had had strong associations with industry and felt it was essential for chemists coming into industry from university to have research experience of working on their own. It was also extremely useful for Oxford in that it gave people like Dorothy Hodgkin a pool of hands to carry out research experiments, while they combined their work with teaching.

Margaret chose to do her research in organic chemistry with Dorothy

Hodgkin, the only chemist of her year to go in this direction. She joined forces with Gerhardt Schmidt, a post-graduate student and a brilliant chemist, then engaged in obtaining his doctorate of philosophy.

The subject of their research was Gramicidin S, an antibiotic which had been isolated in the Soviet Union. Because of the good relations enjoyed between Soviet and British scientists during the war, Richard Synge, then at the Lister Institute of Preventive Medicine in London (who subsequently won a Nobel Prize for his work on this substance), had been able to go to Russia and bring back some of the antibiotic for his research. Knowing of the work Dorothy Hodgkin was doing with penicillin in Oxford, he gave her some of the crystals that he had brought back.

Margaret and Gerhardt's task was to try and work out the protein structures of Gramicidin S, which involved putting X-rays through the crystals and trying to discover from the defraction effects how the atoms were arranged in space. They hoped from this to be able to write a formula for the chemical molecules in the crystals.

But Gramicidin S proved far more complicated than penicillin, on which Dorothy Hodgkin had successfully applied the same techniques. The true form of the structure was only finally solved two or three years ago by Michael Woolfson, Professor of Physics at York University, and then not in the framework of the crystals within which Gerhardt and Margaret Roberts had worked, but in the framework of another derivative that was discovered some time later.

Dorothy Hodgkin has always regretted that Margaret wasn't working on something that she could have solved. Margaret herself, however, was not unduly bothered. Her four years at Oxford had consolidated her passion for politics, and made it very clear to her that she was reading the wrong subject. The obvious way into politics was via the law; that was what most of her fellows in OUCA were reading. Chemistry was fast fading as anything more significant than a means to an end.

There were few people at Oxford who devoted half as much time to OUCA as Margaret Roberts. Whenever anything needed doing, Margaret was there; she would put in the hours and do the jobs that no one else wanted to do, and very soon found herself on the committee, where there were still more routine jobs to do. In her third year she became President of OUCA, the first time a woman had ever been given the position, and she retained it in her fourth year at the university too. It was an undoubted achievement, but it was also her just deserts for years of hard work and dedication to the association, and the simple fact remained that there was no one else to do the job.

Her predecessor as President had been Sir Edward Boyle, whom Margaret admired above all others. He evidently had a very soft spot for her too; when discussing her merits and shortcomings with a colleague, shortly before his death in 1981, he observed: 'People think she's very tough and hard-hearted, and she isn't.'

Nor was Margaret a particularly memorable President of OUCA. Margaret's strength has always lain in her quickness to learn, and she has used this advantage time and time again in her life. In 1946 she had neither the good looks nor the charisma that she enjoys today. Her hair was brown, her face considerably fuller than it is now, her figure stocky, and her style of dress neat but very dull. While she spoke without faltering, Margaret Roberts never aroused much excitement from the floor, and is remembered more for having won the position of president than for anything she ever did or said while holding it.

Nevertheless there were many advantages in being President of OUCA, particularly for someone with an eye on Parliament. Prominent Tory politicians frequently came up to Oxford to address the Association and would be given dinner at the Randolph Hotel beforehand, where Margaret as President of OUCA would act as their host. She was never totally at ease in their company, but Margaret very quickly learnt to appear so. Throughout her life she has hidden her insecurities behind a façade of, at times, overweaning self-confidence. She has learnt over the years to hide every emotion, and there are few who, like the late Sir Edward Boyle, ever reach what lies beneath.

As President and representative of OUCA, she also attended her first Annual Conservative Party Conference in Blackpool in October 1946. She was deeply impressed by the size of the Party, 'and what it meant to be a member of such an organization of people with the same ideals and objectives'.

The Conservative Party was then in Opposition, having lost the July election the year before, at the very end of the war. A Labour Government under Clement Attlee was in power, busy laying the way over the next few years for the introduction of the Welfare State, the National Health Service, and the nationalization of the railways and of the coal, gas and electricity industries.

Margaret had played a small part in the 1945 general election. She had canvassed for Quintin Hogg (now Lord Hailsham) in his successful fight for Oxford against the Labour candidate, Frank Pakenham (now

Lord Longford). Then, when the university went down for the summer vacation, she went home to Grantham, and into battle for the Conservative candidate there, George Worth, who had written to her asking if she would help once the term was over. Local Tories had become quite impressed by Alf Roberts' younger daughter; they would ask after her when buying groceries in his shop, and occasionally invite her in for a glass of sherry when she was home from Oxford. They remember quite vividly how well she could hold her own in conversation with her elders and the clarity of her arguments. After her father's term as Mayor and his work on the Bench, he was quite a notable figure in the town – if not universally the best loved – and it was therefore not incongruous that such people should take an interest in the scholastic progress of his family. This was the way in which she had come to the attention of George Worth, and so she leapt at the invitation to act as his 'pot-boiler' at all the various political meetings in the villages around Grantham. This involved warming up the audiences and keeping their interest and enthusiasm going until the main speaker, the candidate, arrived.

The Conservatives had gone into the election of July 1945 full of confidence. Led by Winston Churchill, who had steadfastly guided Britain through the years of war, they held 432 seats out of 615 in the House of Commons, and were certain that the British public would renew his mandate. But in one of the most surprising upsets in modern political history, the Conservatives were lamentably defeated at the polls, and a Labour Government under Clement Attlee came to power. It was the first time Britain had elected a Labour Government outright; and many people, including Margaret Roberts, were stunned at the result. In Oxford City, Quintin Hogg held his seat, but in Grantham, George Worth lost to the Labour candidate, William Kendall.

By this time Margaret was certain that she wanted to go into politics herself. Schoolfriends recall Margaret at the age of thirteen or fourteen actually declaring that she wanted to be a Member of Parliament – long before her contemporaries in Grantham were wholly aware of what that meant. She herself says the ambition came later. The idea first occurred to her, she says, after a party at a friend's house near Grantham one night, when the hangers-on were sitting around the kitchen chatting and someone turned to Margaret and said, 'I feel that what you'd really like to be is a Member of Parliament.'

Certainly her old friend Margaret Goodrich remembers her walking down Parks Road in Oxford, having just got her degree, saying, 'You know, I oughtn't to have read chemistry. I should have read law. That's what I need for politics. I shall just have to go and read law now.' But both the law and politics required money and, although she had made some good contacts at Oxford, Margaret didn't have limitless funds to go on to further education. Besides, if she had absorbed no other cliché at her grandmother's knee, she had learned to 'Waste not, want not.' She would use her chemistry as a rung on the ladder. She duly signed on, therefore, with the university appointments board, in the hope of finding a job. Thus in early May 1947 a panel of four executives from BX Plastics Limited, a manufacturing company based near Colchester in Essex, interviewed Margaret Roberts and offered her a job in their rapidly expanding Research and Development Department, to start in September at an annual salary of £350.

BX took on three graduates from Oxford that year, and seven from other universities, one of whom left almost immediately. Of the nine that remained, three were women: Margaret Roberts, Audrey Powell and Eileen Rutherford; and they became the first women ever to be employed by the company in this capacity. It was a delicate situation that required tact. Their job was in the field of development rather than research, and involved taking laboratory processes and trying to implement them on a factory scale. The factory, situated some two miles away from the R and D Department, produced celluloid and extruded PVC tubing, and the men who worked on the benches were mostly old diehards who had not encountered women in industry before, let alone women in their early twenties, fresh out of university, who were trying to tell them what to do.

Margaret found it agonizing. She was quite incapable of communicating with the men on the factory floor in any way at all. Where her fellow females might ask 'Hey, Charlie, what about trying this, I think it might work?' and play along with the odd nudge and wink, Margaret would stand rather awkwardly over the man, and in her well-modulated, and now perfected true blue accent, would say, 'Mr So and So, would you mind trying it this way?' This method, as often as not, elicited the two finger response, and earned Margaret the nickname 'Duchess', which stuck throughout three years at BX Plastics.

Another name her colleagues had for her was 'Aunty Margaret', which was more of a reflection on her mental age and her attitude to her contemporaries than any shortcomings on the factory floor. She was yet again the odd one out, just as she had been at school and at

university: a square peg in a round hole. The two other girls shared a
flat; Margaret couldn't understand how anyone could want to do that:
she lived in digs in a respectable house in Colchester with a widow who
cooked breakfast and dinner for her. The two girls let their hair down
if they went to works' parties at Christmas time, drank, and looked as
though they were enjoying themselves. Margaret would arrive wearing
a long formal dress and sit like a pariah at the feast, obviously hating
every minute. They drew the conclusion that she was socially superior,
and quite simply out of her depth. They were quite unaware that her
father was a shopkeeper and had been Mayor. They had no knowledge
of her background whatsoever – they didn't even know she came from
Grantham, because she never ever mentioned her home or her family
to anyone. All she talked about was politics, and with such insensitivity
to the climate of opinion around her, and such total absence of humour,
that once again people sent her up, and once again she would so seldom
be able to see it coming. It was the earnest and dogmatic way in which
she presented her political convictions that put everyone's back up. She
didn't want to explore other people's ideas, never asked what made
them say the things they said, and never conceded that any way that
was different from her own – and hence the Tory Party way – could
possibly have any merit.

She continued in her pursuit of politics with single-minded
dedication from her new base in Colchester. She became actively
involved in the local Conservative Association, where they had a '39–45
Group', a discussion group for ex-servicemen and women who had
returned from the war. But Margaret lived most of all for the weekends
when she would go off on the train to London, or even further afield,
to attend some Conservative function or other, a debating school, a
rally, a conference, or a political get-together, where as often as not,
she would meet old friends from OUCA who were now, like her,
members of the Oxford University Graduates' Association. Someone
she particularly looked forward to seeing at these weekends was Sir
Edward 'Teddy' Boyle, whom she spoke of frequently and of whom
she clearly thought the world.

Margaret was obviously far far happier on her weekends away,
immersed in politics, than ever she was experimenting with polymer
or celluloid at BX Plastics, although they were breaking new industrial
ground every day. She would dash off on Friday afternoons dressed in
a smart black suit with a conservative little hat, specially made for her
by a small milliner in Colchester, 'Minnie Mouse' court shoes, and a

handbag tucked under one arm, looking forty-five if she was a day, and every bit the 'Aunty Margaret' or the 'Duchess' of the factory floor. Ridiculous as she might have seemed to her colleagues in Colchester, Margaret was steering a very clear and precise course, quite indifferent as she always had been to fashion or, indeed, the ways in which other people around her behaved.

Her only concession to what might have been considered normal behaviour for a young woman, was a concern for the way she looked. Her complexion had always been flawless, and while her schoolfriends would be contending with a replica of Mount Vesuvius on their own pubescent faces, Margaret would point to perfect patches of peachy chin and bemoan the advance of a spot. She worried that her legs were too thick, knew her way around the Helena Rubinstein make-up range as well as anyone, and took painstaking care over the clothes she wore. She would never experiment with clothes, and always stuck to rather old-fashioned styles and drab colours. She always wore skirts or dresses, never trousers, but she looked after them well, and never looked creased or dirty. There have been a multitude of other changes in Margaret's life but she has always taken a pride in her appearance.

Margaret's work at BX Plastics was thorough and, according to Stanley Booth, her departmental head, the standard of all the women he employed that year was high. But he was well aware that of the women he had working in the R and D Department, she was the least dedicated. He realized that the only thing she really cared about was politics, and it came as no surprise when she announced, after three years with the firm, that she would be leaving.

With admirable single-mindedness, Margaret had been using her work at Colchester to finance excursions into the political arena. One of these had been to the Annual Conservative Party Conference held in Llandudno in the autumn of 1948, where she was representing the Oxford University Graduates' Association. Her persistence paid off. As Margaret herself has told the story, she bumped into an old Oxford friend, John Grant, who was a director of Blackwell's Bookshop, and they sat down together in the conference hall. Sitting on the other side of Grant was the chairman of the Dartford Association, John Miller. Grant asked Miller who their candidate was, to which the chairman replied, 'We haven't got one, but we're considering getting one.' John Grant then said, 'Would you consider a woman?', and turned to Margaret and suggested she put her name in for it.

Dartford was a tough industrial seat in north Kent, then held by the

Labour MP Norman Dodds with a majority of nearly twenty thousand. It was not the place for a woman of twenty-three, or so the chairman at first thought. But later that afternoon, Margaret was walking down the pier at Llandudno, when she met him again, this time in the company of other delegates from Dartford. They talked for a while, Margaret liked them, they were evidently impressed by her, and when she got back to Colchester a couple of days later, she put in a formal application to be considered as a prospective parliamentary candidate for the seat. There were over twenty applicants that year, of whom Margaret was the only woman, but she was short-listed and, to her great delight, duly selected.

All this happened while Margaret was at BX Plastics, and yet she scarcely breathed a word of it. She always played her cards very close to her chest, and although her colleagues knew she had some special interest in Dartford, they knew nothing of her selection or her plans to find work within easier striking distance of Dartford, where she had agreed to live. A month before she left she announced that she had found herself a Parliamentary seat, a new job with J. Lyons and Company at Cadby Hall in Hammersmith, and was off.

Margaret had found more than a new job and a new place to live. She had at last found an environment in which she fitted. Throughout her early years she had been an ugly duckling in the wrong nest, who was teased for being so different. When she became adopted by Dartford, where she was surrounded by like-minded people who shared her enthusiasm for the Conservative Party and were impressed by her single-minded and earnest approach to politics, she began to emerge as a new woman.

It was at this time that she met Denis Thatcher, someone who, to her ever-rational mind, presented everything she needed. He was ten years older than she, and she had always been more comfortable in the company of older people. He was established in business as managing director of the family paint and wallpaper company, Atlas Preservatives, in Erith in north Kent. He was a fellow Methodist, in name at any rate, he drove a snazzy car – a Jaguar – he was comparatively wealthy, and lived in a flat in Chelsea. Not least of all, he was tall, athletic, good-looking, and very much taken with Margaret.

They had met on the night of her adoption meeting in Dartford. This is the occasion when a candidate that the committee has selected is formally accepted by the rest of the association. The candidate makes a speech, answers questions and is generally very much on public display. Dinner had been arranged for Margaret afterwards and, being short of a man, one of the committee members organizing the dinner had invited Denis Thatcher to make up numbers. He was a business friend of her husband's, and although he didn't live in Dartford, he knew quite a number of people in the association, whom he had met as a result of his factory being sited in Erith.

The adoption meeting went magnificently: all sorts of people turned up, many out of nothing more than curiosity, to have a look at Miss Roberts. Women candidates were a great rarity in 1949 – and they did not find her wanting. The meeting went on a long time and at the end she lingered further to meet and talk to people, quite high on the exhilaration of her triumph. By the end it was late, and the question arose of how she was going to get back to Colchester. The answer was by train, as always. She would take one from Dartford to London, and change there for Colchester. Denis Thatcher offered to save her at least one of the train journeys and drive her to Liverpool Street Station in his car as he was going back to his flat in London. Margaret gratefully accepted, and so began their relationship.

Only one thing made Margaret hesitant about pursuing her relationship with Denis: the fact that he had been married before and was divorced from his first wife. The Methodist church strongly disapproved of divorce, more so thirty years ago than today. So Margaret was faced with a dilemma: whether to forego the strict teachings of Finkin Street, and possibly the approbation of her father which she held dear; or to give up Denis, and all that life with him might promise.

There was no question of Margaret having been involved in the breakdown of Denis's first marriage. He had married Margaret Kempson shortly before the outbreak of the Second World War, and left almost immediately to fight in the army. He served with distinction with the Royal Artillery in France, Sicily and Italy, and was mentioned in dispatches. By the time he returned home, he and the young bride he had left behind were like strangers: typical casualties of the war. They divorced in 1946, there had been no children, and by the time Denis met Margaret Roberts, his ex-wife had been married to Sir Howard Hickman for nearly a year.

Margaret made her decision and, in choosing Denis, for the first time in her life went against the authorities that had hitherto influenced and ruled her every action. She closed her mind to his past, and behaved as though his previous marriage had never existed. She had no curiosity about the first Mrs Thatcher at all. She had never met her, never wanted to, and didn't even know or want to know her name. When once asked she said, 'I think she's a peeress, but I'm not sure.' She didn't even let her children in on the secret; and when the newspapers finally got hold of the story at the time of her bid for the leadership of the Conservative Party many years later, Margaret was utterly devastated.

As the newly adopted prospective candidate for Dartford, Margaret Roberts, like her mother before her, worked all the hours God sent. She moved into digs in the town with a couple who were active members of the Conservative Association, and for two years she left their house at 6.35 in the morning, took a bus to the station, a train to Charing Cross, and another bus out to Hammersmith to put in a day's work in the food research laboratories at J. Lyons. This job, like her work at BX Plastics, represented no more than a means of earning the money to support her political aspirations. She made the same journey in reverse in the evenings, catching the 6.08 train, would then have a quick meal prepared in her lodgings by her landlady, Mrs Woollcott, before embarking on a full evening's constituency work. Once again she would sit up working in her room until late into the night, often until two or three o'clock in the morning, reading, writing speeches and preparing herself.

Given the opportunity to do something which she really enjoyed, at last, surrounded by people who appreciated the Tory Party line she toed with such acceptance, and who shared the interests and convictions that most of the other people she had known had found so boring, Margaret became a far happier person.

She threw herself into the community of Dartford one hundred per cent. It was a big constituency divided into three wards: Erith; Crayford; and Dartford itself. Margaret set about getting to know all the active helpers in each division, and inspiring in them, as she has with the people who have worked for her ever since, enthusiasm, hard work and loyalty. Margaret Thatcher may have created some enemies in her time, but those people who have worked for her most closely have always been her greatest admirers, for the simple reason that she is always prepared to work just as hard if not harder than anyone else. She went to fund-raising functions that they organized, attended rallies, including one for Anthony Eden, where she stood on the platform to offer the vote of thanks alongside Edward Heath, then prospective Tory candidate for neighbouring Bexley.

She spoke at meetings, both within and outside her own constituency. There was one particularly memorable speech she made at a ladies luncheon club in Bexley on the subject of women's rights. 'Don't be scared,' she counselled, 'of the high-flown language of economists and cabinet ministers; but think of politics at our own household level. After all, women live in contact with food supplies, housing shortages and the ever-decreasing opportunities for children, and we must therefore face up to the position, remembering that as more power is taken away from the people, so there is less responsibility for us to assume.' Margaret was always extremely nervous before making speeches and put a lot of work into their preparation, but once she had begun, the nerves evaporated and she could speak clearly and plainly with scarcely a note. She never read her speeches until she was Leader of the Opposition, when she had to do so because the text would be circulated, and it was important that what she said and what she circulated bore some resemblance. Speaking was part of the job she enjoyed. What she found painfully difficult, and continued to do so for a good many years, was to talk to people at the factory gates, which has always been an essential electioneering ploy. She found it no easier to talk to the men spilling out of factories in Dartford than she had talking to the men on the factory floor at BX Plastics. Yet she persevered; she did all that was expected of her, with her characteristic air of confidence, and by the time of the general election in February 1950 she was well known and well supported in the area.

Margaret canvassed high and low, and fitted in as many appearances in the district as she could manage. She was considerably helped on her way by the local press, which gave her unprecedented coverage, as they did in every seat that had a woman standing, because it was such a very uncommon occurrence in 1950. But no amount of publicity or hard work could have won a Tory that seat. She increased the Conservative vote at Dartford by fifty per cent, which was considered a remarkable achievement, and knocked a third off the Labour majority, but still Norman Dodds came romping home with 38,128 votes to her 24,490, as everyone had known all along he would. This result reflected the trend nationwide, and the Labour Party under Clement Attlee were returned to power, but with a very narrow majority. There was every likelihood of another election in the near future.

Margaret was readopted by Dartford after the 1950 election, and fought the seat unsuccessfully a second time in October 1951. This time the Conservatives won the election and Sir Winston Churchill became

Prime Minister for another term.

In the meantime Margaret Roberts had begun to study for the Bar, and to realize the ambition that she had nursed ever since those days at the Quarter Sessions in Grantham. Dartford was obviously a non-starter as far as getting into Parliament in the near future was concerned, and she was still convinced that law was the best route to take. So she enrolled at the Council of Legal Education and studied in her spare time, such as there was, between J. Lyons, Dartford, and additional political jamborees like the National Conservative Candidates Conference held that year in London, where young, pretty and unattached women were very much at a premium. It was there that she first met Airey Neave, who was to play an important part in her life in later years, and Anthony Barber, whose wife-to-be, Jean Asquith, was also standing.

Denis and Margaret announced their engagement on the eve of the 1951 general election. He had actually asked her and she accepted his proposal some weeks earlier, and they had confided the news to John Miller, chairman of the association in Dartford. He advised against making the news public until after the election, lest it have an adverse effect on the voters, who might think that marriage would turn her into a domesticated mother with only a fraction of her time left over for their constituency. How wrong they would have been. However, the news leaked out on the day before polling began, and Margaret Roberts became Mrs Thatcher some six weeks later, on 13 December 1951.

In the meantime she had taken Denis up to Grantham to meet her parents, and various well-chosen friends from her youth, including Canon Goodrich and his wife whose long, low, nicely furnished Elizabethan house at Corby Glen was one she was quite pleased to be able to show to her betrothed. Grantham, and some of the people in it, represented a community from which she had worked hard and struggled to escape. Quite naturally it was to be some years before she was able to look upon the town with much affection.

The wedding was a reasonably quiet affair, with about fifty close friends and relatives in Wesley's Chapel in City Road – the Westminster Abbey of the Methodist church. Alf Roberts gave his daughter away. Margaret's mother also attended the ceremony with Muriel, who, after completing her training in Birmingham, had worked in Grantham as a peripatetic physiotherapist for some years, and was now married to Scots farmer William Cullen. Denis's only relatives were his widowed mother and one unmarried sister, Joy, who lived in Barnes, an upper-middle-class suburb in south London. If Alf Roberts was not best pleased that his daughter should be marrying a divorcee, albeit a Methodist divorcee, Mrs and Miss Thatcher were not overjoyed that their Denis, on whom they both doted, should be pledging his troth to a grocer's daughter from Grantham.

Margaret's decision to break with the strict teachings of the Methodist church brought about a momentous change in her, sharply emphasized in her choice of wedding dress. There was nothing dull and conservative about that: no seemly white, but a long, brilliant sapphire blue velvet dress, the exact replica of an outfit worn by Georgiana, Duchess of Devonshire in a painting by Sir Joshua Reynolds, complete with a little sapphire hat and ostrich feather. Thereafter the colours she chose to wear remained bright and flamboyant.

She never returned to the fiercely strict Methodism of her youth, nor inflicted it on her children. She has always retained her faith, however. As Prime Minister she has taken a far greater hand in the selection of the clergy than the head of state technically should, or has done in the past. Moreover, she has attended the village church at Chequers, the Prime Minister's country residence, more frequently than any of her predecessors. Religious beliefs have very obviously inspired a great many of her actions, both professionally and privately, but she has moved away from the Wesleyan teachings and closer to the Anglican church in her tenets.

The newly married Thatchers went off on honeymoon abroad, first to Portugal, then Madeira, and finally Paris, combining a little of the bridegroom's business with pleasure. They then returned to London to live in Denis's small rented flat on the sixth floor of Swan Court, in Flood Street, Chelsea. He continued to drive down to Erith each day to Atlas Preservatives, leaving early in the morning and not returning home until eight or nine o'clock. Margaret meanwhile spent her days immersed in the law, studying tomes, writing essays and attending lectures at the Council of Legal Education. In the evenings she would cook their dinner, the first time in her life that she had ever had to do so. She had taken domestic science lessons at school, like all the girls at Kesteven, and made her statutory Christmas cake with no apparent difficulty. But thereafter she had always taken accommodation where breakfast and dinner were provided, believing that shopping and cooking were a great waste of time, and not tasks in which women like her should be engaged. Having a husband to cook for was a different matter and she came to enjoy it and learnt to cook well, if never with a great deal of inspiration or imagination. She stuck to simple basic dishes, which looked attractive, tasted good, and could be prepared with the minimum of time and effort.

Where Margaret was really in her element, however, was decorating. She loved shopping for wallpapers and choosing paint colours, then going home, clearing the decks, covering herself up in voluminous overalls, and transforming the face of a room. She did her own decorating in every house that the Thatchers have lived in, right up to the time that she became Leader of the Conservative Party, when there simply weren't the hours in the day to spend on anything other than work. Decorating was one of her greatest forms of relaxation, and she didn't just dabble: she set about it in a planned way, stripped everything down first, and came up with a professional job at the end of it.

A little over a year after they were married Margaret became pregnant, and in August 1953, on the day that England won the Ashes, gave birth not just to the one baby she thought she was expecting, but to twins, Mark and Carol, born at two-minute intervals by caesarian section at Queen Charlotte's Hospital in London. Margaret was delighted with her offspring and has remained in many ways besotted by her children. But she was not one to be over sentimental. Right there and then in her hospital bed she determined to put her name down for the Bar Finals in December, which would force her to complete the course and have the qualification she wanted, twins or no twins.

Decisions of this kind, of course, were made easier by the fact that Denis had a good income, which could support her while she studied and ate the required number of dinners that were part and parcel of the business of training for the Bar. After her final exams there were pupillages to serve under barristers in chambers, and in those days it was the custom to pay a pupilmaster £100 a year and a further ten guineas (£10.50) to the clerk of the chambers. Without Denis's income Margaret Thatcher would never have been able to advance her career so quickly. This was always something she would freely acknowledge: 'It was Denis's money that helped me on my way,' she used to say. And help it did. His income also enabled them to employ a nanny to look after the children, and they had someone permanently living in, initially as nanny and latterly as housekeeper, right up to the time when Mark and Carol went to boarding school.

The advent of the twins and a live-in nanny meant that the household needed extra space. By good fortune they were able to rent the adjoining flat in Swan Court and simply knock a hole in the wall, which gave them double the number of rooms. It was a controlled tenancy for which they paid the princely sum of £7 a week excluding rates. So they remained in Flood Street, as neighbours of the theatrical couple, Sybil Thorndike and Lewis Casson, until Mark and Carol were five. Denis and Margaret lived in the original flat, the twins and nanny lived in the other, with a door connecting the two, and a long corridor down which Mark and Carol would ride their tricycles as they grew older. Initially they shared a bedroom – Mark had blue sheets, Carol had pink – and when they were very small they were dressed in the same colours, always immaculately in clothes very often made for them by their grandmother, Beatrice Roberts. Margaret, who had picked up a great many of her mother's dressmaking skills, also made them clothes from time to time. She was always in despair about the speed with which they grew out of everything, and was not above turning unwanted bits of material into something useful. On one occasion she lined the children's coats with the old nursery curtains.

Margaret passed her Bar Finals in December, and went first into Frederick Lawton's chambers at 5 King's Bench Walk in the Inner Temple, to do a six-months' pupillage in common and criminal law. Michael Havers was also in those chambers, as was Airey Neave, whom Margaret had met three years earlier at the Candidates Conference. From there she went to study chancery law for six months with John Brightman at 1 New Square in Lincoln's Inn. Finally she moved on to tax law in Sir John Senter's chambers in Queen's Bench Walk, again in the Inner Temple, where she remet Anthony Barber, another fellow prospective parliamentary candidate in the 1950 election.

All of this had been mapped out for her by Sir John Senter, an eminent tax barrister who advised the Government in an unofficial capacity, and whom Margaret had sat next to at a dinner in the House of Commons one evening while she was still studying for the Bar. He had been very taken with her, suggesting the chambers she should apply to once she had passed her Finals, the type and length of pupillages she should serve, which included six months in his own, and as good as promised that at the end of her time in Queen's Bench Walk, he would invite her to stay on as a tenant. Without a tenancy a barrister, however well qualified, is not allowed to practise. Unhappily his bond was not as good as his word, and after serving the pupillages he had suggested, and spending six months in his own chambers, Margaret was bluntly informed that there was no room for her and she would have to go.

Sir John Senter was a very unpredictable man, and a lot of his colleagues found him difficult to get on with. At the time Margaret joined the chambers he was going through a period of expansion and had acquired rooms in a building opposite. It was true that he backtracked on this plan, cutting down on the number of tenants he took in, but it would still have been quite possible to keep on Margaret Thatcher had he wanted to. Another casualty at the same time was to be one of Margaret's future Cabinet colleagues, Patrick Jenkin, who was Sir John's own pupil, and he too was pushed out quite unfairly.

There had been a slight atmosphere of unease when Margaret first joined the chambers. Women were tolerated at the Bar provided they kept to subjects they were likely to understand, like domestic problems and divorce. Tax was very definitely considered a male preserve and jealously guarded as such by the clerks of chambers who lived on a commission basis. If work was not going to come to one of their barristers because she was a woman, then they didn't want her in chambers. The problem was exacerbated at Queen's Bench Walk by the belief held by one tenant that a mother with young children, like Margaret, should not be going out to work but should be at home washing nappies. He complained vociferously to several people in the chambers about this before he realized he was fighting a losing battle and settled for it. There was really nothing anyone could pin on Margaret. She was business-like and efficient: she came to work promptly, didn't waste time chattering, got on with the work that had to be done and went home again at 5.30 on the dot. But she was never a brilliantly original pupil. One particular case she worked on involved an allowance to a friendly society. The Revenue argued that this particular society was not a friendly society because it wasn't registered. The relevant question, as her pupilmaster, Peter Rowland, explained was, 'Did friendly societies have to be registered if they had been set up before there was registration?' Margaret was stumped, and had to be led carefully through the stages of research necessary in preparing a defence: she needed to look into the history of friendly societies, the history of the particular society, and the two Acts of Parliament which had introduced the registration, in 1803 and 1842. Margaret worked hard, but Peter Rowland twice sent the case she had prepared back to her to be redone before she delved back far enough to come up with the right answer. It was about ten days' work altogether, and all for the trifling sum of £10, but Margaret won her client the case.

By the time she was told of the outcome she had left the chambers and the Inner Temple, and was installed as a tenant in rather less prestigious tax chambers at 5 New Square in Lincoln's Inn. She had applied first to her old chancery chambers at 1 New Square, but they had no vacancy. Her old pupilmaster, John Brightman, introduced Margaret to C. A. J. Bonner across the Square, and he offered her a place. She remained in those chambers until 1961 when she was given a junior ministerial post by Harold Macmillan; and her name was only finally taken down from the door in 1969.

III

In and Out of the Shadows

Throughout the changes and uncertainties in her legal career Margaret never forgot that her original reason for qualifying as a barrister was to turn her into a better parliamentarian. The Bar was yet another means to the end she had in sight, and she had made no secret of the fact to those people with whom she worked that her first love lay in politics. She had swiftly joined the Society of Conservative Lawyers, where, as always, she worked harder than most, and as a result became the first woman to sit on the executive committee, from 1955 to 1957. Many an hour was spent in her room at 5 New Square searching for a Parliamentary seat, and still more in gloom and despondency at her failure to find one.

In November 1954 there was a by-election in Orpington, another north Kent constituency, and she was short-listed but missed selection. It was the same story two years later in first Beckenham, then Ashford and again in Maidstone; and there were other constituencies, including Hemel Hempstead, where she was not even short-listed. It was not until the summer of 1959 that Margaret struck lucky: Sir John Crowther, Conservative MP for Finchley, announced that he did not intend to stand for the next general election. Margaret applied, and out of two hundred applicants for the seat, the names were finally whittled down until there was a short-list of three, from which Margaret Thatcher was selected as candidate.

It was 'sod's law': when Conservative associations are selecting their candidates, the one factor that very often tips the balance is whether a candidate is prepared to live in the constituency. For this reason, not knowing which seat would come up, Denis and Margaret had delayed buying a house. The situation was somewhat taken out of their hands, however, by the prospect of a sudden and very large rent increase at Swan Court, as a result of the Tory Government's effort to stop restricted rents killing the country's private housing stock. Rather than pay the increase, the Thatchers decided to buy, and settled on a house near Farnborough in Kent – due south of London. A few months later, Margaret won Finchley – due north.

It was as well that Margaret and Denis had found their house no further afield than Farnborough. The Finance and General Purposes Committee in Finchley had made just two stipulations to the selection committee for their choice of new candidate: he or she was to be under forty, and to live within a forty-mile radius of the seat. Dormers fell just within the limit. It was a four-bedroomed, detached house, set in almost an acre of garden, down a private residential cul-de-sac. The Thatchers had chosen it specially because it was within easy reach of the local hospital. At the end of the road there was a wood and a lake which froze over in the winter, and beyond open fields and farmland.

The neighbours were professional people, most of whom daily commuted to London from Bromley Station. Their wives stayed at home and looked after young children, drove the school runs, and kept house, like the majority of middle-class women in the 1950s. Margaret, who drove herself up to Lincoln's Inn every day, was very much the odd one out, and never very well known in the road. Mark and Carol, on the other hand, were very much a part of the community. Road life deputized for home life, and whenever one twin was missing at tea-time or bed-time, the other would be sent off in search on his or her bicycle.

The person cooking the tea would be the nanny. The original nanny who had been with the family in Swan Court moved down to Dormers too, but she subsequently married the gardener and left the Thatcher household for wedded bliss. A new nanny came in her place, a proprietorial old lady known as Abbey, who took over management of both children and house. Abbey was much loved by everyone and became an essential part of the Thatcher household. She remained with them for six years, until Mark and Carol went away to boarding school, and came back thereafter for many more years to look after the family during the school holidays. She was staid and comfortable, providing the twins with much of the warmth and physical affection that, fond though they were of their children, neither Denis nor Margaret found easy to communicate.

Margaret had never been demonstrative about her feelings. Her father once said of her, 'Margaret is ninety-nine point five per cent perfect; the half per cent is that she could be a little bit warmer.' She was formal with her children, Victorian almost; there were no nicknames, she called them 'dear' rather than 'darling', and never played with them for the sheer hell of it or went for a muddy walk in the woods.

Denis was equally formal and rather bluff. He insisted on manners and correct behaviour, would never allow the children to keep pets, wouldn't tolerate slippers and insisted on everything being neat and orderly in the house. The only games he played were ball games in the back garden, where he had set up a cricket net, bowling Mark balls to hit. Denis's first and abiding passion in life was rugby. He had been a first-class referee, although he never played in an international, and in the early days of his marriage he would go off most Saturday afternoons during the season to referee a match. A badly slipped disc unhappily put a stop to his refereeing career in about 1956. A sport he discovered that he could enjoy without upsetting either his back or his doctor, however, was golf, and he has been playing golf almost obsessively ever since.

Margaret, by contrast, has never had a hobby as such and, apart from the hockey she played at school, has not played any sport either. She lives for and thrives on work, and precious little sleep; and if the children had seen little of their mother when she was a barrister, they saw her still more infrequently after her adoption in Finchley.

Margaret threw herself once again whole-heartedly into the constituency; she went there at weekends, giving speeches, attending social functions and bazaars, visiting old people's homes and schools, driving herself across London in her old blue Ford Anglia, and not returning until late into the night. And the people in Finchley were impressed. Each of the thirteen branches in the constituency threw some sort of social function to introduce Margaret to their members, and there was one where the chairman had decided entrance should be free. When Margaret discovered that the chairman was planning to recoup expenses with a raffle, she said, 'I've got a better idea,' and taking a bottle of Scotch from the bar said, 'I'll Dutch auction it.' At the end of the evening, Dutch auction it she did. To the complete astonishment of everyone in the room, none of whom, until a couple of hours previously, she had ever seen in her life before, she called out their names. The price rose in six-penny (2½p) and shilling (5p) bids, and was finally knocked down to someone at £10 – and she didn't get a name wrong once.

Finchley was always considered a safe seat, but Margaret fought the election campaign as vigorously as she had fought Dartford. Thus in the general election of 8 October 1959, five days before her thirty-fourth birthday, with a majority of nearly three and a half thousand votes more than the previous incumbent, Margaret Thatcher at last became a Member of Parliament.

The twins were six, and played no part in the election campaign at all. The first they remembered of it was when they ran out of the house one day and found their mother's car sitting outside, strewn with blue ribbons and posters, and realized that something clearly quite exciting was in the air. They continued to play very little part in their mother's political life, and were never hawked about the streets canvassing. Margaret took Carol with her later that year to open a Christmas bazaar in the constituency, winning a large round of applause when she stood up and said, 'Before I got up on the platform my daughter said, "You won't make too long a speech, will you Mummy?"'

Parliament reconvened on 20 October and Margaret arrived at the House of Commons to be greeted by photographers anxious to snap the new session's intake. Jeremy Thorpe was one of the new arrivals, as were Christopher Chataway and Geoffrey Johnson Smith – both well-known television figures – and Judith Hart. Their pictures duly appeared in the next morning's press. The Conservative Party had retained their power in the general election, with Harold Macmillan as Prime Minister. He was a popular and respected figure in British politics, and someone whom Margaret particularly admired at the time. He increased the Conservative majority in the House in the 1959 election from fifty-eight seats to one hundred, riding on an economic boom with the slogan, 'You never had it so good.' Cartoonists hailed him 'Super Mac'.

Margaret arrived at the House of Commons brimming with confidence and eager to get on with the job. She had organized a secretary for herself, via the senior secretary in the Palace of Westminster who acts as an introduction agency. The girl that met her at the St Stephen's entrance that first day was Paddi Victor Smith, who was already working for another MP and had decided to take on a second to supplement her income.

Paddi, three years Margaret's junior, had fully expected she would have to show her new Member around, teach her the ropes, ease her in gradually; but not a bit of it. Mrs Thatcher knew where she was going and what she was doing right from the start, and her only concern was to get down to work. Arrangements were very primitive in the House of Commons in those days. Ordinary Members had no rooms of their own in which to work. There was a Lady Members' Room where they could leave belongings, but their base was essentially their secretary's desk and the secretaries themselves would be sharing maybe six or more to a room. There were no individual telephones, but a collection of booths lay at one end of the room and whenever a call came through, a steward would call out the name of whoever was wanted. Everyone, therefore, knew everyone else's business and the secretaries inevitably discussed the various MPs they worked for. They were all fascinated by the drive of this newest Member for Finchley, so unlike many of the other Members, who were rather shambolic, enjoyed their pleasures, and were content for things to happen at their own pace. Not Margaret – she made things happen with the same earnest dedication with which she had made everything else happen in her life. From day one, she worked hard and thoroughly, expecting the same of the people who worked for her. But demanding though she was, she was always equitable, fair, and, above all, immensely appreciative of the work she paid people to do. The secretaries who have worked for her over the years have all been completely and utterly devoted to her.

Margaret Thatcher has often been described as a 'lucky' politician, and she certainly does appear to be so, but as it has been pointed out, 'Luck is opportunity meeting readiness,' and when luck did strike, within weeks of her arrival in the House of Commons, she wasn't long in getting ready. At the beginning of every new session of Parliament, back-benchers put their names into a ballot to decide in what order Private Member's Bills should be introduced. There is never time in one session for more than the first five or six drawn out of the hat to be heard, so Members throw their names in without ever giving much thought to what Private Member's Bill they might introduce, should they be given the opportunity. Margaret was no exception. To her surprise she drew second, which left very little time for her to think of a pressing subject, gather support for the idea, do the necessary research, and come up with a sensible proposal and a good speech to send it on its way. Margaret finally settled on a Bill which would give the press access to local council meetings, which had operated hitherto by grace and favour rather than by right. It was a cunning choice, in that it attracted plenty of media coverage, and Margaret Thatcher has never been slow in realizing the value of the press.

This Bill, which she called Public Bodies (Admission of the Press to Meetings) Bill, thus became her maiden speech, delivered to the House one Friday afternoon. This was the custom with Private Member's Bills which were introduced at what was normally a rather quiet time in the Commons, when most of the Members had gone off early for the weekend. Such was the interest aroused by her Bill, however, that the House was very much better attended than usual for such a time.

Margaret stood up, didn't waffle about what an honour it was to represent Finchley as is the tradition of maiden speakers, but came straight to the point and stuck to it. She spoke for twenty-seven minutes – with not a single glance at her notes. Those present were unanimous in their praise for its delivery: 'a speech of front-bench quality', 'a fluency most of us would envy', and 'a maiden speech unlikely to be excelled by any of her contemporaries new to the 1959 Parliament'. There was not, however, unanimous praise for the content of Margaret Thatcher's speech and, after toing and froing and standing committees, the Bill reappeared as the Public Bodies (Admission to Meetings) Bill, altered to allow right of access not only to the press but to the public as well.

It was, nevertheless, quite a triumph, not least because Margaret had brought herself to the attention of Fleet Street, which has always been far more inclined to give space to women politicians than their male counterparts. Photographs of her appeared alongside human interest stories and women's page interviews. Margaret had always enjoyed publicity, and in the early days of her political career had assiduously kept cuttings from the local Dartford and London evening papers, which she once laid out all over the floor for a friend who came to visit. However, the novelty began to wear off once she entered Parliament, and she did not subscribe to the House of Commons cutting service, which for a fee provided MPs with every press reference that appeared about them. She contented herself with keeping the few articles she particularly liked, and let her father be the one who collected and kept any reference he could find.

Mr and Mrs Roberts came down to Dormers very seldom, while Margaret went up to Grantham with equal rarity, although she communicated frequently by telephone and letter. She went through a somewhat uncharitable and rather grand phase of her life, which didn't endear her to many of the people in Grantham. She found the town, and staying with her parents, quite frankly boring, and made it apparent that going there was a chore. If she met an old schoolmate in the street with a couple of children in tow, for example, she would say, 'I simply don't know how you manage. I have to have a nanny for mine.' This was something they of course would have dearly loved, but could not afford. It was some years before Margaret saw the political advantage to be reaped from her humble origins, and began to refer to Grantham with affection. For the time being it remained a boring country town, full of boring country people, and she was pleased to get back to London and the milieu of intelligent minds and more sophisticated lifestyles in which she now mixed.

While Parliament was sitting, Margaret's days were full. Occasionally she would undertake the school run before leaving for the House in the mornings. The only disadvantage about Abbey was that she didn't drive, but there were several other families in the neighbourhood with children at Baston School, the private school the Thatchers had chosen for the twins, and they had organized a lift rota. She would then go straight to the House, arriving soon after ten o'clock most days, and would not be home until ten and sometimes later in the evening. In the mornings she might attend committees, conduct interviews with constituents, wade through her correspondence, dictate letters and write speeches, which she was frequently invited to give in other people's constituencies. She very often took lunch in the canteen or the Members' Dining Room in the House; but wherever she was, she always ate with phenomenal speed, which her companions found impossible to match. Afternoons were normally spent in the Chamber, particularly for Prime Minister's Question Time; and when her turn came round for collecting the children from school in the afternoon, her secretary would very often be dispatched to do so. Squeezed into her diary somewhere amongst all these activities would be hairdressing appointments, where very often her secretary would have to go too, to take dictation while Margaret sat under the dryer. There were more sittings for a bronze head that was being cast (which now sits in the Thatchers' entrance hall in Flood Street, irreverently keeping Carol's woolly hats in shape), and it wasn't long before she was invited to sit on the panel of the Radio 4 programme, 'Any Questions'. Friday evenings took her to Finchley for 'surgery' once a month, when her constituents were able to meet and discuss their problems with her on an individual basis.

The result was there was scarcely a day when Margaret saw the children when they came in from school, and nine times out of ten they were fast asleep by the time she arrived home at night. But she did make it a golden rule to ring the twins at six o'clock every evening to say goodnight to them. Neither twin felt they missed out. They were very well and lovingly cared for by Abbey, who was a constant in their life, who provided the routine, and in many ways took the place of their mother. Mummy was a remote figure, who went off to work every day and some weekends and always seemed to be busy, either as a barrister or as an MP, and they accepted the status quo. In fact, Carol can remember going to her friends' homes and not being the most popular guest by asking, as she sat down to home-made chocolate cake in houses that smelled of furniture polish, what on earth their mothers *did* all day if they didn't go out to work. But if Margaret's children saw little of their mother, so too did her husband.

It was the general consensus of opinion in the secretaries' room at the House of Commons that it would not be long before Mr Thatcher would be off after another woman. Right from the start of their marriage, however, Margaret and Denis had recognized their priorities, and their separate careers came high on the list. Both believed passionately in the family unit, but as an abstract force rather than as a physical bond. Had there been a calamity at home which required their presence, they would have gone at once, and nothing would have been more important. But if life was running smoothly, they were quite content to have Abbey, whom they knew was solid and reliable, run the family. Margaret's attitude, which she instilled in her children from an early age, was 'Life doesn't revolve around your home. Home is a base from which you go out to do your own thing, whether it be work or some other sort of activity.'

As a child, going to stay with a schoolfriend who had the total reverse – a beautiful house with a swimming pool and tennis court, where everything revolved around the home – Carol occasionally used to feel her own home seemed a bit empty by comparison, and to regret the lack of that nucleus. Visits to Margaret's sister, Muriel, who now lived on a farm in Essex provoked the same reaction. With three children, the bustling family life revolved around the farmhouse kitchen where everyone sat down to three meals a day together and had a lot of fun and laughter. Family meals were rare in the Thatcher household. While Margaret spent evenings working late in the House or attending meetings, Denis went to business and club dinners, or ate with golfing friends.

Denis had always positively encouraged Margaret's political aspirations, although he wanted to take no part in them himself. He would appear on parade if needed, but he was far happier leading his own life and pursuing his own interests, which were in most ways vastly different from hers – as they still are. He smokes – she doesn't, and can't stand people around her doing so. He drinks far more than she, and is periodically rebuked. He is passionate about sport, most of which leaves her cold. Although she does utter the odd well-placed 'bloody' when provoked, his language is something that she has never grown entirely used to. Yet their basic philosophy is the same, and though it may never have been a passionate romance, the marriage has worked well over the years.

The one time in the year when the family was together for any length of time was on holiday, a break which in the early days Margaret used to enjoy. The family initially took just one holiday a year, with a traditional bucket and spade affair each summer at the seaside. One year, however, the summer holiday, which they had been planning to spend in Brittany was cancelled because seven-year-old Mark developed chicken pox. To make up for the disappointment, they all went skiing in Switzerland at Christmas instead. It was the most successful holiday the Thatchers had ever had, and thereafter for the next five years, two weeks skiing in Lenzerheid in Switzerland became a regular occurrence.

Summer holidays, taken for three weeks in August, were still spent by the sea, very often at Seaview in the Isle of Wight, where they joined up with other families who regularly spent their holidays there. For some years they rented a flat and did their own catering, for others they stayed in the Pier Hotel, a vast Victorian monstrosity built practically on the beach, which has since been pulled down. It was in the Pier during the August that Margaret had been adopted for Finchley, that the Thatchers were to meet some of their firmest friends, John Stebbings, a solicitor, and his wife, Tricia, now Sir John and Lady Stebbings. The word had gone out that 'the most super young barrister with her husband and twins' was staying in the hotel, whom the men were all dying to meet. One evening, down in the basement over the ironing board Tricia and her cousin Pam met another young mother who, when they all returned upstairs to join their husbands, announced herself as Margaret Thatcher. They all had dinner together that night, and so entranced were they by this 'super young barrister', that within a very short time John Stebbings was to be seen emerging from the sea with one small twin clutched in each hand, while Pam's husband Frank had been put on to Jaguar washing duty. They would picnic on the beach, swim, sail, and Denis would be detailed to take assorted children off for a ride in his speed boat. Occasionally there would be fancy-dress competitions for the children, and Margaret once devised an 'Invisible Man' costume for one of the boys, which involved wrapping him up in yards and yards of bandage, and won him first prize.

Margaret still found the company of men preferable to that of women, for, by and large, the former talked about the things that interested her. Not many people described her as a social snob, but there are few who deny she is an intellectual snob. Much of the time, the women she would meet socially were not up to her intellectual capacity. Friends say she used to be a difficult person to invite to a dinner party. She would talk even the men under the table, and the women just gave up.

The usual chatter of young mothers was unknown to her, and any discussions about children would be of a serious nature. The twins' education, for example, was something that occupied her mind, and she gave careful consideration to the schools they chose. Woe betide any headmaster or mistress that was not doing as he or she ought. The first to experience her wrath was the woman who ran the little kindergarten off Sloane Square in London, where the twins went each morning in the days that they lived in Swan Court. Each child was given a turn at being class leader, which involved handing round the pencils in the mornings and the like. Mark was made leader, but Carol never was. Margaret, ever conscious of the difficulty inherent in bringing up twins, thought this insensitive and monstrous, and went directly to the woman and told her so. She was to have a run-in with another of Carol's headmistresses, never leaving anyone in doubt about who was in charge of the Thatcher childrens' education.

It was a joint decision, however, to send the twins to boarding schools, and one made early on. Margaret was of the opinion that a good boarding school was better than any sort of day school, but that a good day school was better than an inferior boarding school. Denis had been public-school educated himself, at Mill Hill, and strongly believed that boys, at least, should go away to school. Given their fractured home life, it seemed sensible to send Carol away too. Margaret and Denis looked at several, putting the children's names down for more than one. But finally they settled for Mark on Belmont, the preparatory school for Mill Hill, followed by Harrow, and Queenswood near Hatfield for Carol.

Margaret was in no way an uninterested or neglectful mother, and Mark and Carol were never left with the impression that they were unimportant in her life. Far from it; she would fuss over them, worry about them, and be ever anxious that they were getting enough good nourishing food to eat. Carol went away to stay with a schoolfriend on one occasion, and came back pleased as punch because she had been given 'bubble and squeak' for supper. Margaret was horrified. 'That's the last time Carol is going to that house,' she said. 'I'm not having my daughter fed on left-overs.'

Denis used to say that the twins were spoilt. Outside observers suggest that it was Mark that was spoilt. Mark was very much Margaret's favourite, and she pampered him as a child, fetched and carried for him when she was at home and seldom corrected him. As a result he went through a phase of being an odious little boy. On the other hand, Carol, undoubtedly the brighter of the two and always something of a rebel by nature, had a much tougher time from her mother, but was invariably the favourite of their friends and acquaintances. The two had quite different personalities from the start, and were never especially close. Margaret herself always used to say that the twins were 'mortal enemies'. Carol was much more like her mother in character, as well as looks, while Mark was always very much more like his father. He used to imitate Denis, and amongst other characteristics that he adopted was the habit of picking up the telephone and saying 'Thatcher' with a loud bark. It was an unprepossessing way for an adult to answer the telephone in a private house, but for a child it was insufferable, as Margaret was wise to see, and she did eventually tell Mark to stop.

Margaret was determined to give her children the things that she never had as a child, including dancing lessons. While they were living in London, Carol and Mark attended Miss Vacani's famous dancing school in the Brompton Road. In Margaret's own childhood, dancing had been forbidden, and the first time she ever stepped on to a dance floor was at Oxford. When they were in Farnborough the twins had riding lessons at a nearby stables. Although there was a ban on household pets, dolls and furry bears were allowed including one bear that Margaret herself was particularly fond of, called Humphrey. On the twins' birthdays they had large tea parties with games in the garden, which, although their mother would be there, were usually prepared and organized by Abbey. It always astonished Margaret, however, that the twins should get so excited. On their tenth birthday, when asked if there was great excitement in the house, she replied, 'Yes, extraordinarily enough, there is. I thought they'd be too old to get excited about their birthday by now, but they do seem to be.' Never having really enjoyed a childhood herself, she found it difficult to understand her own children. On one occasion when Mark and Carol were both away at boarding school, Margaret went through their toy cupboard and gave away a vast amount of their toys, because she decided they had outgrown them. It never crossed her mind that they might have wanted some say in the matter, or might have been particularly attached to some creature that she was irrevocably passing on as jumble.

Mark was dispatched to boarding school in September 1961 at the age of eight, two years ahead of his sister, and just a month before Margaret was summoned to Number Ten by Harold Macmillan and given her first junior post in the Government.

In the two years that she had been in the House, she had involved herself in a number of controversial issues, including the Criminal Justice Bill calling for the reinstatement of corporal punishment. For this she was branded 'reactionary'. She had no time, as she made clear to the standing committee, for the bleeding hearts brigade whose prime concern was for the rehabilitation of the criminal. It was the Government's duty to protect the public from a new breed of criminal that had emerged in recent years, one 'who uses violence for the sake of violence,' who 'causes pain as a form of pleasure'. He should be given the choice between jail and the birch.

In the spring of 1961 she weighed in against Chancellor Selwyn Lloyd's Budget. She welcomed his reduction or surtax, 'because it will help married women teachers who want to return to the profession', but pointed out scathingly that middle-class wives in Britain who went out to work were still taxed more heavily than any of their European counterparts. She argued against the increased tax imposed on companies, because it would be inflationary, she said; and showed chapter and verse how the Inland Revenue already possessed powers that they were not using to tax capital gains.

Whenever Margaret made speeches in those days she would do all the research herself, which frequently involved long hours in the House of Commons Library. Homework was always something she had been good at – what she lacked in original thought, she made up for in study – and she never embarked on anything without being properly and thoroughly prepared. In addition to the work she put into the job, however, she did and does have the most extraordinary ability to see figures and memorize them, and to pick out and remember the relevant points in boring, weighty reports. She would write out her speeches in longhand, very often then transferring the headings on to a smaller piece of paper to have by her in note form. But she invariably delivered her speeches without the aid of her notes, except perhaps when she was quoting a string of figures which she might need to check. Margaret was a great one for blinding the Opposition with strings of figures and statistics, which no one was ever in a position to argue with since they seldom had the faintest idea whether she was right or wrong. Yet, for all her confidence in the course of a speech, she was always very nervous beforehand, and this is something that she still has not overcome.

Margaret used to have lunch with her sister Muriel periodically when she came to London for the day, and it was on just such an occasion that she received a message summoning her to Number Ten. She went into the Prime Minister's study with a hunch that she might be asked to propose or second the Loyal Address after the Queen's Speech for the opening of Parliament that was coming shortly. She left with the job of Parliamentary Secretary at the Ministry of Pensions – a junior Government post after just two years in the House.

Sadly, it was an achievement that her mother never lived to see. Beatrice Roberts had become ill with cancer, and had been in and out of hospital in Grantham for some months before she finally died at home in December 1960. Margaret was very upset: death is something that always shocks her very deeply, irrespective of whether it is someone she knows intimately or not. She becomes very quiet and pale, looking quite visibly shaken. But as with every other emotion, she very quickly masters herself, setting it at the back of her mind, as something that crying won't make any better. She is tolerant of other people breaking down, however, and is gifted at finding the right words to comfort. Carol, then eight, burst into tears when she was told the news of her grandmother's death. She remembers her mother very sweetly saying, 'Don't worry; Grandma will go to heaven.'

Margaret went up to Leicester, where her mother was cremated, there meeting Muriel who, in the later stages of their mother's illness, had been helping to nurse her. The Roberts were by this time living in the house they had bought at the end of the war, across the road from the shop, in North Parade.

Alfred Roberts stayed on there by himself after his wife's death, still making the occasional but increasingly infrequent trip to Kent to visit Margaret and Denis at Dormers. He was always a welcome visitor when he did come, particularly with his grandchildren who delighted in his tireless enthusiasm for playing snakes and ladders with them. Visits from Denis's family, on the other hand, were less welcome. Margaret found her in-laws a bit of a strain.

Life as a Parliamentary Secretary at the Ministry of Pensions involved a mixture of finance and welfare, and on the whole Margaret was happy there. She made her debut at the Despatch Box during Question Time on Pensions in November, and gave her first speech in a major debate as a Junior Minister the following March. The latter was in answer to a Labour motion of censure, deploring the Government's failure to raise pensions. Margaret had done her homework; she had worked out the comparative value of pensions in 1946, 1951, 1959 and 1962, the cost of living in smoking and non-smoking households, the total sums spent on pensions, the total sums raised in surtax and the comparative amounts spent on pensions abroad. She rose to her feet and hurled statistics into the stunned and silent air.

Junior ministers do a lot of hard work for very little glory and, tucked away in their ministries with the civil servants, are out of the general swim of life in the House. Margaret served under three different ministers at Pensions: John Boyd-Carpenter, Neil MacPherson and Richard Wood, and her most valuable discovery in three years at the job was the way in which the civil servants treated their minister. She observed how they tailored their advice to suit the man to whom they were proffering it; and giving only suggestions which they knew would please him. It was the beginning of a long-standing distrust of the civil service.

In April 1962, Margaret's secretary Paddi left to get married, and Diana Powell, who shared the same room in the House of Commons, took her place. By this time Paddi had been working full-time for Mrs Thatcher, having found there simply weren't enough hours in the day for two MPs, particularly when one worked at Margaret's pace. Diana had been working part-time for Megan Lloyd George, filling in with Mrs T – as she called her – when Paddi was on holiday, so they already knew each other to some extent. Diana was ten years older than Margaret, and remained with her for seven years. They had a perfect working relationship; Diana Powell is one of the few people who has been able to extract a sense of humour from Mrs Thatcher; and one of the many people who has come away devoted to her.

Paddi was married in the Church of the Sacred Heart at Henley-on-Thames. Her groom was John Lilley, who worked in the Government Statistical Service at the Department of Trade; and one of her bridesmaids was to have been Carol Thatcher. Carol, however, was so overcome by excitement and nerves that she made herself ill and had to stay at home. To make up for the disappointment, Carol was asked to be a godmother when their daughter, Rosemary, was born one year later.

The next two years were politically uncertain and difficult. Harold Macmillan, ' Super Mac', was reaping the effects amongst other things of excessive Government spending, in which he had gone against the advice of his Chancellor, Peter Thorneycroft, who had thus resigned his office. The Britain that had never had it so good, was now suffering the reverse: the economy had begun to slump, unemployment had risen; and the Prime Minister, having enjoyed a popularity rating of seventy-nine per cent in 1960, was now held to be the most unpopular Prime Minister since Neville Chamberlain was attacked for 'appeasing' Hitler in the Munich Agreement of 1938. In an attempt to regain favour, he gave in to members of the Party who were calling for an increase in Government spending, and in order to get the measures accepted by his colleagues in Cabinet who disagreed, engaged in a massive reshuffle, which became known as 'the July Massacre'.

Macmillan had further gone out on a limb over the European Economic Community, formed in 1955, to which he had submitted Britain's first application to join. Leader of the Opposition, Hugh Gaitskell, had spoken vehemently against the proposal. Such a move, he declared at the Labour Party Conference in October 1962, would go against a thousand years of British history – providing the perfect cue for Home Secretary, R.A. Butler, at the Conservative Party Conference the following week. 'For them a thousand years of history books,' he proclaimed. 'For us the future.' It was a good line, in a good speech, and the Government took the Conference with them. But early in 1963, President de Gaulle of France dealt a crushing blow to both Macmillan and his Government when he voted against Britain's entry to the Common Market.

Still more embarrassment to the Tories came with a spate of security scandals: Blake, Lonsdale and Vassall were soon followed by the case that really shook the Government to its roots – Profumo. In the early summer of 1963 John Profumo, a Minister at the War Office, was accused of having had an affair with the prostitute Christine Keeler, who had a tenuous connection with the Russian Embassy. Mr Profumo publicly denied the affair in the House of Commons, and Macmillan duly accepted his word. Days later, John Profumo admitted that he had lied to the House, and resigned his post. The wolves began to bay for blood and a strong 'Macmillan must go' movement sprung into action on the Tory back-benches. On the eve of the Conservative Party Conference in Blackpool that October, the matter resolved itself when Harold Macmillan became seriously ill and resigned as Leader.

The Conference was thrown into confusion, and a number of contenders for the leadership stepped forward. The most prominent of these were Home Secretary, 'Rab' Butler, Chancellor of the Exchequer, Reginald Maudling, and Lord President of the Council, Lord Hailsham, who announced that he intended to forfeit his title and revert to Quintin Hogg. One other contender with a lot of support from the delegates (and whom Macmillan favoured for that very reason), if not so much from the Government, was the Foreign Secretary, the Earl of Home.

Margaret supported Rab Butler, but Macmillan felt that he was neither tough enough for the job, nor commanded sufficient support from within the Party, and it was his wish that prevailed. The system of choosing a Leader of the Tory Party at that time was a totally undemocratic process known as 'emergence'. The current Leader took soundings in Cabinet about whom its members would most like to see replace him, and the man with the greatest support won. Butler had a certain amount of support in Cabinet, and could have put up a fight and possibly become Leader, but for the sake of the party unity he backed down and accepted Macmillan's choice.

Thus, on 18 October 1963, Lord Home became Leader of the Party and Prime Minister. He, too, put aside his title and was acceptably renamed Sir Alec Douglas-Home, by virtue of the legislation brought in just three months previously to enable Labour acolyte Anthony Wedgwood Benn to revert from Lord Stansgate into a commoner.

Less than a year after he became Prime Minister, Sir Alec decided to call a general election. Following the death of Hugh Gaitskell, in January 1963, the Labour Party had a new leader, Harold Wilson. Wilson was a brilliant political manipulator, who promised to take Britain out of the decline of thirteen years of Tory rule, 'thirteen wasted years', and bring to its people the fruits of the scientific age, of technology, and enlightened leadership. And in the election of October 1964, Harold Wilson scraped home with a Labour lead of just four seats in the House of Commons, and became the new Prime Minister of Britain.

The election campaign had been great fun up in Finchley, but Margaret did not enjoy a walkover as in 1959. This time local issues were in earnest. There was trouble at the golf club: people had been refused entry because they stated on their entrance forms that they were Jewish. The Liberals in the constituency made great capital out of this, stirring up the sizeable Jewish community in Finchley and, with a candidate by the name of John Pardoe, were set to pose a serious threat to Margaret's majority.

Margaret Roberts with her sister, Muriel, four years her senior. Margaret was a pretty, neat little girl, invariably dressed in clothes made by her mother, an expert seamstress

The little grocer's shop in Grantham where Margaret Roberts was born in 1925, and where she spent her childhood

Margaret Roberts (*back row, extreme left*) with her class at Kesteven and Grantham Girls School

Dorothy Gillies (*right*) with a colleague. This strong-minded lady became headmistress of Kesteven in 1939, and was to prove a formidable, yet ultimately unsuccessful, opponent to Margaret Roberts' ambitions

Miss Kay (*centre*), the science mistress at Kesteven who inspired Margaret Roberts to specialize in chemistry in the VIth form, and to read the subject at Somerville College, Oxford

Margaret with her parents and her sister, Muriel. This photograph was taken in 1943, the year that Alfred Roberts served as Mayor of Grantham

Somerville matriculation photograph for 1943. Margaret Roberts is in the back row, fifth from the right

Margaret in October 1951, the prospective Conservative Parliamentary candidate for Dartford. She had fought the seat unsuccessfully in the 1950 election, and although in 1951 the Conservatives won nationally, she was never to become Member for Dartford

Margaret Roberts talking to the dustmen of Dartford in her election campaign in October 1951. She found electioneering a difficult task, but realized that it was essential. In the many election campaigns of her political life, she has developed into an expert canvasser, as witness her performance in the 1983 general election

The marriage of Margaret Roberts to Denis Thatcher in London in December 1951

The first Mrs Margaret Thatcher: Lady Hickman in a photograph taken at her home

Margaret Thatcher proudly holding her twins, Mark and Carol, born in August 1953

Margaret with Denis and the twins in 1959. In the summer of that year, she had been selected as the Conservative candidate for Finchley, and her Parliamentary career was about to take off

One of Margaret Thatcher's few recreations: skiing in Switzerland in 1962

Home life: (*above*) One of Margaret's favourite occupations, redecorating the flat at Swan Court, aided and abetted by Denis; (*below*) Margaret, newly appointed joint Parliamentary Secretary to the Ministry of Pensions, reading with her eight-year-old children

Margaret Thatcher attending the wedding of Paddi Victor Smith at Henley in April 1962. She is seen here with Bert Blatch, chairman of the Finchley Conservative Association, Mrs Blatch, and Paddi's successor as her secretary, Diana Powell. The one person unable to attend the ceremony was Carol, chosen to be a bridesmaid, but struck down by nerves

Margaret Thatcher arriving at the House of Commons in October 1961, ready to take up her appointment as a junior minister

It wasn't the first time the Liberals had caused concern in Finchley. When Margaret had come before the selection committee as one of twenty-one potential candidates back in the summer of 1958, the Tories were in trouble on the Council, where they were rapidly losing seats to the Liberals. Each candidate had been asked how they would stop the rot. Margaret was the only one who came up with the impressive answer: 'There's only one way, you've got to go out on to the streets and fight them, and be Conservative, and you will win in the end.' And that, six years later, was precisely what she did do.

The Party workers in Finchley have always found Margaret hectic to keep up with when she is canvassing. She whizzes up and down streets like greased lightning, diving into people's homes, sitting down for a moment, leaping to her feet, lunging at a hand here or a wheelchair there, and stopping to talk to shopkeepers about their prices. Much of the time she would have her secretary Diana for company on these sorties. They would go and have lunch in the pub' over a few beers with Margaret's agent, Roy Langston, and other members of the committee, including Bert Blatch, then chairman of the association, future chairmen, Ron Thurlow and John Tiplady, and big bearded Vic Usher. Then there would be more hands to shake, more meetings to address, and more faces to recall.

One of Margaret's greatest assets in politics has been her ability to remember faces and names. It is a particularly feminine gift, and one that she has in abundance. Her performance in the Dutch auction at the social evening soon after her adoption in Finchley was no fluke. Margaret remembers not only the face and the name, but also whether they have an arthritic knee, a house with rising damp, or a daughter in South Africa. Moreover this does not apply only to constituents whose votes she is after. She knows the names, and the names and particulars of the spouses, of more members of her Party in the House of Commons than any previous Leader.

Another peculiarly feminine characteristic is her concern that people should have enough to eat. Anyone coming to her house was – and still is – always provided with sustenance of some sort or another, even if it was nothing more exotic than a packet of chocolate biscuits or a slice of Fullers Walnut Cake, which she always kept on hand in her larder. The compulsion to feed people went further than her own circle of acquaintances. Margaret Thatcher has inherited from her father the fundamental belief that people should stand on their own two feet and not be molly-coddled by the state from birth to death, but she does believe quite genuinely in charity, and puts her money where her mouth is. For example, Margaret came to hear about one woman in Finchley, who had suffered a series of mental breakdowns and was going through a very tough period in her life. Quite anonymously, Margaret arranged for food parcels to be sent to this woman, paid for out of her own pocket.

Most of the routine work of Members in the House of Commons is to do with the constituency: dealing with people's problems over housing, schooling and the state of the pavement outside their front door. Occasionally people write wanting their MP to make an appeal on their behalf for children who are in trouble with the law or for husbands who can't find work. Margaret Thatcher had to deal with the case of a boy who wanted to be a postman, but was being turned down on the grounds that he had a police record, earned for stealing a milk bottle when he was ten years old. Another case, of a more serious nature, involved a constituent called Gerald Brooke, a lecturer in Russian at the Holborn College of Law, Languages and Commerce, who had been arrested by the KGB in Moscow early in 1965 and imprisoned on a spying charge. The Russians would not allow the British consul to see Brooke and refused to detail the nature of the charges against him. Margaret leapt to his aid, pestered the Foreign Office to take action, led a protest in the House over the Russians' behaviour, and in due course, although by no means immediately, Brooke was released. This was an exceptional case, and one which inevitably earned her a degree of kudos and publicity, but the unglamorous, routine welfare side of her job was something that Margaret Thatcher enjoyed. Even those constituents who detest her politics and would never vote for her, do admit that she has always been a very good constituency MP.

In 1965 there was another change of leadership in the Conservative Party. Sir Alec Douglas-Home had neither the ambition nor the stomach for leadership, particularly at a time when Harold Wilson, at the head of the Labour Government, was gaining so much ground with the electorate. A number of Tory MPs began to say out loud that Sir Alec's image was not the right one to counter Wilson, and he duly stepped down. Before doing so, however, he introduced a new system for choosing the Party Leader, which hitherto had operated by selection rather than by formal election. The procedure he created was a two-tier ballot: in order for a contestant to win the first round, he had to have a lead of fifteen per cent over his nearest rival. If no one was sufficiently ahead of the field, then there would be a second ballot, for which new candidates could put their names forward.

The three contenders that stood for election in July 1965 were Edward Heath, former Minister for Labour and Lord Privy Seal in charge of Britain's application to join the EEC, Reginald Maudling, former Chancellor of the Exchequer, and Enoch Powell, who had been Minister of Health. Margaret cast her vote for Ted Heath and, although he didn't get a clear fifteen per cent lead over the other two, Maudling and Powell conceded victory. There was no second ballot, and Ted Heath became Leader of the Conservative Party.

Like Margaret, Ted Heath was a product of the grammar school, and there was much comment in the newspapers about this being the first time that the Conservative Party had not had a member of the Establishment at its helm. Like Margaret, he had also gone to Oxford, albeit on a scholarship, and he too had been President of the Oxford University Conservative Association. Ted Heath was also a loner; he possessed a wealth of talents, excelling in everything he turned his hand to – from sailing to conducting, from writing to politics – and yet his great failing was an inability to communicate with people, either individuals or the public. This was made even more evident by the way he spoke, with an accent which sounded phoney, like the proverbial plum in his mouth.

They were never close friends, but Margaret liked Ted, and would often say how good he had been to her. Over the next five years he put her into a variety of shadow ministries, giving her an opportunity to see the working of far more departments, and their individual problems, than the average politician experiences in fifteen years. She began at the Ministry of Housing and Land in October 1965, having nursed Pensions the while. Five months later, in March 1966, she was moved to the Treasury, where she became Number Two spokesman. In October 1967 she was brought into the Shadow Cabinet, as Shadow Minister of Power, and in October of the following year, Margaret became Shadow Minister of Education.

Life at home during that time also went through a series of changes. Carol went away to boarding school in the autumn of 1963, so Dormers was bereft of children during term time. With the increase in Margaret's work load over the next couple of years, Kent seemed an excessively long way to travel home every night. She had, furthermore, just suffered a bout of pneumonia, and decided that if she was going to carry on she would have to take a flat in London. Farnborough, moreover, had always been the wrong side of London for Finchley, and was rapidly losing its charm. During the years the Thatchers had lived there, the village they had known had vanished and the area was being considerably built up. So Denis and Margaret began to look around for another house in Kent, meanwhile buying a London flat in Westminster Gardens, a large mansion block in Marsham Street not far from the House of Commons. It was to be two years, however, before they found the perfect replacement in Kent. In the meantime they rented a cottage in good golfing country in Horsmonden, near Tunbridge Wells, which they used for weekends and school holidays.

Margaret generally enjoyed the constitution of an ox, but did succumb to the occasional human condition. She fainted in the House once; she caught mumps from the twins; and during her first ten years in Parliament, she suffered quite acutely at times from hay fever. She also suffered from bad posture. She would walk, as to some extent she still does, with one shoulder leading. Diana Powell's mother, a physical training teacher, attempted to correct this. Margaret was quite receptive to her advice, trying hard to improve her walk, but it was a habit she had adopted as a child, and it proved difficult to lose. Diana would constantly have to remind her to stand properly – and to stop scratching her eyes when the hay fever was bad.

But while Margaret kept good health, her father, who had been fit all his life, fell ill with bronchitis. After one particularly fierce attack he had been unable to get downstairs to the telephone. The minute she heard, Margaret left for Grantham and, pulling all her Parliamentary strings, organized a second telephone to be installed by his bed, so that he would always be able to telephone for help if he needed it again.

Old Alf Roberts was well into his seventies by this time, still living in the house across the road from the shop. Then suddenly, to everyone's surprise, he announced that he was getting married again. His bride was Cicely Hubbard, a fellow Methodist and mother of four grown-up children, whose husband, a farmer, had been killed in a motoring accident some years before. She lived in the little village of Eaton, ten miles or so out of Grantham. This had been one of the places where Mr Roberts had so often preached, and as they were both Methodists, this was how they had first met. Cissie was a small, gentle mouse of a woman, with no pretensions of any sort. In 1965 she and Alfred were married, and lived thereafter in his house in North Parade.

That same year the Thatcher family firm was taken over by Castrol, which Denis joined as a director. Within months Castrol was in turn taken over by the large Scottish company, Burmah Oil, and Denis again found himself on the board. It was a welcome step financially, and Denis now drove around in a smart Daimler with the registration DT3.

In the same year, the Thatchers moved out of their little rented cottage in Horsmonden and into a house they had bought called The Mount, Lamberhurst. It was a large, imposing house with magnificent views set in three acres of garden, with its own driveway, a grass tennis court and a swimming pool. A further attraction was that it was close to the golf course at Lamberhurst, of which Denis had grown rather fond. Despite these attractions, it was never altogether a wise buy. Mark and Carol were away at school for almost nine months of the year, and The Mount was really a house which cried out for a large live-in family, with a stack of coats and Wellington boots at the back door, and muddy paw prints all over the kitchen floor. But the Thatchers were essentially suburban people, with suburban tastes. Their houses were immaculately neat and tidy, with no pets allowed by order of Denis, and no comfortable chaos. Mark and Carol were the only people who played on the tennis court and, for the most part, it was only they who swam in the pool. Denis always complained that it was freezing, and Margaret didn't much like what it did to her hair-do. While Denis loved the country and longed for the chance to escape from London, he liked his country to be ordered. Margaret had never much liked the great outdoors, and found every excuse to be busy inside: decorating, cooking, dressmaking or getting on with the ever-increasing load of political work.

By March 1966, the country entered into the second general election campaign in two years. Harold Wilson, a man convincing to many and a great orator, was riding the crest of the wave; new technology was going to sweep the board, and bring a new bright and prosperous future to Britain. Tory popularity was low, and with the slogan, 'You know Labour Works', the Socialists had a head start in the race for the polls. Margaret was returned safe and sound in Finchley, but the result overall was a victory for Labour, returned to power with a much improved majority of ninety-seven seats. Most Conservatives had known from the start that they didn't stand a chance. It was a contest of economic mud-slinging. Labour accused the previous Tory Chancellor, Reginald Maudling, of being responsible for a £750 million deficit in the balance of payments, which for argument's sake, was rounded up to £800 million. Their own economic record was looking good. Although incomes had gone up, productivity had not, but these were not the sort of facts people wanted to hear. The Tory Manifesto 'Action not Words' fell on deaf ears; particularly when the Chancellor, Jim Callaghan, was promising that personal income tax would not be raised in the forthcoming Budget.

The Chancellor was true to his word. What he did instead, however, in a desperate bid to collect the vital revenue he needed without breaking his election pledge, was to introduce a tax on employers called Selective Employment Tax. Employers would automatically pay a fixed sum per employee on the pay roll, which six months later would be paid back as was, be paid back with a bonus, or not be paid back at all, depending upon the nature of the industry the employer was operating.

Even before Parliament was reconvened, Margaret was on her way to the Treasury to work under Iain Macleod, as shadow spokesman, in preparing an attack on the proposed Bill. Margaret went away and did her homework, and three weeks later she returned to the House for the Budget debate. She listened patiently as John Diamond, the Chief Secretary to the Treasury, extolled the workings and wonders of the proposed SET. Then very quietly she rose to her feet, and proceeded to pour such scorn on Mr Diamond and his tax which involved so much giving and taking to get right back to the place they both began from. 'Oh that Gilbert and Sullivan should be living at this hour,' she cried, warming to her theme, 'This is sheer cock-eyed lunacy, absolute lunacy. I really think the Chancellor needs a woman at the Treasury.' She then proceeded to announce, while jaws dropped in astonishment around her, that she had read every Budget speech and every Finance Bill since 1946, and that not even the most grasping Chancellor had failed to make at least one minor concession on the social side. Not, that was, until Chancellor Callaghan.

It was a memorable speech, which won her some much deserved praise, and left poor Mr Diamond with little choice but to crawl away under a stone, where he would have been well advised to stay, for the lady was not through. She weighed into the tax yet again in her speech at the Tory Party Conference in Blackpool later in the year, with the same scathing ferocity, earning her a standing ovation. When Selective Employment Tax was introduced in the autumn, it was not without a great many amendments.

Margaret found making speeches of this kind, particularly in the House where she could see the sparks fly, the most exhilarating and exciting part of the job. Insults in the corridor or out in the street would have cut her to the core, but insults in the House fell off her like water off a duck's back. She had the masculine ability of being unemotional, of being able to disassociate the insult from the man, which all successful politicians must have, and once out of the Chamber of being able to go and chat over a drink in the bar like old friends.

Margaret had one or two friends on the opposite side of the fence, including the late John Mackintosh, the Labour MP for Berwick and East Lothian, who had frequently sought out her company during their days in obscurity on the back-benches. Now on the opposition front-bench, she was regarded as a good sparring partner, and her opposite number on the Labour side would sometimes telephone to let Margaret know what he was going to say in his speech, so that she might be able to go prepared.

There were occasions, on the other hand, when Margaret had not much more than an hour's notice that she was going to have to speak at all. She might be told at lunch-time that she had to make the first speech of the afternoon because someone was ill. She never panicked, she would say, 'I must just have ten minutes', and would collect her thoughts, jot down a few notes on the back of an envelope or a piece of paper, and turn out a perfectly competent speech.

Margaret never visibly panicked or flapped about anything, either political or domestic. Having heeded the words her grandmother doubtless taught, she would not cry over spilt milk, but quickly set about mopping it up. The first time she went to America, for example: it was an English Speaking Union lecture tour, and she was very excited to be going. She was no seasoned traveller. The first time she had been abroad in her life was on honeymoon, and the furthest she had travelled since then was Switzerland, on their family skiing trips. Denis and her secretary Diana had come to see her off, and they had all arrived at Heathrow Airport in plenty of time. They checked into Terminal Three, when, looking over her documents, Margaret suddenly discovered that her passport was out of date. Diana had asked her some weeks previously if it was all right, and Margaret had said it was, so she had nobody to blame but herself, and didn't blame anybody else. She didn't even swear. Denis got a little excited; Margaret simply exclaimed, 'How stupid I am' and, leaping into a taxi with Diana, drove back into London to the Passport Office in Petty France. The airport meantime telephoned to say she was on her way, so the Passport Office was expecting her, and she was in and out with a new stamp on her passport in under half an hour; and miraculously caught her plane.

Margaret's crack during her speech in the Budget debate about the Chancellor needing a woman at the Treasury was pure rhetoric, but it did belie her real ambition in politics at that time – to be the first woman Chancellor of the Exchequer. It was a standing joke with Diana Powell. 'Of course, when I'm Chancellor...' she would say. The ambition and the joke, however, lasted longer than that particular stay at the Treasury. After twenty months, which she enjoyed more than any other – not least because of the man she had been working under – she was moved on to the Opposition Ministry of Fuel and Power. She had found Iain Macleod a joy to work with, and admired his convictions.

She arrived in 1967 to shadow the Ministry of Fuel and Power just in time to take part in the debate on the Aberfan disaster. An enormous slag-heap dominating the tiny Welsh mining village became dislodged and buried the small village school, killing one hundred and sixteen children and twenty-eight adults. Margaret was deeply shocked. 'I remember that mother,' she said, 'who had sent her son off to school after a bit of a row. It was one of those mornings when everyone was a bit on edge, and they hadn't parted friends. Ever afterwards she'll be haunted by the thought of him going off to his death like that.'

The Labour Minister she shadowed at Fuel and Power was Richard Marsh, another new boy to the 1959 Parliament, who coincidentally had drawn first in the Private Member's Bill ballot, in which she had drawn second. And by an even greater coincidence, he then moved to the Ministry of Transport, where Margaret soon followed.

At the Party Conference in October 1968, the same month in which she moved to Transport, Margaret was invited to give the annual lecture at the Conservative Political Centre's meeting. This is a branch of the Conservative Party Organization, responsible for passing on high thoughts and ideals from the top of the Party to those at the bottom, and the invitation to address them is considered something of an accolade. Margaret followed in the footsteps of such illustrious names as Rab Butler, Quintin Hogg, and her political mentor, Sir Edward Boyle.

Margaret's lecture was entitled, 'What's Wrong with Politics', and was a statement of her fundamental beliefs which have scarcely changed a jot in the last fifteen years. What was wrong with politics she averred, was too much Government interference in people's lives, too much bureaucracy. 'People should be encouraged if necessary by taxation incentives to make increasing provision for themselves out of their own resources,' she declared. She abhorred Harold Wilson's prices and incomes policy, and 'the totally unacceptable notion that the Government shall have the power to fix which wages and salaries should increase.' 'There is nothing wrong with people wanting larger incomes,' she said. 'It would seem a worthy objective for men and women to wish to raise the standard of living for their families and to give them greater opportunities than they themselves had. . . . What is wrong is that people should want more without giving anything in return.' Margaret then went on to quote the philosopher, John Stuart Mill: 'The only freedom which deserves the name is that of pursuing our own good in our own way so long as we do not deprive others of theirs, or impede their efforts to obtain it. . . . Mankind are greater gainers by suffering each other to live as seems good to themselves than by compelling each to live as seems good to the rest.' 'No great party can survive,' she concluded, 'except on the basis of firm beliefs about what it wants to do. It is not enough to have reluctant support. We want people's enthusiasm as well.'

Margaret's political career was gathering momentum, but she never shone like a super nova. She was recognized as being able and hard working, yet she was not a particularly dazzling speaker, and when invitations came they would often be for the sheer novelty of having a woman, and there weren't many around. The Conservative Party was still very much of a male preserve in the House of Commons, and there were a great many Members who thought that was just the way it should be. Her most notable predecessor, Florence Horsburgh, blazed the trail, but she was much older than Margaret, and never noted for her femininity.

Margaret, on the other hand, made a concerted effort to retain her femininity. She loved clothes, and was always immensely keen to show off any new purchase. In those days she could and did shop anywhere, and most of her clothes were bought off the peg. Some, however, were cast-offs from her sister Muriel, who took one dress size larger than Margaret, and would always pass on anything which she thought might suit her. Margaret could then alter or adapt garments in no time. And if she didn't want something for herself, she would pass it on to her secretary Diana, who was much the same size and shape.

Margaret has never had any compunction about wearing other people's belongings, or indeed lending her own. She herself had very little jewellery: a double string of cultured pearls which Denis gave her when the twins were born, a few costume brooches, and artificial pearl earrings. Once, when she was going to a reception at Canada House, she was wearing a black dress and didn't like the look of anything she had of her own against it. Diana therefore suggested she might borrow some jade that she had been given for her twenty-first birthday, knowing how fond she was of green. Margaret duly went off adorned with her secretary's jade and diamond earrings, with a matching necklace and brooch.

On another occasion, it was Diana who was in need. She was going off on a boat trip to Norway and needed an anorak. 'Don't think of buying one,' said Margaret as soon as she heard, 'borrow mine.' And Diana was dispatched with a very expensive pale blue anorak which Margaret normally wore skiing at Christmas.

In addition to her Parliamentary work, Margaret was always punctilious about her children, writing to them every week, turning up to speech days and other school events, and trying to organize trips round the school holidays. Mark had gone to Harrow at thirteen, where he shone at sport, particularly racquets, but not much else. Margaret was very concerned before he went that Mark should be no different from the other boys. She went to consult with the Stebbings, whose son, Richard, was at Harrow, to know how much pocket money he should be given. But for all her efforts, Mark had a tendency to behave as though his mother was already Prime Minister. He was not enormously popular, and generally considered to be rather pompous.

Pomposity was a feature of Mark from a very tender age. Although Margaret had stopped him answering the telephone with his surname, she hadn't gone far enough. There was an occasion when she had taken both the children to visit an old friend, who had children of much the same age as the Thatchers. While the mothers talked indoors, the children all played together in the sandpit outside. When the time came to leave Mark, dressed as he invariably was like Little Lord Fauntleroy, didn't volunteer any farewells to his host in the sandpit. When instructed to do so by his mother, he regarded scathingly this child who looked appropriately grubby for the end of a day in the garden, and said, 'Oh no Mummy, I couldn't possibly say goodbye to someone so scruffy.'

Carol had always been a much more sympathetic character; much stronger, and far less inclined to drop her mother's name. At the age of twelve, she used to say, 'When I am grown up I shall leave home as soon as I can.' She was rebellious and not always very popular with the staff at her school, but well liked by her peers. At sixteen she left Queenswood, where Margaret had never much cared for the headmistress, and went to study for 'A' Levels at St Paul's School for Girls in London.

A month after Carol started at St Paul's, Margaret was moved by Ted Heath from Transport to become Shadow Minister for Education. Her philosophy about schooling and where her own children went to school suddenly became public knowledge. The world of education was in a volatile state; there was student unrest in almost every university, and growing concern over falling standards in schools. The Labour Government had come into power in 1965 on the promise to 'eliminate selection and separatism in secondary education'. In their 1966 Manifesto they had pledged 'to abolish the 11-plus – that barrier to educational opportunity', and to reorganize secondary education on comprehensive lines. Although they hadn't had the money to implement much change in the intervening years, most local authorities had already submitted long-term plans of how their schools should be reorganized. By October 1969, when Margaret came to the job, the current Secretary of State for Education, Edward Short, was intent on forcing unwilling authorities to submit their plans by law with a Compulsory Comprehensives Bill.

Margaret, following Sir Edward Boyle in the shadow ministry, made it clear that the Tories would fight Short's Bill tooth and nail; that she personally had nothing against such schemes in some circumstances. 'Indeed I know many parents prefer them,' she said on her first day. 'I certainly don't propose to unscramble plans that are already in existence. I am not a reactionary.' But as an ex-grammar-school girl herself, she was the last person to sit back and let anyone destroy the very system that had given her the opportunity to advance in life. Sir Edward Boyle, Eton-educated, had not felt so passionately and had upset a great many in the Party by appearing to be almost agreeable to Labour's scheme. He was thus reshuffled out of Shadow Education by his ex-grammar-school Leader, and went off to become Vice Chancellor of Leeds University. Margaret was left with the task of preparing the Conservative election programme on education.

There was as yet no date for an election, but the Labour Government had been going through some troubled times. The economy had been going steadily downhill since they took office, and Harold Wilson had finally been forced to give in to pressure to devalue the pound. The power of the unions meanwhile had been inexorably on the increase, and Wilson's attempt to curb that power, by proposing legislation to make the strike vote secret, had been firmly squashed by his own party.

Confidence was temporarily restored as the effects of devaluation began to show so, while the sun was shining in June 1970 and the country was feeling good, he called a general election. But the rot ran deeper than the sunshine, and shortly before polling day the Government had to release figures which showed that the balance of trade was in the red, that unemployment had risen, and the number of working hours lost by strikes had set a new record.

Ted Heath and the Tory Party offered a better deal; the terms of which had been worked out one weekend in February when the Shadow Cabinet and senior officials from Tory Central Office met at the Selsdon Park Hotel, in Croydon. The outcome was a determination to get away from state intervention and return to a state of free enterprise.

Harold Wilson seized on the name and christened Ted Heath 'Selsdon Man', like some archaeological find, who embodied the bad old days of Tory rule, of class, of greed and of ineffective government. But the smear failed to stick. The package Ted Heath promised was a clean break with the past, a 'quiet revolution' with no more unwieldy bureaucracy, no more Government-imposed wage freezes, and no more Socialist interference in people's lives. 'Stand on your own two feet,' was the slogan with which he went to the polls, and the country responded.

It was a bizarre campaign, with the opinion polls showing Labour firmly ahead of the Tories. Yet when the votes were cast, it was the Conservatives who won by a majority of thirty seats, and Ted Heath became Prime Minister.

Margaret retained her portfolio at Education, and thus became the second woman in the history of the Conservative Party to be a full Cabinet Minister. The first was a predecessor at the Ministry of Education, the late Florence Horsburgh, 'The face that sank a thousand scholarships,' as she had been tagged for her unpopular measures during the time that she held the post in Winston Churchill's 1951–5 Government.

Tragically, Margaret's father, the man who had been the single greatest influence in her life, her mentor and guide up the ladder from Grantham to Westminster, never lived to see the election. Alfred Roberts died in 1970, just a few months before she became a member of the Government. He had been ill for some time, and although Margaret realized he couldn't go on indefinitely, the blow was nonetheless devastating to her. He died in his bed at home in North Parade: Muriel had telephoned with the news and spoke to Carol, who in turn told her mother when she came home.

Margaret went straight up to Grantham, where Alf was cremated and his ashes buried in the garden of remembrance. Margaret missed her father enormously. She refers to him as 'Pa' nowadays, not 'Daddy', and still mentions him quite frequently. It is a great regret in her life that he never lived to see her become a Cabinet Minister, or indeed Prime Minister. But the day she first stepped into Number Ten as premier nine years later, she paid tribute to him.

'He brought me up to believe all the things I do believe, and they're the values on which I fought the election,' she said. 'It's passionately interesting to me that the things I learned in a small town, in a very modest home, are just the things that I believe have won the election . . . I owe almost everything to my father.'

Shortly after Alf Roberts' death, Margaret's secretary Diana left. Her elderly father, whom she had been looking after for some years, also died. At fifty-five, having spent all her working life in London, she decided to sell the family home in Oxted, from which she had been commuting at some pains, and go to live in Brighton. It was a difficult decision, but she had been with Mrs T for seven years, and devoted though she was to her, she was sick to death of London.

With Margaret as a Minister all sorts of changes occurred to the Thatcher household. The most dramatic of these was their housing arrangements. Margaret felt she simply couldn't cope with a large country house any longer, and so The Mount was sold. In place of the flat in Westminster Gardens, they bought a terraced house at 19 Flood Street, directly opposite Swan Court, where they had lived when they were first married. For a year or more they had no house in the country at all, and Denis hated it. He didn't like living in London – it was far too far from the golf club and all his friends – and he wasn't particularly fond of the house in Flood Street anyway. In time he found the ideal solution: a pretty flat in a large square house called Court Lodge, which sat right on the golf course at Lamberhurst, not two minutes' walk from the first tee. The flat had a three-year lease, and he had all he needed; although Margaret was never very happy living in rented accommodation. She much preferred living in a house that she owned.

Life as a Minister was very different from life in Opposition. Margaret moved out of a small cramped room in the nether regions of the House of Commons into a large air-conditioned office in the Department of Education and Science, then housed in Curzon Street, in the West End. She sat at a large desk, with any number of civil servants at the end of a telephone, there to do her every bidding. A large car with a driver took her to and from Cabinet meetings in Downing Street, the House of Commons, Finchley or anywhere else she had occasion to visit. Her secretary, now Elizabeth Williams, no longer had all the tasks that Diana had tackled. She was there to buy the Sunday joint and deal with Finchley; everything else was taken care of by the Ministry.

Margaret embarked on the job with the same energy, dedication and attention to detail that she had shown everywhere else in her life. There were certain fundamentals that she believed in about education, and she stuck to them through thick and thin. She believed that there should be freedom for parents to send their children to the school of their choice; that enough money should be available for education at all stages, so that every child should be able to develop their abilities to the full; that more money should go into primary education, 'the foundation on which all later education and training is built'; and that local authorities should be allowed to decide what kind of system was best for their area, taking into account the wishes of the parents, the travelling distances involved and the suitability of the existing buildings. She also believed that children should not be allowed to leave school until the age of sixteen.

Margaret has always based her beliefs on a mixture of instinct and personal experience, or the experience of those people whom she meets and talks to, and this was no less true with her theories about education. Her own father chose to send her to the school at the opposite end of the town rather than the school round the corner, because he preferred the former. The school he had chosen for her was better, to a large extent, because more money had been spent on the building. And she had friends at Kesteven who had been forced to leave school at fourteen or fifteen, with no chance of further education, because their parents had been unable to afford to keep them there any longer.

There is a distinct pecking order in Cabinet, and the Minister for Education resides somewhere in the lower echelons. They are not normally expected to peck except by express invitation, and on the specific subject of their Ministry. Margaret was either unaware or, as is more probable, unimpressed by such convention. She was not afraid to speak up, and not just on matters that concerned education. What is more, she never spoke unless she was certain of her facts and figures, and as ever she had always done more homework than virtually anyone else around the table. In a very short time she was exceedingly unpopular, both with Ted Heath and with the rest of his Cabinet.

Ted Heath disliked two things almost above all else: people who disagreed with him; and women. Margaret was both. But for all his failings, Ted Heath was not stupid; he recognized her ability and her value to his Government, so he kept her there, though not with very good grace. To be fair, he was not alone, and Margaret was left very much out in the cold. Even in 1970, the Parliamentary Conservative Party was still intensely chauvinistic, and remarks that Margaret had made in public had not done much to soften attitudes. 'If you want something said,' she had told five thousand members of the National Union of Townswomen's Guilds in the Albert Hall in 1965, 'ask a man. If you want something done, ask a woman.' Just before she was appointed Shadow Education Secretary, replying to a motion in favour of more equal rights for women during the Party Conference, she closed with a quotation from Sophocles: 'Once a woman is made equal to a man, she becomes his superior.'

Margaret seldom says things she doesn't mean, with the result that she had few friends in Cabinet. She wasn't part of the old boy network, didn't understand the rules, and wasn't interested in learning them. She argued her point like a terrier with a rat, refusing to let go, and showed up a great many of her male counterparts for the talkers they were. But it was a lonely situation to be in. If Denis was unable to attend some evening function with her, for example, the rest of her colleagues would go off in small groups together to have dinner in a restaurant, and were it not for the sensitivity of one or two more considerate members, Margaret would frequently have been left on her own.

Denis had never much enjoyed the company of politicians, but he did try to accompany Margaret to functions when he was not tied up with his own business. He became fiercely protective of her. He worried that she was being overworked, invariably taking her home before the end of a party, so that she wouldn't be tired out. He was quite bossy in those days, and although Margaret was never an acquiescent wife, he was seen to be the one in charge, something that as her confidence has grown, he has been happy to relinquish.

Her confidence grew, to a large extent, out of her relationship with Denis, who has remained her best friend in life. Where his money had helped to start Margaret off on her career, it was his support and total loyalty towards his wife which boosted her for the climb. She complained about him from time to time – to some very well-chosen ears – grumbling about his language, his golfing cronies, or his penchant for the odd 'snifter' too early in the day, in much the same way that any spouse grumbles about the other after twenty odd years of marriage. But he always thought she was wonderful, and buoyed up by this knowledge, she could withstand any number of cold shoulders turned against her.

During her three and a half years at the Ministry of Education, Margaret needed that support more than ever. She was not only isolated in Cabinet, she was also unpopular in many parts of the country and was harshly criticized by the left-wing press. Her first action on taking office was to withdraw compulsion on local authorities to submit plans to turn comprehensive. Labour's document insisting upon this had been called Circular 10/66. Margaret scrapped that and put out her own, Circular 10/70. It was nothing more or less than she had promised in the Tory Election Manifesto, and yet the National Union of Teachers, who were officially in favour of Labour's plan, kicked up a tremendous fuss about it, and took Fleet Street with them. When schemes came into her department from local authorities, Margaret scrutinized them, and some she let through, others she blocked. She was accused of 'sabotaging' dozens of schools to prevent them becoming comprehensive. In fact out of four thousand proposals, she vetoed less than four hundred. Authorities complained that her guidelines were unclear, and so she took the opportunity of spelling them out in a speech to the NUT's annual conference in 1972. Hundreds of teachers got to their feet and walked out in protest.

One authority whose scheme she blocked was Surrey County Council, within whose boundaries fell two large grammar schools in Epsom, one for girls, one for boys, both with very high academic reputations. The Council wanted to absorb both into a comprehensive system, but twenty-four thousand parents and electors were opposed to the idea out of a total electorate in Epsom of eighty thousand. Margaret's decision was that the grammar schools should remain unchanged and should retain full capacity.

Her critics quickly argued that she had said in her Election Manifesto that local authorities would be given the freedom to decide for themselves what was the best system for their own areas. Margaret replied that she had also said the wishes of the parents and local voters must be taken into account too, and in this instance they had clearly not been. Her decision was final.

Another promise on which the Conservative Party had come to power was a reduction in tax. But if income tax were cut, the revenue that would have come from it inevitably had to be found elsewhere. Jim Callaghan, as Labour's Chancellor, had tried to find it by imposing Selective Employment Tax. The Heath Government, with Iain Macleod initially as Chancellor of the Exchequer, found it by insisting that Government spending be cut. His target was a cut of £300 million, a sizeable chunk of which was to come from the Education Budget. Each Minister whose department was ordered to be thus pruned, fought hard to shift the cuts to someone else's department. Margaret fought for Education harder than most, but something had to go.

At the end of the day, one of the sacrifices was the free milk provided daily in primary schools for children from the ages of seven to eleven, which cost the Government £8 million a year. The philosophy behind that decision, as she later explained, was that cuts in the budget should not affect the children's education:

> 'I took the view that most parents are able to pay for the milk for their children, and that the job of the Government was to provide such things in education which they couldn't pay for, like new primary schools. The previous Labour Government had stopped free milk in the secondary schools, and though some on their own side objected, there was no great storm over that. The important thing was to protect education, and that's what we did. Indeed, we expanded it.'

But storm there was. There was outrage of a quite unprecedented nature, whipped up by newspapers like the *Sun*, who called her 'The most unpopular woman in Britain'. Margaret was labelled, 'Mrs Thatcher, milk snatcher', and the slogan stuck. She was slammed for increasing the price of school meals to sixty pence a week. She was attacked for handing out a £2 million subsidy to direct-grant schools for the better-off (which she did in order that they might cut their fees), while refusing an inquiry into slum schools, (which she did because she thought the resources needed would be better spent on building primary schools). In the House all manner of abuse was hurled at her. She was the 'Minister of Lost Opportunity,' shrieked one; 'Mrs Scrooge with a painted face,' cried a second; 'A reactionary cave woman,' and an 'ideological elitist,' shouted others. And whenever she rose to her feet to speak, they would chant 'Ditch the bitch'.

Greatest fury of all, however, came from the students. It had become apparent that student union funds were going towards all sorts of diverse causes, such as paying members' court fines, and supporting African freedom movements and Upper Clyde strikers. Because union dues were compulsory in many universities and polytechnics, they were thus ultimately being paid by the local authorities which provided the student grants, which, in effect, meant that ratepayers and taxpayers were paying for causes they may not have wanted to support.

Margaret's scheme was that the university or polytechnic authorities might take over responsibility for funding the student unions themselves; and the suggestion went down like a lead balloon. Students jeered and chanted at her everywhere she went. She was mobbed and abused. At the South Bank Polytechnic in London students refused to come forward to receive awards from her. Some walked out of the hall, while six students who were to have had lunch with her left before the first course was served, having given her a note which said, 'We have lived with the lies of you and your so-called democratic Government for long enough.' She made her speech, nevertheless, and was not deterred by the chants of 'If you all hate Thatcher, clap your hands,' from outside.

The abuse was not always confined to words. In June 1971 she walked into another angry demonstration by polytechnic students in Liverpool. Her speech was drowned by shouts of 'What about school milk?' and 'Tories out', paper darts were thrown across the hall, and when her host proposed a vote of thanks for a speech of which no one had been able to hear a word, someone produced a loud burp. She was finally led out of a side entrance to avoid the crowds that were still chanting at the front.

Margaret arrived at the sanctuary of Guinevere Tilney, wife of the local MP, whose house she was using as a base during her visit, looking pale and shaken. Guinevere asked how it went. 'It was a very rowdy meeting,' said Margaret, and when pressed for more details, pulled back her blouse to reveal an enormous bruise on her chest, where someone had hit her with a stone egg. Guinevere was horrified and immediately asked what she could do to help. 'Nothing,' said Margaret, 'I've got two more engagements this afternoon. Give me a nice hot cup of tea.'

'Did it hurt?' asked her hostess.

'It did hurt like mad,' she admitted.

'And what did you do?'

'I went on speaking,' said Margaret. 'What else could I do?'

Margaret was not the only member of her family that came in for abuse. Her period at Education unhappily coincided with Carol's years at the University of London, where she was reading law. Carol was treated quite abominably by her fellow students, who harangued and ostracized her for everything her mother did.

It reached the stage where Denis was saying that perhaps the time had come for Margaret to give it all up. She has never been as tough as she likes to appear, and the unpleasantness upset her enormously, although she has always been far too self-controlled ever to let emotions of that sort show. She confessed later that she was almost broken by the experience, and when she has said in subsequent interviews with the press that she is not all iron, that there have been times when she has cried in private, those were the times. But thoughts of giving it all up were not for her. She was bitterly distressed that her children should be made to suffer because of what she was and did, but she believed in what she was doing, and believed that it was right for the greatest number of people. Nothing would have made her abandon ship because the seas were rough.

Within the higher regions of the Tory Party she was as unpopular as anywhere else, but the moment the Opposition started baying for her resignation, Ted Heath dug in his heels and insisted that she stay. Tory wives disliked her, and when challenged about their feelings, one wife snapped, 'It's no wonder when the only thing she ever talks to us about is the price of beef.' But even they might have felt remorse had they been present during a formal lunch at Downing Street one day. The room fell suddenly quiet just as an eminent guest was asking if there was 'any truth in the rumour that Mrs Thatcher is a woman?' Margaret, sitting just a few chairs away, pretended not to notice. Her colleagues were caught between mortification and hysteria.

The charge that Margaret only talked to Tory wives about the price of beef is easy to believe. She had nothing whatever in common with them. They tended to be middle- and upper-class ladies who had been to public school, had been reared with privilege, rode horses, owned large houses in the country, spoke in rather loud Knightsbridge voices, gave 'At Homes', and felt ostracized without at least one society party a week. On top of which, a lot of them were snobs, as was most of the Tory Establishment. They recognized Margaret for the shopkeeper's daughter she was, detected that the accent was phoney, and didn't much want to be friends with her, whatever she was like. She, in turn, recognized their hostility, saw that they had nothing whatever in common, predicted that they weren't up to talking about politics, which left the subject of beef.

Inside the Department she was a hard taskmaster, who expected everyone to work as hard as she did. When she encountered sloppy thinking or cutting of corners, she came down on the culprit with all the wrath and scorn that she had reserved in the past for spokesmen introducing senseless bills in the House of Commons. The whole Department found the Minister a strain to have around the place. They felt it was becoming impossible to have a rational conversation with her. So when she announced that she was going off to Corsica for two weeks' holiday, they all heaved a massive sigh of relief at the prospect for them of two weeks' peace. Imagine their dismay when, ten days later, she was back, having had enough of Corsica and raring to get back into harness.

To help defuse the hostility between Margaret and the student population, Ted Heath appointed Norman St John-Stevas as her Number Two at the Department of Education. He reached the entrance to the office at nine o'clock on his first morning in the job to find Margaret Thatcher waiting to greet him at the front door, palm outstretched. He went on to become a friend, one of the few she had at that time. He took over far more of the public ministerial duties than an Under-Secretary is normally wont to do, in order to take the heat off Mrs Thatcher, and to try to bridge the widening gap between her and the educationalists and the press. She was so upset for a while that she refused to talk to the press at all, and when she did, treated every question as a trap.

There was one occasion when Norman was due to make a reply on Education in the House in the early afternoon. He was busy in a committee room in the basement working on his speech and, because there was no television monitor in this particular room (as there was in most) which would have told him what stage they had reached in the Chamber, Norman missed the debate. Margaret, who had been out shopping over lunch and returned clutching Harrods carrier bags, realized that Norman was not there to make the reply, and did it for him off the top of her head. She never mentioned what she had done, nor reproached Norman. Neither spoke of it at all.

By this time Margaret had a new secretary, Alison Ward, who had joined her in January 1971. Alison, aged twenty at the time, had heard on the House of Commons grapevine that Mrs Thatcher was looking for a secretary, but, with only three months' experience as a political secretary, thought a Cabinet Minister would be more than she could manage. However, she was persuaded to meet the Minister. There was no interview; Mrs Thatcher took one look at Alison, and asked her if she could start on Monday. Margaret is a woman of great instinct, with the particularly feminine tendency to judge a person at first sight, largely on nothing more scientific than whether she likes the look of them or not. If she does, she is friendly and relaxed, and the chances are the feeling will be mutual. If she takes against someone, she makes no attempt at pretence, and there is no frost more chilling than the brand reserved for people Margaret dislikes.

For all Mrs Thatcher's problems, which did attract a disproportionate share of the headlines, the entire Heath Government itself was in trouble. Inflation was soaring with no apparent means of stopping it. Wage claims had led to one strike after another, disrupting every section of the community. And in 1972, going against every principle in the manifesto on which the Tory Government had come to power, Ted Heath announced a compulsory incomes policy.

Far from pulling out of industry, as he had pledged, and abandoning those 'lame ducks' that couldn't stand on their own two feet, he increased Government subsidies to ailing companies, such as Govan Shipbuilders on the Upper Clyde, and nationalized Rolls-Royce. He brought about a series of U-turns which shocked not only those people who had believed his Manifesto in the last election, but several members of his Cabinet too. For although those involved share responsibility for decisions taken in Cabinet, it is in practice only a limited few who take the decisions. There is no democratic system of voting in Cabinet. Provided the Prime Minister has the support of his most senior colleagues, he will do as he pleases. If any member finds that decision offensive to his principles, then the onus is on him to resign.

Margaret seriously considered this option, but loyalty is something she values above all else, and she determined to be loyal to her Leader. She also realized, quite rightly, that if she did leave the Cabinet, she might be a long time returning. Thus she decided to stay where she was and accept her share of the collective responsibility for the Heath U-turns.

The Government had been cursed with a great deal of bad luck, as well as self-inflicted trouble. It had inherited a situation of wage inflation from the previous administration, and Ted Heath had done what Harold Wilson had wanted to do, pushed through an Industrial Relations Act designed to limit the ease with which trade unions could use the strike weapon. Not surprisingly the unions were incensed, but failed to stop the Bill going through Parliament. Once it had become law, they flouted it, with the result that one of the biggest unions, the Amalgamated Union of Engineering Workers, was fined £75,000 by the specially set up National Industrial Relations Court for refusing to comply with an order banning strike activity. AUEW President, Hugh Scanlon, responded by calling for a one-day stoppage, which successfully closed shipyards, factories, newspapers and many power stations. Thereafter, he called one-day strikes throughout the autumn, plus a ban on overtime. Without engineers to run them, power stations began to reduce their output, which meant a shortage in electricity. Meanwhile the Arabs imposed an oil embargo following the Yom Kippur War of October 1973 in the Middle East, to try to dissuade Western powers from helping Israel, and the price of oil quadrupled. This effectively wrecked the Government's economic policy of expansion, announced by Chancellor Tony Barber in the spring Budget of 1971.*

The coal miners then rejected repeated pay offers, determined to hold out for a thirty-one per cent increase, which was quite contrary to the Government's restraint on wage claims. They enforced an overtime ban like the engineers, and stopped doing safety work on the pits. The Government responded by declaring a state of emergency and restricted the use of electricity. It launched an advertising campaign with the catch-phrase SOS, which stood for Switch Off Something. Illuminated signs were switched off, thermostats in official buildings were turned down to 63°F, and a speed limit of fifty m.p.h. was imposed on the roads. By December, the train drivers too had imposed a ban on overtime and Sunday working, and on 1 January, in a last effort to conserve fuel and ration scarce supplies to industry, the Government introduced a three-day working week. Finally in February 1974, after a cold, dark winter of disruptions, with 2.2 million people unemployed – the most since the Great Depression – the pound at its lowest since the war, and long queues at every petrol station, talks between the Government and the miners' leaders broke down, and Ted Heath decided to go to the country. Two days after he announced a date for the election, the miners voted by an overwhelming majority of eighty-one per cent to come out on strike.

The Conservative slogan in the election of February 1974 was ' Who Governs?' Laurence Daly, General Secretary of the National Union of

---

* Tony Barber had taken over the job after the sudden death of Iain Macleod in July, shortly after coming into office.

Mineworkers, and its Communist Vice Chairman, Mick McGahey, had boasted openly that their industrial action could 'break' the constitutionally elected Tory Government.

In their Election Manifesto, Labour declared that they would reject 'the policies of confrontation and conflict and fight-to-the-finish philosophies,' and offered 'a way out of the crisis'. Harold Wilson promised to draw up a 'social contract' with the unions, based on 'justice, equality, concern for the low-paid'. He promised to cut taxes for the poor, raise them for the rich, and scrap the Industrial Relations Act.

At the polls there was no clear-cut winner. Labour emerged the victor with just five seats more than the Conservatives, but they were thirty-two seats behind all the other parties combined. Heath explored the possibility of forming a coalition with the Liberals, but failed to reach agreement with their Leader, Jeremy Thorpe, so the idea floundered and Ted Heath handed in his resignation to the Queen. Harold Wilson thus returned to Downing Street, though such a small majority meant that his chances of getting any unpopular measure through Parliament would be quite hopeless. But the immediate crisis was soon over. He made a new, higher offer to the miners, which was accepted, and the country returned to a full working week.

The Conservative Party had been in power for just forty months. Although they were much troubled months, and personally nightmarish for Margaret Thatcher, the Tories did achieve results which have had a lasting effect. Britain became a member of the European Economic Community, the coinage was decimalized, and one new rate of Value Added Tax replaced the muddled system of Purchase and Selective Employment Taxes.

But not all of their achievements, it has to be said, were totally popular within the Tory Party. The measures which alienated a great many of their own supporters lay in the field of housing and home ownership. Heath's Government had lifted the restriction on the sale of council houses and removed the control of credit, so in theory more people were in a position to buy their own homes. But at the same time not enough new houses were being built in the private sector. Mortgage interest rates rose drastically, as did the cost of houses and, with demand exceeding supply, the practice of 'gazumping' became commonplace (where there was no deal that couldn't be broken by a better offer). The result was that young couples could no longer afford to buy. On top of this, the Heath Government's reorganization of local government had increased rather than lightened the weight of bureaucracy in that area, involving higher running costs which in turn were paid for by higher rates.

This was the mess to which Ted Heath assigned Margaret soon after the election by appointing her as Shadow Minister of the Environment. It was a role in which she undertook some of her hardest work, and made a good name for herself. Gone was the office in Elizabeth House with the staff to take care of everything; and gone was the chauffeur-driven car to whisk her from place to place. Opposition was a very different proposition. She was back to a small room in Star Court in the House of Commons, with her secretary, Alison Ward, who was now assigned to every duty under the sun.

The Environment was a vast brief, and during the few months that she held the post, Margaret spoke more frequently in the House than any of her colleagues. The work load was phenomenal, and yet, on top of it all, Margaret insisted upon maintaining an active role as wife and mother. She might not be there to cook meals in the evening, but she would make absolutely certain that there was something to eat in the house and, more specifically, something cold to carve from in the fridge. She did all her own shopping, as often as not from the Safeway supermarket in the King's Road, and she bought in bulk, so that the household would never run out of lavatory paper, cereals or soap. She had resisted the freezer revolution as long as she could, but it eventually became the most sensible way of running her life. The Sunday joint, however, did still come fresh, whenever possible from a small butcher in the King's Road.

In 1974 Burmah Oil moved its head office from London to Swindon, which meant a journey of sixty-five miles each day by car for Denis. He would leave the house at 6.30 sharp every morning, having eaten breakfast at six o'clock, and there was not one morning when Margaret wasn't up to make breakfast, when most nights she wouldn't have been in bed before one or two o'clock. She used to worry about the dangers of him driving so far every day, particularly when the roads were bad in the winter; but it was senseless to move the whole family out to Swindon when she needed to be in London at such outlandish hours. Because of the whip system in the House, she might be called upon to vote any time in the evening up till midnight, and travelling anywhere after that was out of the question.

Whatever time she went to bed, however, Margaret never failed first to take off her make-up and hang up the clothes she had stepped out of. Leaving her clothes in a pile and crawling exhausted into bed was not her style. It was all part of the basic good housekeeping philosophy that had been learnt at her grandmother's knee: take care of things and they will last. She hadn't used soap and water on her face since she was a child, when she had an old china washbowl and stand in her bedroom. Since then she had always taken her make-up off with remover and put a good moisturiser on afterwards. On the other hand, she had retained the childhood habit of washing her hair once a week, and if she wanted to cheer it up in between washes for some function or other, she would use heated rollers.

Carol was still studying law at this stage. Having been away at school since the age of ten, Carol chose London University so that she could live at home for a while. But the choice of degree had been Margaret's suggestion. Carol was uncertain what she wanted to read, and her mother suggested law on the grounds that it would be 'much more useful than the arts'. While she hadn't interfered in either of her twin's careers, she did feel it was very important that they should both qualify for a profession. When Carol finished her degree, Margaret was insistent that she go on further and qualify as a solicitor.

Mark had always been academically rather lazy – possibly aware that his greater gift was for sport – and when he emerged from Harrow with a collection of mediocre 'A' levels, he followed in his father's footsteps and joined a firm of chartered accountants in the City of London. He was no more popular there than he had been at Harrow – again because he aggrandized himself. Nor was he any more successful academically: he was to have three attempts at the second part of his final exams, failing to qualify each time.

How her children fared both academically and emotionally was always a source of great anxiety to Margaret. However many hours a day she put into politics – and these were to increase with her rise up the ladder – there was always a reserve of energy for her family. When Carol in later years asked her how on earth she did it, Margaret replied, 'Don't forget I've been going flat out for twenty years. People think you wake up one fine day and find yourself Prime Minister, having had a sort of laid-back existence. I've never had a laid-back existence: I've always been immensely busy.' This was no less true in the nurturing of her family than of her career.

IV

Leader Amongst Men

Before Parliament broke up for the summer recess in August 1974, Margaret had to prepare her part of the Election Manifesto. She was well aware as they all were that, shackled by such a small majority in the House, Harold Wilson would have to go to the country soon. Having done as much, and fought her proposals every inch of the way through the Shadow Cabinet, she went off to Kent for a two-week holiday, and a well-earned break. On the first day she had no less than five telephone calls from Conservative Central Office, and by the second day she was back in London, recalled first to announce her proposals to a press conference and then to turn them into a short film to be shown as a party political broadcast on television at the end of the month.

Her proposals in the field of housing appeared to go against all the ideals of non-Government intervention in which she, as one of the Selsdon Man brigade, believed. She promised that the Conservatives would bring the mortgage interest rate down to a maximum of nine and a half per cent; first-time buyers would get a grant of £1 on every £2 they saved for a deposit, up to a certain ceiling; and council tenants of three years' standing would have the absolute right to buy their homes at two-thirds the market value, on a one hundred per cent mortgage from the council with no deposit. Labour denounced it as 'Margaret's Midsummer madness' and a blatant 'electoral bribe', which in the event didn't come off. On the day Wilson chose to go to the polls, 10 October, the electorate once again rejected the Tory Party and all their bright hopes for the future. Harold Wilson was returned to power with a small, but this time workable, majority.

In politics, no less than in any other business, it is always the man or woman at the head that takes ultimate responsibility for the success or failure of the enterprise. In the aftermath of two lost elections, it was inevitable that the Party should start questioning the fitness of their Leader to continue in the job. Ted Heath, however, was in no great hurry to go. He very much enjoyed the position, and now that he had tasted premiership with all that it provided, he was all the more loath to give it up. One particular sadness would be the loss of Chequers, a magnificent house in the Buckinghamshire countryside that had been given to future prime ministers of all complexions by Lord Lee of Fareham in 1918. Heath's attachment to it was all the stronger because of his background; previous Tory prime ministers had usually possessed a similar house in their own family, but a grammar-school boy from Broadstairs did not.

The Conservative Party is traditionally quite dispassionate in the way it treats its leaders who fail to bring home the goods. Ted Heath had provided further ammunition to his critics in the Party by announcing his intention, should they have won the election, to form an all-party coalition, 'a National Coalition Government involving all the parties until the crisis is mastered'.

Senior-ranking friends and close colleagues like Lord Carrington and Jim Prior advised Ted Heath to offer his resignation, if only so that he might be re-elected and his critics silenced. Failing that, they could get someone of a like mind, such as William Whitelaw, into his place before someone of a less sympathetic stance came forward to challenge. But Ted Heath was unreceptive to their advice. He believed that he had fought both elections on the right policies, and that when the dust had settled they would be seen to have been the right policies.

Speculation about a successor was rife, not only within the Party, but also in the press, and the name which recurred most frequently was that of Keith Joseph, who had been Minister for Health and Social Security in the Heath administration. During that time he had been totally absorbed in the enormity of his job, and it was only once the Tories were pushed into Opposition that he had a chance to reflect on what he and the rest of the Party had been doing in the past forty months, and to discuss it with his friends in the Party:

> 'I realized that we had allowed our good intentions to run away with us, and I was anxious to try to learn the lessons of what had happened, and in particular why the Germans had done so well with their social market philosophy. . . . 'When Mr Heath offered me a position in his Shadow Cabinet, I asked him to let me have a place without portfolio so that I could set up a little research body to find out the lessons from Western Europe, and to find out why their prosperity was so much better than ours.'

Mr Heath agreed, and thus was born the Centre for Policy Studies, in which right-wing *Daily Telegraph* journalist, Alfred Sherman, Margaret Thatcher, and Ted Heath's nominee on the Board, Adam Ridley, played leading roles. The Centre rapidly ceased to focus on western Europe, and started to try to apply the lessons of social market philosophy to their own thinking in Britain. In a speech delivered in Preston on 5 September 1974, Sir Keith Joseph introduced the new economic theory of monetarism into politics for the first time in this country, and paved the way for the revolution that Mrs Thatcher's brand of Conservatism brought with it.

Successive governments since the Second World War had based their economic policies upon the thinking of John Maynard Keynes. He frowned upon the existing wisdom for curing unemployment, which was to lower wages and cut everything in sight. He argued that the only way to reduce unemployment and depression was for the Government to intervene and remedy the defects in the economic system, to increase demand by fiscal measures and by public investment. Monetarism, on the other hand, as expounded by its great advocate, Professor Milton Friedman, is a return to the nineteenth-century economic philosophies of David Ricardo, and enlightened self-interest: each man was the best judge of his own interests and, provided laws were obeyed and contracts kept, the division of labour and the market would together produce the optimum economic result, with no need for Government interference whatsoever. Twentieth-century monetarism is based on much the same idea. Inflation is caused, its proponents say, by excessive money stock; and Government shouldn't interfere in unemployment or output, but should remain as unobtrusive as possible in both the economy and industry.

Espousing this theory in his speech at Preston, Sir Keith denounced Keynesianism, as 'the method that successive governments have used to reduce unemployment – namely, expanding aggregate demand by deficit financing – which has created inflation, and without really helping the unemployed either'. He was thus blaming the Tory Chancellor, Tony Barber, for his expansionist policies and his increase in Government spending, which he felt had caused the present inflation. This didn't go down well with Mr Heath.

Tony Barber had by this time retired from politics, and Ted Heath needed to find a replacement Shadow Chancellor. Keith Joseph was the man best qualified for the job, but with his views, and the fact that he posed the only obvious threat to Heath's position as Leader, Sir Keith Joseph was not the man that he was keen to put into the Number Two job in his Shadow Cabinet. So, when he came to put together a team after the October defeat, Heath chose Robert Carr for the Treasury, with Margaret Thatcher as his Number Two, to have 'particular responsibility for financial legislation and public expenditure'.

This turned out to be a grave tactical error. Margaret went into the job, where she was presented with a Labour Finance Bill to fight and where she excelled herself, just at the moment when her colleagues were looking round for someone to nominate as Leader.

Long before this, however, an awkward situation had arisen between Ted Heath and the 1922 Committee. This body, actually founded in 1923, stemmed from the revolt of Tory MPs who ousted Austen Chamberlain as Party Leader. Its function today is to take care of administrative matters affecting back-benchers, and to ensure that their views are brought to the attention of the Party Leader. It is run by an elected eighteen-member executive, chaired in 1974 by Edward du Cann. It was at his London home that the executive had arranged to meet on 14 October, four days after the election, to deal with normal business before the start of a new session of Parliament. By the time the meeting occurred, however, there was more than the odd rumbling of discontent about Ted Heath's leadership. Members of the executive had been deluged with demands from their fellow back-benchers that something be done about it. So when they met, the matter that they discussed was not the business that had been scheduled, as a great many people, including half of Fleet Street, were aware. When the eighteen arrived at Edward du Cann's house that night, although the meeting was supposed to have been a private affair, they encountered a barrage of reporters and photographers, all eager to know if another 1922-style revolt was in the making.

It wasn't. What the back-benchers agreed amongst themselves was that there must be a new leadership election, not necessarily to be rid of Heath, but to reaffirm his position and to put an end to the criticism and unrest. Du Cann was dispatched to explain the situation to Ted Heath, and report back to the executive the following day. Ted Heath took the news badly. He refused to see the logic, failed to appreciate that anyone might be on his side, and took the whole thing as a personal betrayal.

Wanting to avoid the publicity that the meeting the previous night had attracted, Edward du Cann set up the second meeting, where he was due to report back on his conversation with Ted Heath, at Keyser Ullman, the merchant bank of which he was chairman, in Milk Street. Once again the press knew the game plan and were there waiting with cameras. 'Milk Street Mafia,' ran the headlines in that evening's papers, with an embellished tale about the plot to bring Heath down.

Heath was not amused. He refused an invitation to meet the executive face to face to discuss the matter, on the grounds that it was customary to re-elect the executive after every new Parliament and, as this had not yet been done, he was not going to deal with the present incumbents. A full meeting of the 1922 Committee went ahead without him, in which his leadership was discussed, and the full executive was returned without a single change – the first time in memory that it had been so. But Heath refused to heed the warnings, adamant in his belief that he was the only person capable of leading the Tory Party.

When Sir Alec Douglas-Home had reformed the procedure for electing a Leader of the Party (a procedure which Ted Heath himself used to oust its architect in 1965), he had not foreseen the occasion arising in which the current Leader might not want to budge. New rules, therefore, had to be worked out. When Heath realized that he faced a full-scale rebellion if he didn't agree, he appointed a ten-member rules committee, chaired by Lord Home, to make recommendations. It came back with its proposals just before the House broke for Christmas. When the Party was in Opposition, new leadership elections should be held every year. In addition, to win outright in the first ballot, a candidate would need not just to lead by fifteen per cent of the votes cast, but by fifteen per cent of the total electorate, which was then two hundred and seventy-six. The proposals were accepted, and Heath agreed to hold an election as soon as could be arranged to get the whole business over and done with. The date was set for 4 February 1975.

Who should stand as candidates in that election, of course, had been the most common topic of conversation since the Tory defeat in the October general election. Sir Keith Joseph had begun as the most favoured contender. Quite a sizeable number of back-benchers were keen that Edward du Cann should stand but, having just been re-elected to serve another year as chairman of the 1922 Committee, whose task it was to be returning officer in an election, there were obviously complications. There was also a small question mark about his suitability, since he had not been an enthusiastic supporter of Britain's entry into the EEC. One or two people suggested Margaret Thatcher, including Fergus Montgomery, who had entered the House at the same time as her, and served as her Parliamentary Private Secretary at Education. She turned the suggestion down flat, on the grounds that, as she had already said several times in public, including on the BBC TV children's programme, 'Blue Peter', she didn't think the Tory Party was ready to have a woman at the top. 'It will be years before a woman either leads the Party or becomes Prime Minister,' she had said. 'I don't see it happening in my lifetime.' Her choice for Leader was Sir Keith Joseph, and she made it quite clear that she would support him.

But the picture soon changed. Keith Joseph made the most appallingly ill-begotten speech to Edgbaston Conservatives on 19 October, in which he seemed to be suggesting that the lower classes – those mothers in 'socio-economic classes four and five' who, because of their own deprivation, were least fitted to bring up children – should be given free contraceptives to stop them breeding so prolifically. 'The balance of our population, our human stock, is threatened,' he said; casting his name, his reputation and, to a certain extent, his spirit into the lions' den. He was accused of advocating 'master race' theories, and wanting 'pills for the proles'. And, despite a week of desperate denials about how his speech had been misinterpreted and about what he had really meant, his chances of ever leading the Tory Party were finished.

At this point Margaret began to think seriously about putting herself forward. But it was not until November, when Sir Keith had said for once and for all that he would not stand, that she announced her intention to do so.

Margaret reached her decision to challenge Ted Heath for leadership of the Conservative Party alone and unaided. There were no family discussions about what it would mean if she won; nor, indeed, about what it would mean if she lost. The latter would almost certainly have meant the end of her career on the front-bench. These were not considerations that she dwelt on. Margaret looked at the state of the country, at the state of the Tory Party, at the people around her who might lead it, and decided that none of them was capable of doing what she believed the country needed to make it right. If anyone ever says she's a Joan of Arc, she replies, 'I don't want to be burned at the stake', but the parallel is there.

Her explanation of why she had stepped forward was, 'Because I'm a true Tory, and I believe they can rule this country better than anyone else. And because I saw the Tory Party going much too much to the left, and there didn't seem to be anyone who had the thoughts and ideas I had, and it seemed to be absolutely vital for the country that I stood.'

Yet, while Margaret saw that her country needed her, there were many in the country who had scarcely heard of Margaret Thatcher. Certainly she had been unpopular over the milk-snatching episode, to anyone vitally interested in politics she had made some memorable speeches, and her colleagues had seen her capacity for hard work and detail, but to the average man in the street she was a nobody.

Bernard Levin, writing in *The Times*, said that she was every bit as cold and aloof as Ted Heath, 'and there's no point in the Party jumping out of the Igloo and into the Glacier'. She was certainly not a politician who fired the popular imagination. Moreover, there were more than a few people on both sides of the House who thought she was a boring, middle-class suburbanite, of very limited intelligence.

But Margaret had her supporters; a few people who saw something there that the others had missed. One was Gordon Reece, an ex-journalist, ex-ATV producer, at the time working for EMI promoting video cassettes – a good few years ahead of the boom. One of his sidelines, however, was making party political broadcasts for the Tory Party, and it was in this capacity that he first met Margaret and became spell-bound. He recognized qualities of integrity and leadership in Margaret that others were to take months or even years to find, and he decided to back her, offering his expertise and knowledge of the media to help in the campaign. At the time there were people who thought he was committing professional suicide. If Margaret's bid for the leadership had failed and Ted Heath had been returned to the job, Reece's neck would have been on the chopping block. But he thought she was a remarkable woman, who exuded enormous strength and magnetism, and he backed his instinct.

Another person who saw some special quality in Mrs Thatcher was Airey Neave, a relatively little known but highly respected back-bencher, whom she had first met when they were candidates together in the 1950 election. They met again when he was a junior tenant in Frederick Lawton's chambers in the Inner Temple, where Margaret did her common and criminal law pupillage in 1953. They had been friendly to some extent ever since and he had watched with interest her performance since her arrival in the House. He had initially supported Edward du Cann for the leadership, but in January du Cann announced that he was definitely not going to stand, having been in a state of some indecision over the previous few months. If he had stood and become Leader, he would have had to give up the bank, which he was loath to do. There was also some suggestion that close scrutiny of Keyser

Margaret Thatcher as Secretary of State for Education in her new office on the twelfth floor of Elizabeth House, near Waterloo Station, where the Department moved in October 1972

Margaret **Thatcher** with **Prime** Minister Edward Heath at the annual Tory Conference in Blackpool in 1970. Relations were not to be so cordial in later years

Margaret Thatcher found herself in the news in November 1974 when she advised pensioners to stock up on high-proteined tinned food to keep abreast of inflation: (*left*) Jon of the *Daily Mail* took advantage of this controversy, coinciding as it did with Margaret's challenge to Heath for the leadership of the Conservative Party; (*below*) Meanwhile, Fleet Street photographers delighted in depicting her en route from the King's Road to Flood Street with her shopping basket brimming

'Mrs Thatcher? This is THE grocer.'

The past and the future of the Conservative Party. Margaret with Alec Douglas-Home, Harold Macmillan and Edward Heath: all four were to enjoy prime ministerial rank

Margaret Thatcher returning to Flood Street in the early hours, having won the contest for the leadership of the Conservative Party, 12 February 1975

Daily Mail cartoon for 29 November 1974, showing Margaret's rise to the leadership of the Conservative Party

Margaret Thatcher, new Leader of the Opposition, awaiting the arrival of Black Rod to summon her to the Lords for the State Opening of Parliament. Around her are her Shadow Cabinet: *from left to right*, Norman St John-Stevas, Geoffrey Howe, Keith Joseph, William Whitelaw, James Prior and Francis Pym

In March 1979 the Tories forced and won a motion of no-confidence against Callaghan's Government and Parliament was dissolved. But all too soon, Margaret Thatcher's elation was turned to sorrow by the assassination of Airey Neave, one of her closest political friends. She is shown in this photograph at Airey Neave's funeral on 6 April at Longworth in Oxfordshire

The men in Margaret Thatcher's public life: Triumph at the Tory Party Conference in 1975. As Margaret holds aloft a blue feather duster, she is applauded by her colleagues. *From left to right*, Ian Gilmour, Reginald Maudling, Keith Joseph, William Whitelaw, Peter Thorneycroft (Chairman of the Party), Peter Thomas (Chairman of the Conference) and Colonel Alastair Graesser

Margaret Thatcher in light monetarist conversation with Keith Joseph

Margaret Thatcher in deep contemplation with her Home Secretary, William Whitelaw

The man who created the image of Margaret Thatcher. Gordon Reece, her personal adviser through two general elections

Ullman's affairs might prove a little embarrassing to a potential Prime Minister – a suggestion subsequently proved correct. In May 1979, a Department of Trade report accused the bank's directors, headed by du Cann, of incompetence over an improper £17 million loan made in 1973. In the end his wife tipped the balance of his indecision by saying she didn't want him to stand. At this point Airey Neave transferred his support, and that of a great many back-benchers who trusted his judgment, to Margaret Thatcher.

Politics is a dirty point-scoring business at the best of times. When a politician is fighting for his job, it becomes even dirtier. In November 1974, Margaret was once again in the firing line for what at the time had seemed a perfectly innocuous suggestion she had made to help elderly people keep abreast of inflation and make their pensions go a little further. Her advice was to stock up on high-protein tinned food, such as salmon, sardines and ham: buy a tin a week over a period of years, because they would keep for ever, and were bound to go up in price. She had done much the same thing herself, she said. All this appeared in a magazine called *Pre-Retirement Choice*, to whom she had given an interview on the grounds that Denis would be reaching retirement age himself the following year. Labour seized on this, as did the cartoonists, who depicted Margaret Thatcher surrounded by a mountain of tins, which she had taken out of the mouths of starving pensioners. Her opponents in the Tory Party made capital too, and some would say instigated a lot of the furore: here was proof of just how out of touch she was with ordinary people who couldn't afford to stock-pile tins of salmon and ham. The whole episode was deeply suspect, as Patrick Cosgrave, writing in the *Spectator*, demonstrated. A Mr Tallis, who had rung a radio chat show claiming that Mrs Thatcher had tried to buy a large quantity of sugar from his shop in the Finchley Road during the sugar shortage, turned out to be bogus. Mrs Thatcher seldom, if ever, shopped in the Finchley Road, and Mr Tallis didn't trade there anyway. It was upsetting, but Margaret had developed a tougher hide than she had possessed in her days in Education. 'They broke Keith,' she said, referring to his Edgbaston speech, 'but they won't break me.'

Margaret spent Christmas with the family at Court Lodge, their flat on the golf course at Lamberhurst, and saw friends such as Bill Deedes and his wife in nearby Aldington. Bill, MP for Ashford, and editor of the *Daily Telegraph*, is the recipient of the regular 'Dear Bill' letters in the satirical magazine *Private Eye*, purported to have been written by

Denis Thatcher. The fictitious letters were later adapted into a play called 'Anyone for Denis' and Bill Deedes is indeed the great golfing chum of Denis that both versions portrayed. Evenings with Denis's golfing friends are not something that Margaret has ever greatly relished. Golf bores her witless, although rumour has it that she did, just once in her life, walk round a course with Denis. The moment the subject of golf comes up in conversation she makes her exit. However other friends that they habitually saw over Christmas were the Josephs, and with them Margaret found much more to talk about.

Soon after her return to London, Edward du Cann made his decision not to stand for the leadership, and made it clear that his vote would now be cast for Margaret Thatcher, swinging the mass of support which had been behind him to her cause. Airey Neave offered his services as campaign manager with William Shelton, a colleague from Ministry of Education days as his deputy, and the race was on. Airey Neave was to prove Margaret Thatcher's greatest asset. Having trained women agents during the war, he had a very high regard for women and their courage. He was an exceptionally brave man himself: the first Allied officer to escape from Colditz, the German prisoner-of-war camp, he then went back to organize a highly successful exit route for other escapees. What he saw in Margaret, as he later said, was 'the first real idealist politician for a long time. Margaret is a philosopher as well as a politician'.

But the race to the ballot, and the need to convince sufficient Tories of these qualities, were by no means all that Margaret had to think about on the cold dark days of January and early February. As Number Two at the Shadow Treasury, with special responsibility for financial legislation, Margaret had a great deal on her plate: namely Chancellor Denis Healey's Finance Bill which was ripe for demolition. And it was her demolition of this which really made people in the House, and outside it, sit up and take notice, and begin for the first time to take seriously Margaret Thatcher's bid for the leadership.

After her first speech on the subject in December, Frank Johnson, then political sketch writer with the *Daily Telegraph*, wrote: 'Mrs Thatcher became the first Tory front-bencher in this Parliament to win from Tory back-benchers a cheer promoted by enthusiasm rather than hope of distant knighthoods or peerages. . . . Mrs Thatcher proved, as was once said of a deceptively easy-going operatic prima donna, that she has dimples of iron.'

'There are four ways of acquiring money,' she remarked scathingly to millionaire Socialist Harold Lever, who led the debate, 'Make it, earn it, marry it, and borrow it. The Right Honourable Gentleman seems to know about all four.'

Then, moving from Mr Lever's own finances to those of the nation, she said: 'Yesterday it was suggested that there should be a penalty on companies which went beyond the Social Contract. It seems very odd that employers who were not party to the Social Contract pay a penalty if the Contract fails, but those who were parties to the Contract seem to take no party in the penalty.'

From there she turned her gaze to Mr Healey, and weighed into him for the glib remarks that he had made in his Budget speech about accumulation of material goods not bringing happiness. She produced a newspaper cutting in which the Chancellor was quoted as saying that he never saved, and that whenever he got any money he would 'go out and buy something for the house'. Mr Healey leapt to his feet and demanded to know the source of the quotation. 'The *Sunday Telegraph*,' replied Mrs Thatcher. And Mr Healey sat down, muttering some rather hollow denials and the odd 'preposterous'.

She was back in fighting form again in January, two weeks before the leadership ballot, when she heaped her scorn on Labour's Capital Transfer Tax – which would be imposed on gifts and bequests, even to charities. Mr Healey came in for another roasting. She accused him of being the first Chancellor of the Exchequer to put a tax on doing a good turn. 'You apparently do not understand the effect your tax will have on the lives of individuals, the economy, or indeed on a free society in general,' she said.

The next day Healey was back to defend his corner. 'Mrs Thatcher,' he said, 'has emerged from the debate as La Pasionaria of Privilege ["pasionaria", meaning passion flower, the nickname given to a fiery Communist woman orator from the days of the Spanish Civil War]. She has shown she has decided to see her Party tagged as the Party of the rich few, and I believe she and her Party will regret it.'

Nothing concentrated the mind quite like personal abuse. Margaret rose calmly to her feet and said that she would like to have begun by saying that Mr Healey's remarks had not done him justice. Unfortunately, they had. She continued:

> Some Chancellors are micro-economic, some Chancellors are fiscal. This one is just plain cheap. When he rose to speak yesterday, we on this side were amazed how one could possibly

get to be Chancellor of the Exchequer and speak for his Government knowing so little about existing taxes, and so little about the proposals which were coming before Parliament. If this Chancellor can be a Chancellor, anyone in the House of Commons could be Chancellor. I had hoped that the Right Honourable Gentleman might at least address himself to the practical effects, because they will affect . . . everyone, including people born, as I was, with no privilege at all.

It was a triumphant diatribe, bringing rapturous applause from her colleagues in the House and the media, which thrives on exchanges of this sort. The timing could not have been more perfect, nor more devastating for Ted Heath. Those people who had thought her challenge not worth taking seriously, suddenly saw that she could pose a very real threat. As Frank Johnson wrote at the time: 'Reluctant though I am to risk the lady's wrath by questioning her undoubted femininity, let it be said that the Tories need more men like her.'

From that debate she went from strength to strength with the help and guidance of Airey Neave, who managed a brilliant election campaign on her behalf. Every Sunday evening he, William Shelton and Keith Joseph, acting in the role of senior adviser, met over supper in Flood Street, where Margaret was candidate, cook, hostess and washer-up-of-dishes all rolled into one. They made an excellent team, with contacts in all the right places. With Alfred Sherman at the Centre for Policy Studies and Gordon Reece also working closely alongside her, they had the media well under control.

Margaret Thatcher was not initially very well disposed towards Fleet Street, having suffered so badly during her years in Curzon Street, but she didn't need anyone to tell her just how important a good relationship with the press was now. In earlier days she had been infuriated by the way she was attacked for her style of dress, her penchant for 'a little black dress and pearls', the caricature of the Tory lady. 'I don't know why the bloody hell I shouldn't wear these pearls,' she had retorted at a dinner in the Carlton Club, where she was guest one evening. 'They were a present from Denis.' 'Mrs Thatcher,' said Ronnie Millar, who was part of the Party communications team, 'if you'd go on television and say that, you'd have the country at your feet.'

'Oh, do you think so?' she said, but never heeded the advice.

She now assiduously set about wooing the chauvinist editors of Fleet Street, who were every bit as sceptical about the idea of a woman leading the Party as were her colleagues in Parliament. Many of them were, moreover, loyal supporters of Ted Heath. She took them to lunch, stared them straight in the eyes, and spelt out her ideas for the Tory Party and for getting Britain back on its feet, in straight-from-the-heart, plain English, which is a way of speaking not often given to politicians. She presented an intriguing combination of feminine looks with a masculine mind. And it was over the lunch tables of London, at meetings set up by Gordon Reece, that some of her most valuable supporters were won.

The ticket she was travelling on was that government was about people. In January she spelt out her precise vision in a leader page article in the *Daily Telegraph* entitled 'My Kind of Tory Party'. She accepted collective responsibility for losing two elections, and said:

> To deny that we failed the people is futile, as well as arrogant. Successful governments win elections. So do parties with broadly acceptable policies. We lost. . . . Yet two lessons do emerge from our own experience. The first is that in the long run rapid inflation is the worst enemy. The second is that we must never again allow a preoccupation with macro-economics and industrial growth to blind us to the day to day problems of ordinary people, in all walks of life. My kind of Tory Party would make no secret of its belief in individual freedom and individual prosperity, in the maintenance of law and order, in the wide distribution of private property, in rewards for energy, skill and thrift, in diversity of choice, in the preservation of local rights in local communities.

As the date for the ballot drew closer, a third name entered the running, that of Hugh Fraser, then married to historian and author, Lady Antonia Fraser. He was a senior back-bencher of some standing, but hardly leadership material. He did, however, provide an alternative for anyone who wanted to oust Heath, but couldn't bring themselves to vote for a woman.

On 3 February, just one day before the first ballot, Margaret's prospects were looking gloomy. Seventy per cent of the rank and file members of the Conservative Party throughout the country were said to be in favour of Heath staying on as Leader. In the House the figures were less certain, but later that day Lord Home, the very man whom Ted Heath had unseated ten years earlier, came out in support of him, which added considerable weight to his cause. With the exception of

Keith Joseph and one other member who intended to abstain, the entire Shadow Cabinet was also behind Ted Heath.

He went to cast his vote the following day in Committee Room 14, thus reasonably confident of victory. His campaign managers had told him that he could expect between 138 and 144 votes, which could give him a clear victory in the first round. Margaret's team had played cautious all along. She should think in terms of a tie, with something in the region of 122 votes each, she had been told.

She too voted soon after the ballot opened at noon, and then went off to the City for a working lunch, coming back to wait nervously for the result in Airey Neave's office in the House of Commons. Down the corridor, Ted Heath was waiting less nervously in his own office, accompanied by his old friend, Lord Aldington. Voting closed at 3.30, and at four o'clock, Edward du Cann emerged from Committee Room 14 into the corridor outside, now seething with lobby correspondents, and announced the result: Margaret Thatcher – 130, Edward Heath – 119, Hugh Fraser – 16, and there were eleven abstentions.

Margaret was stunned. Ted Heath was even more shocked. 'So,' he said, 'we got it all wrong,' and set about writing his resignation. But there was no knowing what proportion of the votes cast for her were an indication of positive support for Margaret Thatcher, and what proportion belonged to people who were placing their vote anywhere just to be rid of Heath. She didn't allow herself to bask in success for long. The second ballot was set for a week hence, and there was no knowing how many names would come out of the woodwork now that there was no longer the risk of losing to Ted Heath and the retribution that would bring. For instance, William Whitelaw, ex-Northern Ireland Secretary and now Party chairman, was a dedicated Heathite who had refused to stand while Heath did. But now he would see it as his duty to come forward in the hope of preserving the Heath tradition of leadership. Other names to come forward were Geoffrey Howe, former Solicitor General and chairman of the left-wing Bow Group, also ex-Prices Minister in Heath's Government; Jim Prior, once Ted Heath's personal assistant, and John Peyton, Shadow Leader of the House. Maurice Macmillan and Julian Amery also toyed with the idea for a while, but decided against running.

The week between the votes was agony, and Margaret couldn't wait for the period of waiting to be over. Several people who had supported Heath now came over to her side; one of the most significant of these was Norman St John-Stevas, her flamboyant Number Two from

Education, who had christened her 'The Blessed Margaret'. He was now a fellow member of the Cabinet, shadowing Education, and his declaration for Margaret brought with him a large section of the Party's moderate centre, diluting Margaret's reputation as a right-wing radical.

It was a curiously amicable week, with none of the character assassination that had gone on before the previous ballot, culminating in a Young Conservatives' meeting in Eastbourne, where both Margaret and Willie Whitelaw had been invited to speak. There had been a lot of work to do in the meantime, a lot of active canvassing for support, and with four candidates in the field, there was scarcely a corridor in the House of Commons where there wasn't a campaign worker discreetly hustling those members who had not yet decided which way they were going to vote. As one young MP afterwards remarked, he wished the whole thing could have gone on to the hundredth ballot, because he had never had so many invitations to dinner in his life.

Through it all Margaret was still busy on the Finance Bill which was now at the committee stage. She worked like a Trojan on the Bill, and earned the respect of all of the people who worked on it with her. Economics was the area in which she felt most at home, and she grasped and understood the most intricate details.

But there was more than the leadership election going on at the same time. Carol was sitting for her law finals at London University, and Margaret was desperately worried that her activity in the leadership campaign might have some adverse effect on her daughter. Her whip in the Finance Bill was Cecil Parkinson, who seven years later became chairman of the Conservative Party Association, and one of her most trusted Cabinet colleagues. He would drive her home at night on occasions when they had both worked late, and was quite astonished at how, having had her head deep in complex figures and the intricacies of the Bill, she would suddenly turn into the worried mother, suffering nerves for her daughter in the midst of exams.

Finally the day dawned, a tense one in the Thatcher household all round. Carol still had two more exams to do and, sitting in the kitchen at Flood Street, she admitted she was jolly nervous about them.

'You're not as nervous as I am,' said Margaret, 'I'm nervous too.'

'Do you think you're going to win?' asked Carol.

'We don't know if we've got the numbers.' Later that afternoon, at the end of a three-hour exam, one of the invigilators came up to Carol and asked, 'Do you know the results?'

'No,' responded Carol rather tetchily, 'of course I don't, I've just spent the last three hours pouring my heart out about Equity.'

'Your Mum won,' he said quietly, and a shiver ran down her spine, '146.'

None of the family really believed that Margaret was likely to win. They had all been astonished by the outcome of the first ballot, and held out little more hope for this one. So, when the news finally came from the Committee Room at four o'clock, just as it had the week before, they were all utterly flabbergasted. The results were: Margaret – 146, Willie Whitelaw – 79, Geoffrey Howe – 19, James Prior – 19, and John Peyton – 11. As Norman St John-Stevas, would-be confidant of popes and queens, said later, 'It wasn't an election. It was an assumption.'

It was also history. Margaret heard the news herself from Airey Neave. She had once again been waiting in his small room in the House, consumed with nerves, when he came in and said quite simply, 'It's all right. You're Leader of the Opposition.' It was the most tremendous moment. Everyone who had worked so hard all those months, who had pored over the opinion polls, helped with speeches and articles, tramped the corridors of Westminster seeking support, stayed up round the clock planning the strategy, were rapturous. It was all over; Margaret Thatcher, the grocer's daughter from Grantham, had miraculously conquered the most chauvinist, Establishment Party, years before even she, with all her determination, thought it would ever be possible.

The campaign was over, but the work was about to begin, and with typical single-mindedness, she settled straight down to write a few notes in preparation for the press conference that followed. 'To me it is like a dream, that the next name in the list after Harold Macmillan, Sir Alec Douglas-Home and Edward Heath is Margaret Thatcher,' she said to newspaper, television and radio reporters packed into the Grand Committee Room off Westminster Hall. 'Each has brought his own style of leadership and stamp of greatness to his task, and I shall take on the work with humility and dedication.' She then thanked all the people who had helped her, and said, 'It is important to me that this prize has been won in open electoral contest with four other potential leaders. I know they will be disappointed, but I hope we shall soon be back working together as colleagues for the things in which we all believe. There is much to do, and I hope you will allow me time to do it thoughtfully and well.'

That evening when Carol arrived home, having walked in the rain all the way from Marble Arch, wrapped in thought about the enormity of what had happened, the house in Flood Street was under siege. People with cameras, flash-bulbs popping, were everywhere waiting for Margaret to come home, and they were there to stay. There was going to be little chance of getting any sleep at No.19 that night, so to escape the hordes, the family slipped away and spent the night with neighbours at No.31.

With more exams to do the next morning, Carol had a quick look at the press conference on television and went to bed. It was past midnight when Margaret finally arrived home and came into Carol's room to say goodnight. She was looking radiant, blue eyes shining bright. Gone were the nerves of the morning and the knowledge that her future hung in the balance with the ballot – it had been a brutal case of all or nothing: Leader and potential Prime Minister, or a lifetime on the back-benches. It had turned out to be all.

During the leadership election, when Margaret Thatcher looked likely to succeed, a group of Labour MPs became involved in an argument in the Smoking Room in the House of Commons. 'If she wins,' said one, 'it will be the best news for the Labour Party ever. We will be in power for ever and ever.' Amongst the group was someone who knew her better. 'You're quite wrong,' he said. 'That woman is the bees' knees; she is the most remarkable woman alive. She is the best man there is.'

It was a while before anyone else came to agree with him, or indeed before many members of the general public came to see that she was anything more than a caricature. A great deal of public relations work had to be done. But first, with the question of leadership over, Margaret had to set about finding a team to lead. High on the list of priorities was the tricky subject of how to deal with Ted Heath. She had been to see him as a matter of courtesy way back in November when she had decided she would stand, but he had taken her gesture ungraciously. On this occasion she went round to his house in Wilton Street – without the official car and driver that went with the job, as he had not yet given those up – and offered him a job in her Shadow Cabinet. He said no thank you very much. That, at least, is her version of what happened. Ted Heath claims that she never offered him a specific job of any sort. And there is yet another version of the episode, namely that Margaret never saw Ted at all. She went round to his house, was shown into a waiting room on the ground floor, and Ted, who was upstairs, kept her waiting such an intolerable length of time that she finally got up and walked out.

There is no doubt that he was very very bitter about what had happened. It was bad enough losing, it was worse still losing to a woman, and to crown it all he had lost to the one woman he could stand least of all. And there is equally little doubt that she was well aware of his intense dislike of her and didn't frankly want him anywhere near. He was a peculiarly cold fish; with no distinct sexuality. Margaret once said that when she was with Ted she didn't feel as though she was talking to a man at all. Both felt awkward in the other's company, and so Ted opted to retire to the back-benches to think dark thoughts, with every intention of keeping his criticism to himself. But it wasn't many months before the temptation to say what he thought of his successor overcame him.

He would snipe at her in the House and in private, but it was years before Ted Heath could bring himself to mention Margaret Thatcher's name in public. The day she was officially adopted as Leader by the Conservative Party as a whole (as distinct from the Parliamentary Party), nine days after the ballot, in the Europa Hotel in London, Heath contrived to be on holiday in Spain. He sent a telegram instead, in which he sounded as gracious as he could. It was read out by Lord Hailsham, who had proposed the motion accepting Margaret. 'It is an immense privilege to be elected to this office and to be able to serve the Party in it. Grave problems face us as a nation and as a Party, which will not be overcome simply or easily, and which will need both skill and determination for their solution. Margaret Thatcher has both, and I sincerely wish her well.' When, a year later, he was asked by a television interviewer if he had anything nice to say about his successor, he replied, 'When she became Leader of the Party I wished her well and I wished her every success. I don't think anyone can do more than that.'

Ted's feelings for her were irrelevant for the time being. He had turned down a post in her Shadow Cabinet (or the opportunity to be offered a post), and there were still twenty-two places to fill, and this was the priority that occupied her mind immediately. She knew well enough what she wanted in the long term, but Margaret was a relatively inexperienced minister. She had moved about in a number of junior ministries, as many people had, but she had never held any of the posts in Cabinet which are normally considered essential for a potential leader, such as Chancellor of the Exchequer, Home or Foreign Secretary. Indeed, she had only been a member of the Cabinet once, and then as Minister for Education, which was considered to be a very minor rung on the ladder. Not surprisingly, she lacked the confidence to bring out the long knives.

The Tory Party was something she still held in awe, and while she didn't think a great deal of a great many of the people at the top of the ladder, she recognized at this stage that she needed them. So, she retained a large proportion of Ted Heath's old friends. There was more than a little of the feeling that enemies can do less harm if they are standing where you can see them.

Deputy leadership thus went to Willie Whitelaw, closest of all Heath's allies, and her leading opponent in the ballot. Whitelaw had opposed Margaret because he had felt she was too right wing, too doctrinaire and lacking in any feeling for people or compassion. He was also dead set against having a woman at the top, being very much of the old school. But having lost, he acted to type; ex-Scots Guards, officer and a gentleman, he did the right and proper thing. Margaret had won by a fair process, and he saw it as his duty to get on with her, to fall in behind the Leader, which he did. And he says:

> If you make up your mind that you want the Conservative Party to run this country, and you have a contribution to make, the only way of making it is through the person that leads it. It's no use trying to think that you're going to make it by waltzing off on your own and arguing with them all the time. If you have any power and if you have any position, then you've got to wheel it in behind them. Anything else is silly.

However, Margaret did bring in some of her own supporters as well; Keith Joseph, who became Number Three in the Shadow Cabinet with a special brief on policy and research; and Airey Neave, whom she appointed to shadow Northern Ireland. In addition, she felt the need at that early, rather insecure stage, for another woman in the Shadow Cabinet, and invited Sally Oppenheim to be in charge of consumer affairs.

Much of the advice about who should go where came from Airey Neave, who was also responsible for setting up her private office and recruiting staff. It was he too who suggested some of the reorganization that went on at Conservative Central Office, which she now took over as Leader. Chairman of the Conservative National Union is traditionally the appointment of the Leader, and the team who work

97

under him will be the Leader's men, working together to further that Leader's policies. In this case, where the new Leader's policies were quite different from those of her predecessors, it was inevitable that she should effect a clean sweep in Smith Square. Margaret has always found dismissing people the hardest part of her job, and it was a very fraught and unpleasant time, in which she relied heavily on Airey Neave. Out went the uppermost layer of officials in the building and in came friends, headed by Lord Thorneycroft.

Peter Thorneycroft had served under Churchill and Macmillan (from whose Cabinet he had resigned because he disagreed with his economic policy). He had retired from politics and was working in industry, as chairman of Trusthouse Forte amongst other things. His deputy was Angus Maude, another one-time member of a Cabinet who had disagreed with his Leader; on this occasion Ted Heath in his Shadow Cabinet in 1966. Margaret offered the appointment of vice chairman to Baroness Young, an old acquaintance from Oxford, where after university she had spent many years in local government. She was also a close friend of Airey Neave, whose constituency was close by in Abingdon. Since becoming a life peer in 1971, she had been active in the House of Lords as whip in the Heath administration, then Parliamentary Under Secretary, and in this role had come to know Lord Thorneycroft too. Gordon Reece was persuaded to give up his job at EMI and join the Party full-time as director of publicity.

On the other hand, seven key officials were shown the door at Central Office including one of the treasurers, the head of research and the director-general. Such dramatic axing at Smith Square brought much criticism from certain sections of the Tory press. *The Times*, which had backed Heath for the leadership, called it 'the act of a downright fool,' but as Alan Watkins in the left-wing magazine, *New Statesman*, gleefully observed, 'Those that live by patronage shall surely perish by patronage.'

Someone who survived the purge and came up smiling was playwright Ronald Millar, a Noël Coward-like figure who had been advising and writing speeches for the Party under Ted Heath's administration on an unpaid freelance basis since 1969. He had been close to all of Heath's men – Tony Barber, Willie Whitelaw, Lord Carrington – and had been especially close to Ted himself in the last few months, working on campaign speeches and helping with his television appearances.

Margaret, thus far in her career had had no need for speech writers, but as Leader of the Party this would change. Furthermore, she had to step straight into Ted's shoes and deliver speeches that had been scheduled for him. One such speech was due to be given a week after she took over, and it was duly shown to her. She immediately asked who had written it for Ted, and then said, 'Well I'd better meet this man.' Ronnie Millar was summoned, and was in some indecision about where his loyalties lay. He was fond of Ted, but he finally decided that he had gone into the job in the first place not because of a burning desire to go and fight for Heath, but because he couldn't stand Harold Wilson any longer, and if he was going to go on living in Britain, felt he had to do something about it. There was therefore no real conflict; his ultimate loyalty was to the Conservative Party. So he went to meet Mrs Thatcher in the Shadow Leader's room in the House of Commons.

The meeting was very guarded, each was highly suspicious of the other, and Ronnie went away promising to give the job a try. The speech in question was a five-minute party political broadcast. Ronnie was in the midst of rehearsals at the Haymarket Theatre at the time, and he sat in the darkened stalls with one eye on the actors and the other on what he was writing for Mrs Thatcher. When he reappeared some time later to show her what he had written, the meeting was equally guarded. Ronnie read the speech out to her, on the grounds that politicians have a tendency to read things in a very strange way. The speech ended with a quotation from Abraham Lincoln:

> You cannot bring about prosperity by discouraging thrift.
> You cannot strengthen the weak by weakening the strong.
> You cannot help strong men by tearing down big men.
> You cannot help the wage-earner by pulling down the wage-payer.
> You cannot further the brotherhood of man by encouraging class hatred.
> You cannot help the poor by destroying the rich.
> You cannot establish sound security on borrowed money.
> You cannot keep out of trouble by spending more than you earn.
> You cannot build character and courage by taking away man's initiative and independence.
> You cannot help men permanently by doing for them what they could and should do for themselves.

Margaret listened in stony silence. When he was finished, she said nothing, but bent down and reached into the portmanteau by her feet, inside which was a handbag, and from the handbag she pulled out her wallet, and from the inside compartment of the wallet she produced a torn and yellowing piece of paper, which she handed to Ronnie. It was the Abraham Lincoln speech he had just read to her. 'I never go anywhere without it,' she said.

The friendship was sealed, and Ronnie Millar, knighted in the New Year's honours list in 1980, has been a trusted favourite ever since. Margaret's very first private engagement after becoming Leader of the Opposition in February 1975 was to take the family to the first Saturday night performance of the play he had written – and had been rehearsing while writing that first speech – at the Haymarket. After the show, they all went off to Annabel's nightclub, where Mark was a member; Margaret saying they would be able to talk a bit there. It was obviously her first – and very probably her last – visit. The noise almost deafened her.

Ronnie wrote major speeches and conference speeches, but the day-to-day political speeches were written by a variety of people, sought out by those now running her private office. These included Richard Ryder, a young journalist friend of Neave's who worked on the Peterborough column of the *Daily Telegraph*, and who recruited some of his old colleagues to submit speeches. It would be Margaret's habit initially to have four or five speeches to choose from for one particular occasion. She would read them, choose the one she liked, and then call in the author to go over it with him. But she never took the decision on her own. Everything went to Airey Neave for his approval, and often to other colleagues, like Leon Brittan, Angus Maude and Jim Prior, by whom she was quite easily swayed.

Margaret was now installed in the Leader of the Opposition's room, a large office not far from the Chamber of the House, overlooking the Commons car park. She instantly set about having it redecorated – alas, there was no time to do it herself, although she chose the colour scheme. She moved in a few creature comforts, a glass-topped coffee table, some comfortable chairs, and a brass table lamp. Her secretary, Alison Ward, took over a room adjoining Mrs Thatcher's, which she shared with Caroline Stephens, one of the few people that Margaret took on who had formerly worked for Ted Heath. Caroline subsequently married Richard Ryder.

One other person, whom as Leader of the Opposition she automatically inherited, was the official driver, George Newell. He had been with Ted Heath on and off, as he had progressed up the ministerial ladder, for nearly fifteen years. The relationship between minister or shadow minister and his driver is a close one. He is on hand to drive the minister from the time he leaves home in the morning until he goes home in the evening, which can be any time up to and sometimes after midnight. Because drivers are employed by the civil service, they then have to take the official car back to the central garage and get themselves home after that under their own steam. They might then be expected to be back on duty again at nine o'clock or even earlier the following morning. Considerate ministers tend to let their driver go earlier in the evening, and if they are going to be sitting late in the House, make some other arrangement to get home. Not all ministers are so thoughtful. Ted was, and if he did keep George late then he always showed his appreciation. As a result George was tremendously loyal to Heath, and was not at all pleased when he was dislodged as Leader.

Within weeks, however, he was utterly devoted to Mrs Thatcher. He and his wife, May, lived in Sydenham; they had no children, and so Margaret was always anxious when she kept him away from his wife, particularly at weekends. If she went off on a tour, or to some function where she was presented with flowers, she would always give George the prettiest bunch and tell him to take them home to May, and apologize for keeping him so long.

With the job came police protection too, and again Margaret very quickly won enormous affection from her detectives from the Special Branch, because she was so considerate. She would always enquire about their wives and children in a motherly way, and unlike so many other politicians who might also ask, she always managed to sound as though she were really interested in the answer. In all the years that she has now had protection – and official drivers – not one has asked for a transfer.

But while she was winning converts in her own personal circle, there was still a lot of work to be done in the country to dispel the unfortunate image she projected of the archetypal 'plummy' Tory. At the instigation of Gordon Reece, the entire persona underwent a refit. Her voice was her biggest enemy. She had always said how lucky she was to have been able to lose her Lincolnshire accent, and though she didn't much like doing it, she could be persuaded to say a few sentences in her old accent from time to time. But what she had acquired in its place sounded affected. No one told her quite that, but they did say the pitch was too high for public speaking – she sounded positively shrill at times – and she was quite prepared to accept that her voice could do with improvement. With Ronnie Millar's connections in the theatre, voice lessons were therefore organized with the teacher at the National Theatre, and with practice her pitch came down.

Her dress was another problem. She had never got out of the 'little black dress and pearls' style, which had been so ridiculed in her days at the Department of Education and Science. With the number of engagements that she now had to perform, she needed a bigger wardrobe and someone to advise her generally on what to wear when. She therefore enlisted the help of her friend Guinevere Tilney, with whom she had served as co-chairman of the Women's National Commission. Between them they tried and tested several hairdressers, make-up artists and fashion houses, from whom she was still buying off-the-peg clothes.

Her hair was at this time being dyed blonde, something she had started when she first began to grey at the temples some years before, and something she felt quite passionately every woman should do. 'Margaret,' she howled in horror when she saw her old Grantham friend, Margaret Wickstead (née Goodrich), for the first time after some years. 'What on earth's happened to your marvellous red hair?'

'It's going grey,' responded Margaret simply.

'Well you must dye it,' said the other Margaret.

'Oh, I can't be bothered,' said Margaret Wickstead.

'You should,' declared Mrs Thatcher emphatically, 'you should.'

Margaret did dread the idea of growing old, although there were precious few people with whom she would ever discuss anything so personal. She also dreaded falling prey to the diseases of middle age, such as hysterectomies; she worried that her neck gave her age away, and began wearing high collars and bows; and she was conscious of varicose veins in her legs. The nearest she ever came to a panic would be over some feminine vanity, such as if she didn't have the right shoes to go with a dress.

With the job of Leader came the need to travel, both at home and abroad, something which Margaret had done very seldom in the past. She had been on an English Speaking Union lecture tour to the States, attended a Parliamentary Commonwealth Conference in the Bahamas, and she'd visited Russia with a group of MPs, but Abroad was still very foreign to her, and it was a long time before she became confident away from home. She also stepped up travel at home: within days of the election she was whisked off to the industrial north of England and

Scotland, places where it was felt she had least sympathy. Yet she went down exceptionally well, partly no doubt because of the novelty value in being the first woman Leader, and people came out of curiosity. In what remained of 1975, she made twelve forays around Great Britain, and several abroad: to Luxembourg, France, Germany, Rumania, Canada and the United States.

Margaret was nervous abroad for two reasons. First, never having held the post of Foreign Secretary, a common grounding for leaders of the Party, she was ignorant of foreign affairs. Her forte had always been economics, and she was painfully aware of her shortcomings. Second, unlike her public-school-educated colleagues, who had learnt several languages at school and spent holidays on the Continent, she knew the scantiest amount of French, not a syllable of anything else, and had not set a foot outside England until she was married.

She did, however, have one huge advantage over her colleagues: she was a woman, and as such attracted massive interest abroad, particularly in America where the women's movement was far stronger than in any other country. Margaret had never been very impressed by feminism, and made no bones about it when asked, as she invariably was, whether she owed at least part of her success to Women's Lib. 'Some of us were making it long before Women's Lib was ever thought of,' she snapped, adding that all the political leaders she had so far met had 'just accepted me as a politician and got on with business'. The fact that she happened to be a woman, she said, was 'something that never bothers or concerns me'. This was a little less than the truth. Margaret is very conscious of being a woman, and thoroughly enjoys being treated and appreciated as such. She likes people to flatter her, she enjoys dressing up, loves clothes and jewellery, she takes care about her weight and how her hair looks. In short, she loves being told she's looking nice – provided she is told in appropriate circumstances, and not when she has come to talk business.

Despite her hectic schedule, Margaret still tried to keep up with the family and, by dint of organization and forward planning, managed to see them from time to time. She had made it a rule never to go off on trips when Mark or Carol were on holiday, and she continued, whenever possible, to plot all her engagements around the family. Alison Ward managed her diary, and Denis had an equally efficient secretary at Burmah, Phyllis Kilner, who had been with him for twenty-five years and ran his life with wizard precision. She told Alison months in advance when Mrs Thatcher would be needed for a Burmah dinner, and Alison likewise warned Phyllis when there was some occasion on which Denis would be needed. But in 1975 Denis retired from Burmah, at the age of sixty, taking with him a Rolls-Royce, which he still has discreetly parked underground at the House of Commons.

Denis's retirement was something Margaret had been dreading. 'I don't know what I'm going to do when Denis retires,' she had once said. 'He can't retire. He must find some other work to do.' In fact, he did continue to work; he remained on the board of two companies as non-executive director, and as chairman of the chemical firm, Chipmans Limited. So her fears were abated for the time being. It did mean, however, that he was more available to accompany her when necessary, and no longer had to face the gruelling drive at 6.30 every morning out to Swindon.

At much the same time the lease on the flat at Court Lodge expired. The Thatchers therefore moved off the golf course, which was a security man's nightmare, and into another flat nearby, in the wing of a National Trust-owned property, Scotney Castle. Scotney is a magnificent house, set down a winding drive lined with rhododendron and other trees, and amidst acres of well-kept gardens and farmland, with a ruined fourteenth-century castle and lake in the grounds. Before the National Trust took over ownership, the house was in the Hussey family, and Mrs Christopher Hussey still lives in the main part of the house, administers the farm that surrounds it, and feeds the swans each evening.

As it is a National Trust property, the grounds are open to the public at certain times and so security is still not perfect, but the place is mainly kept as a bolt-hole for Denis, to escape from London and from politicians. Immediately after the leadership election he told reporters, 'They say I am the most shadowy husband of all time. I intend to stay that way and leave the limelight to my wife.' Thereafter he stuck to his word. He recognized that once he gave an interview to one newspaper he would be bounden to give one to every other paper that asked, and it was simpler to give a blanket no. He made an exception just once to talk exclusively about business, but he has never discussed his personal life nor politics. This was no bad thing: Denis Thatcher's views are well known to be extremely right wing. His language is also famous for its colour, and what he says in private is enough to make even Mrs Thatcher's hair curl.

By the time Carol had passed her law exams, she had had enough of living at home. Unlike her brother, she shrank from publicity, and had always found being Mrs Thatcher's daughter hard to take. Margaret, however, was very insistent that even if she didn't want to practise law, Carol should qualify as a solicitor, which involved serving time as an articled clerk. She sought the advice of their old friend from Isle of Wight days, John Stebbings, who agreed that Carol should be articled, but pointed out that there was the whole country to choose from; and between them they settled on Chichester.

It had been Margaret who had persuaded Carol to go to university in the first place, saying that in the future it would be vital to have a degree in order to get a good job. She would have liked Mark to go to university too, but as an alternative had arranged for him to join IPEC, an Australian firm run by a friend of Denis's, to study accountancy – Denis's own professional training. Mark scraped through the first part of his finals, but repeatedly failed to get any further, and it was a great worry to Margaret that he couldn't pass exams.

Mark had developed an interest in motor racing, and two years previously with a couple of friends had founded his own team which he called Mark Thatcher Racing. Initially people seemed prepared to give him cars to drive, which made Margaret both nervous for his safety and suspicious of his benefactors and their motives. But as time went by, and his driving record proved less than ace, British sponsors became thin on the ground, and Mark was tempted to look elsewhere, namely Japan.

Margaret herself had never been the slightest bit interested in cars. She saw them as a means of travelling from A to B, and no more. While Denis had had a succession of fancy cars, she had owned two in the last twenty years: the old blue Ford Anglia, which Paddi Victor Smith had driven; and when that expired, she bought a little white Vauxhall Viva, which she passed on to Carol when she went off to Chichester.

Despite all her own worries as Leader of the Opposition, she still behaved like a mother hen where her children were concerned, even though they were by now quite grown up. When Carol went off to Chichester, Margaret was worried sick about whether the digs she was living in were cold, whether she was getting enough to eat, or whether she was going to run out of money. On one occasion Margaret had been taking part in 'Any Questions' on Radio 4, travelling down that day from the Midlands. She had no car to get home and was planning on taking the train. A fellow panellist offered her a lift as far as Hertfordshire, and after giving her a cup of tea, lent her his car and driver to take her home. She asked to be taken to one of the mainline stations instead: Carol was due to arrive on a train at 1.30 in the morning and she wanted to be there to meet her.

Margaret's first Party Conference as Leader in October, was a make-or-break occasion. She had convinced half of Europe and a good section of America that she was a good leader for the Tory Party, she had impressed President Gerald Ford and Secretary of State Henry Kissinger, and come away confident: 'I feel I have been accepted as a leader in the international sphere – the field in which they said I would never be accepted.' But in the constituencies of Great Britain she was still an interloper – cold, affected, and unacceptably right wing – and the opportunity to change their minds lay in the Conference. Once again it was held in the seaside town of Blackpool: a week-long affair with speeches in the main hall all day, followed by group meetings, societies and fringe conferences in smaller rooms, lasting well into the evening, and finally, receptions, parties, dinners and dances, to complete the night. With the media encamped for the week and television teams with interview rooms set up, every hour of the day was filled. It was a hectic, exhausting week, culminating in the Leader's speech on the final Friday morning.

Ted Heath, still very much the darling of the delegates, arrived a day after Margaret, and was given a tumultuous reception as he walked into the main hall at the Winter Gardens. He noticeably avoided the new faces sitting at the front of the platform. That evening, over drinks in the bar with a couple of journalists, he spoke his mind. Keith Joseph and Margaret Thatcher were a couple of fanatics who were going to damage the country and ruin the Conservative Party. And with that, having ensured that the morning's papers would lead with his views, he issued a pre-emptory denial, and returned to London.

It was all the more vital that Margaret's speech on the Friday should go well, and as the week progressed she grew increasingly anxious. The speech had been written by two members of the research department, Adam Ridley and Christopher Patten. But as the delivery date drew closer, she decided that she wanted Ronnie Millar to come up and have a quick look at it. He was duly telephoned and arrived in Blackpool, where he set the cat well and truly among the pigeons by saying he didn't much care for the speech. And so they all sat down in Margaret's suite at the Imperial Hotel, and wrote another one. Margaret kept coming in and out, adding a few thoughts while doing a quick dress change, before dashing off to the next function she had to attend. It was late at night before she could give it her undivided attention. Denis, dressed in a dinner jacket, sat perched on the window ledge, listening while the others worked on the speech, reading and re-reading it out loud. Finally Margaret said, 'No, no, I don't think you've got the peroration right,' whereupon Denis spoke for the first time in about two hours, and said, 'Dear, I think it's right.' 'Do you?' she said, and the peroration stayed.

It was a long hard night with scarcely any hours for sleep. The next morning Margaret was a bundle of nerves. She was due to speak at 11.30, and was dressed and ready long before it was time to go. Ronnie Millar was still working away at the final touches to the speech, changing the odd word until he was entirely satisfied that it was perfect. Having bounced in and out of the room, Margaret finally came and knelt down on the floor beside him to see what he was doing. 'I can't sit,' she explained, 'because it will ruin my dress. Go on, go on, go on.'

Just as they were about to leave for the Winter Gardens, the phone rang. It was a message from the Conference: some idiot had got up unexpectedly, which was making them run over time, and could she please delay leaving for another eight minutes. 'No, no,' she protested, 'I don't mind waiting down there for an hour, but I'm not going to stay in this damned hotel shaking with nerves for another minute.'

Chairman of the Conference that year was Margaret's old friend, Peter Thomas, and it was he who introduced her with an excellent speech. As he spoke, however, Margaret played a stroke of pure genius. A moment earlier an old woman in the audience had presented her with a blue feather duster. She seized the duster, flicked it quickly round the lectern, and fleetingly across Peter's nose; and the hall was won. They roared with laughter; and suddenly the nerves vanished. Margaret rose to her feet, and started to speak. She began by paying tribute to previous leaders of the Conservative Party:

> I know you will understand the humility I feel at following in the footsteps of great men like our Leader (in the year I first attended a Party Conference), Winston Churchill, a man called by destiny to raise the name of Britain to supreme heights in the history of the free world. . . . Of Anthony Eden, who set us the goal of a property-owning democracy. . . . Of Harold Macmillan, whose leadership brought so many ambitions within the grasp of every citizen. . . . Of Alec Douglas-Home who earned the affection and admiration of us all . . . And of Edward Heath, who successfully

led the Party to victory in 1970 and brilliantly led the nation into Europe in 1973.

. . . they all had one thing in common: each met the challenge of his time. Now, what is the challenge of our time? I believe there are two challenges: to overcome the country's economic and financial problems; and to regain our confidence in Britain and ourselves.

She explained why she had criticized the country when she was abroad:

It wasn't Britain I was criticizing, it was Socialism; and I will go on . . . because it is bad for Britain. Britain and Socialism are not the same thing, and as long as I have health and strength they never will be.

No country can flourish if its economic and social life is dominated by nationalization and state control. . . Something else is happening to this country. We are witnessing a deliberate attack on our values . . . on those who want to promote merit and excellence . . . on our heritage and our great past. And there are those who gnaw away at our national self-respect, rewriting British history as centuries of unrelieved gloom, oppression and failure – as days of hopelessness, not days of hope.

Let me give you my vision: a man's right to work as he will, to spend what he earns, to own property, to have the state as servant and not as master: these are the British inheritance. They are the essence of a free country, and on that freedom all our other freedoms depend.

When she sat down the delegates from the constituencies cheered until they were hoarse. Later that evening she said, 'Now I am Leader.' She was still not a totally confident Leader, however, and not all her speeches were as well received as that at Blackpool in October. There was one occasion when she made a very poor speech in the House, and she knew it had been poor. 'I don't mind admitting to you,' she told a friend, 'I do feel depressed.'

'These are the sort of experiences from which you must learn,' said the friend firmly. 'You are depressed, you haven't done yourself justice, but when you're Prime Minister you're going to have to face far worse than that, and often these things are a test for later on in life.'

She found Prime Minister Harold Wilson particularly unnerving in the House. He was masterful in knowing just where to put in the knife, and had managed to rattle her. When he once teased her for her inexperience, she retaliated, 'What the Prime Minister means is that he has been around for a long time – and he looks it.' She hated the way he refused to answer questions directly; and she reached the stage where she once said she didn't want to open a debate censuring the Government; she wanted to speak later, so she could see how Wilson was going to defend himself first. Airey Neave took her gently aside and said, 'But Margaret, when you're Prime Minister you'll have to open debates quite often.'

Harold Wilson was always there to remind her of her inadequacies. When she made a weak speech, he would leap to make capital. One of his hobby horses was Russia. It was his cordial relationship with Russia that had made him so loath, when he was in power in 1964, to protest about her constituent, Gerald Brooke, being held by the KGB. When he returned from a trip to Russia, firmly committed to detente between East and West, and she challenged him about the wisdom of such a policy during Prime Minister's Question Time, he slapped her down by suggesting that she should leave foreign policy to someone with a little more experience. She determined to do some more work on the subject, and the speech she delivered in Kensington Town Hall in January 1976 touched a raw nerve:

> The first duty of a government is to safeguard its people against external aggression; to guarantee the survival of our way of life. [The present Government] is dismantling our defence at a moment when the strategic threat to Britain and her allies from an expansionist power is graver than at any moment since the end of the last war. Russia is ruled by a dictatorship of patient, far-sighted men who are rapidly making their country the foremost naval and military power in the world. They are not doing this solely for the sake of self-defence. A huge, largely land-locked country like Russia does not need to build the most powerful navy in the world just to guard its own frontiers. No. The Russians are bent on world dominance, and they are rapidly acquiring the means to become the most powerful imperial nation the world has seen. They put guns before butter, while we put just about everything before guns. They know they are a super power in only one sense

– the military sense. They are a failure in human and economic terms. If we cannot draw the lesson of what they tried to do in Portugal and are now trying to do in Angola, then we are destined – in their words – to end up on 'the scrap heap of history'.

Russia responded with remarkable speed. Tass, the official Soviet news agency, called her an 'Iron Lady', 'the Cold War Warrior', and embarked upon a campaign to discredit her in Russia. Cartoons appeared of Margaret sitting astride a broomstick, flying over the House of Commons, with the caption, 'Wicked Witch of the West'. It was Guinevere Tilney who first told her that the Russians had called her 'Iron Lady', and she was absolutely delighted. 'That's the greatest compliment they could ever have paid me,' she said and proceeded to boast about it in public speeches: 'The Russians said I was an Iron Lady,' she said in an election address three years later, 'They were right; Britain needs an Iron Lady.'

She was not so delighted, however, when politicians in the House employed it as a cheap jibe, and the British press used it in reference to her own personality. This was particularly galling when she had gone along, at such pains, with Gordon Reece's scheme to let people see the human side of her. She hated being interviewed and loathed television. 'Winston was never interviewed on television,' she complained, but was sensible to the changed roles of both television and the politician, and with Gordon's help allowed herself to be given the soft sell. She talked about the feminine side of her life, the dress sizes she took, the way she cared for her skin, how she felt about combining motherhood with a career, and whether she ever cried. It was all sham. These were not subjects which Mrs Thatcher would have chosen to talk about, certainly not to a stranger from the national press. But it was a quid pro quo. Favours in the media all came at a price, and if they were going to support her politically, which would be vital in the next general election, she had to give her pound of flesh from time to time on the women's pages.

There was a brief respite from the attentions of the press, however, in the spring of 1976, when Harold Wilson stunned both country and colleagues by suddenly resigning. He went into a Cabinet meeting on 16 March, and proceeded to read out an eight-page statement which began, 'I have just returned from an audience with the Queen.' He went on to say that he had informed her of his irrevocable decision to abdicate power and return to the back-benches, repeating the promise that

Stanley Baldwin had made when he handed the reins of government over to Neville Chamberlain in 1937: 'Once I leave, I leave. I am not going to speak to the man on the bridge and I am not going to spit on the deck.'

It was not clear at the time, and has never been made clear since, why Wilson decided to quit. He was a totally political animal, loved the House, loved the job, and on his own admission was 'as fit as a flea', and only sixty years old. Labour was at a low ebb in the country, it was true, and had lost a series of by-elections which had cut their majority in the House to one, but there had been no major confrontations with the unions and inflation appeared to be well under control. There would, Wilson announced, be no need to call a general election, and the Party should simply choose his successor and carry on.

Since there was every likelihood that his successor would be Foreign Secretary James Callaghan, who presented the toughest proposition of all the contenders, and there was a good chance that if they went to the country, Labour would lose the election, Margaret was naturally unhappy with Wilson's decision, and lost no time in saying so. When he appeared in the House for the first time after the announcement, Margaret wished him well in retirement, and demanded that his successor call a general election immediately. Wilson accepted her good wishes, but with customary agility rejected out of hand her demand for an election. Who, innumerable Tories asked, would be his successor? 'We have long had a practice of democratic election,' said Wilson, 'not the scatty system you introduced, but for which the Right Hon. Gentleman the Member for Penrith [Willie Whitelaw] would have been leader.'

As predicted, the following week, Jim Callaghan did become Leader and thus Prime Minister, beating the more left-wing contenders for the post, and presenting as tricky an opponent as Margaret had feared. He very quickly isolated what irritated her most – namely to be condescending to her sex – and proceeded to be so for the next three years, while she bided her time awaiting his job. But his three years were not all plain sailing. Despite great Parliamentary cunning, he ran into some bad luck. No sooner was he installed in Downing Street than Labour lost its majority seat in the House, and the economy began to fall around his ears.

Wilson had succeeded in persuading the unions to accept a voluntary six per cent ceiling on pay rises, and it was this which had reflected so well in the level of inflation. This deal, however, was shortly due to expire, and Callaghan and his Chancellor, who continued to be Denis Healey, worked out a new plan which involved asking the unions to accept a three per cent increase in return for £1.3 billion in tax cuts. And if they didn't like the idea, then it was up to them to come up with an alternative.

Margaret complained bitterly that it was a sell-out to the unions, and when a deal was struck, which worked out at a four and a half per cent ceiling, the pound crashed to an all-time low. She introduced a motion of no confidence in the Government, saying that Callaghan was presiding over 'drift, debt and decay'. 'Now, now, little lady,' goaded Callaghan, after defeating the motion by calling on the support of the minor parties in the House, 'you don't want to believe all those things you read in the newspapers about crisis and upheavals and the end of civilization as we know it. Dearie me, not at all.'

Margaret called a second motion of no confidence nearly a year later, in March 1977. The Devolution Bill, which Labour had pledged itself to in its Election Manifesto, was opposed by a whole range of Labour rebels, joining forces with anti-devolution Tories. Shortly after that, the left wing revolted over spending cuts that Callaghan badly needed to push through Parliament in order to satisfy the International Monetary Fund, from which Healey had borrowed a colossal amount some months earlier in a desperate effort to keep the economy afloat. The Conservatives were fast winning favour in the country – the latest poll had shown they were in the lead by fifteen points; so it was vital for Callaghan that he should defeat the vote of no confidence. He therefore approached the Liberals, who held thirteen seats in the House, and negotiated what became known as the 'Lib-Lab Pact', of mutual back-scratching, with their Leader, David Steel. The vote of no confidence was thus defeated by 322 votes to 298.

The Prime Minister's troubles were by no means over. The pact was not a great success, and the Labour Party itself was growing increasingly rebellious and fractious. Callaghan finally had to gather his MPs together and tell them to make up their minds: 'Our present difficulties are not caused by the Tories,' he bellowed, 'they are caused by ourselves. Either this Government governs or it goes.'

It chose to govern. In the meantime Margaret embarked on more foreign travel. She had received a great many invitations since becoming Leader: the world had been fascinated right from the start to see for themselves the woman who could become Leader of the Conservative Party. But once the Russians had labelled her the 'Iron

Lady', the interest was considerably heightened. China had issued an invitation immediately after the Tass report and, although Mrs Thatcher had to defend her decision to go to a country with a regime in every way as totalitarian as the Soviet Union – which she did on the grounds that it was not expansionist like Russia – a trip had subsequently been worked out where she would visit China, Japan and Hong Kong.

Carol had by this time finished her stint in Chichester and decided that she could no longer bear to live in a country where she was inevitably tagged Mrs Thatcher's daughter, and stood no chance of being accepted as plain Carol Thatcher. She had been bitterly unhappy at university because of her mother's politics, and now that Margaret was Leader, every move either of her children made was chronicled in the diary pages of the daily press. Her much publicized romance with Jonathan Aitken, a young Conservative MP and nephew of the late Lord Beaverbrook, was the final straw. Margaret, whose morals were founded on Victorian principles, was reported to be very unhappy about the activities of her unmarried daughter. What she was most unhappy about, in fact, was the publicity. In the end Carol decided to get away from it all and go to stay in Australia for a while, where she had a number of friends, including Elizabeth Stebbings, daughter of John and Tricia. She travelled with her mother to the Far East, and while Margaret attended talks, Carol went sightseeing. They parted company in Hong Kong: Carol flew on to Sydney, where she had planned to stay six months, and ended up living for five years, while Margaret flew home to London. There was no acrimony. Carol was hugely fond of her mother, and in many ways is like her. But there is no doubt that Margaret Thatcher is a very dominating personality, and Carol was suffering from a desperate need to get out from under her influence.

Fiercely moral though she was herself, Margaret took the attitude, once the twins were grown up, that how and with whom they spent their time was none of her business. Mark's predilection for young women is legendary. He was often to be seen at Queen's Tennis Club, where he seemed to be far more interested in sizing up the female talent than improving his game. The comings and goings of his girlfriends were inevitably well catalogued by the press. Margaret was remarkably *laissez faire* about it all. And yet, she still believes strictly in the code of morality with which she and her parents' generation were brought up. She was quite shocked when she went round a College of Education last year, and told a friend, 'I found that the students had no rules – they didn't have to be in by a certain time of night.'

Mark was very much the apple of his mother's eye, as he always had been. He didn't abuse that position in that he was devoted to her and always totally loyal, but she did become quite worried that he might get into deep water. 'You know, the trouble with Mark is he just can't pass exams,' she told a friend over a drink in her room at the House of Commons one day. 'And the difficulty is, people are offering him jobs right and left. And you know I cannot accept a job for him just because he's my son.'

Margaret's Far Eastern tour went well, and she was accorded the reception normally extended to a head of state, rather than the leader of a party in opposition. China was a great treat for her, for she has always been very fond of Chinese art. Her dining room at Scotney was entirely Chinese in theme, with a Chinese rug on the floor and prints on the walls; she had more Chinese prints hanging in the living room at Flood Street. Her other great love is porcelain, and once again both homes were filled with plates and other pieces collected over the years, some from this trip in 1977.

Later in the year she returned to America, where she had scored such a success the previous September. Everywhere she went, she spoke confidently about leading a Conservative Government. 'The question is not whether we will win,' she told crowds in New York, 'but how large the majority will be.' And in Washington she met the new President, Jimmy Carter, who had just declared that he couldn't receive the French Opposition Leader, the Socialist, François Mitterand, on the grounds that he was only able to meet heads of state. That Margaret should have been swept so smartly into Carter's Oval Office in the White House was a sign that world leaders were taking her seriously.

The more success Margaret experienced abroad, the more confidence she exuded at home and in her Shadow Cabinet, and the more convinced she became that her vision for the future was the only way to get Britain back on to its feet. This wasn't mere power play. David Wolfson, today one of her special advisers, said once that he divided all the people he knew into kings, prophets and judges. Margaret, in his opinion, was a prophet. Patrick Cosgrave, another of her advisers at one time, labels people as warriors and heavers, and he placed her as a warrior. She was both prophet and warrior: she passionately believed that she was right, and if the British way of life, which she valued above all else, was going to be saved from destruction, then there was need for radical change, and it was her duty to bring that about. She spelt out this ideal when she was invited to address the Zurich Economic Society in March 1977:

> In September 1946 Winston Churchill called for an act of faith in recreating the European family. It is an act of faith too, which is required today by all of us in restoring the free society. The new renaissance . . . was perhaps best described by Kipling:
> 'So when the world is asleep, and there
>   seems no hope of waking
> Out of some long, bad dream that makes
>   her mutter and moan,
> Suddenly, all men arise to the noise of
>   fetters breaking,
> And everyone smiles at his neighbour
>   and tells him his soul is his own.'

Rudyard Kipling has always been one of Margaret's great heroes and favourite authors, whom she loves to hear quoted. She prides herself in knowing every sentence of his work, and it has always been something of a challenge to Ronnie Millar, who also admires Kipling, to find a quotation she doesn't know. He once did. 'No,' she said in disbelief. 'That can't be Kipling. I know it all,' and went straight to the bookshelf to look up one of her many volumes of his work.

Margaret had always seen things in black and white. She would become quite irritated if people complicated the issue with grey. What she saw, she spoke about quite bluntly, and what she said, she stuck to. This has been the hallmark of her politics all along, which was quite revolutionary in itself. Politicians are past masters at sitting on the fence, hedging their bets, and never giving a straight answer. When she first became Leader of the Party she held back, and when Jim Prior, for example, thought that speaking out about the evils of the union practice of operating a 'closed shop' in industries was unwise, she went along with it. She lacked the courage of her convictions. As time passed, she gained that courage, and when one of her Shadow Cabinet thought she was going too far, she argued with him.

One such issue was immigration. This potentially explosive subject had already lost the Conservative Party Enoch Powell, one of its most brilliant men. He had made a speech ten years earlier in 1968 in Birmingham, in which he forecast a race war in Britain if the

Government didn't do something to curb immigration. 'As I look ahead,' he said, 'I am filled with foreboding. Like the Romans, I seem to see "the River Tiber foaming with much blood".' This was considered so insensitive and radical, that Ted Heath had sacked him from his Shadow Cabinet. In the end such was his disgust with the way the Party was going, particularly when the Tory Government joined the Common Market, that Enoch Powell left the Party altogether. He had since become quite a supporter of Margaret, however, and they still meet and talk quite frequently.

The immigration laws introduced in 1968 had quite considerably restricted people coming into the United Kingdom: anybody applying for admission had to prove that one parent or grandparent was born in Britain. But when President Idi Amin expelled Uganda's entire Asian population in 1972, the Heath administration was obliged to relax the laws on humanitarian grounds and allowed all those with British passports to immigrate, regardless of their parentage. When Margaret became Leader, she reaffirmed that the Party would continue to honour Heath's pledge.

By the late 1970s, however, with the gradual deterioration in national morale, with unemployment and violence on the increase, and housing becoming scarce, there was a growing wave of racial unrest. This to some extent focused round the National Front, a fascist organization which openly preached racial hatred and vowed to make Britain white again. While the vast majority of people in the country abhorred all that the National Front stood for, the organization did attract a lot of publicity, and began to draw a growing number of supporters.

Margaret had an instinctive feeling that many people in the country were anxious about immigration, and that the time had come for the Conservative Party to say something, and stop pretending that the problem didn't exist. The moment arrived when she was invited to take part in a Granada Television 'World in Action' programme in January 1978, in the aftermath of a riot in Wolverhampton, in which about two hundred black youths fought everyone in sight after being provoked by a gang of whites. Many Britons, she said, were afraid of 'being swamped by people with a different culture' and, for the sake of good race relations and maintenance of the 'fundamental British characteristics which have done so much for the world', it was the duty of the Government to 'hold out the clear prospect of an end to immigration.'

'Every country can take some small minorities and in many ways they add to the richness and variety of this country,' she added, 'but the moment the minority threatens to become a big one, people get frightened. We are not in politics to ignore people's worries; we are in politics to deal with them.'

The programme caused a stink. She was condemned from every quarter, from the Labour front-bench, immigrant leaders, community workers, the Church, and even from some members of her own Party. She was accused of 'moving towards the attitudes and policies of the National Front', of 'making racial hatred respectable'. The matter was provocative enough to make even Ted Heath break his vow of silence. She had caused 'an unnecessary national row', he said; and the Right Reverend David Young, Bishop of Ripon, warned, 'You are playing a dangerous game. You are fostering emotions and feelings of prejudice, fear and hatred which can only be destructive to our society.'

These outbursts, particularly those from her own side, only served to confirm Margaret's belief that she was surrounded by mealy-mouthed moderates, who were so terrified of rocking the boat and losing support that they didn't have the guts to do what had to be done. She had already moved Ian Gilmour, one of Heath's supporters, whom she had initially made Shadow Home Secretary, to Defence, because he didn't agree with her support for reintroducing capital punishment. She sacked Winston Churchill as Opposition spokesman on Defence when he too defied her voting orders in the House. Now she began to work round them, making decisions in smaller groups where she knew she had support, before presenting ideas to the full Shadow Cabinet. She brought in advisers from the City; professional managers like Sir John Hoskins, who became head of her policy unit, Norman Strauss from Lever Brothers, Sir Derek Rayner from Marks & Spencer, and Robin Ibbs from ICI. These were all people with new ideas and the expertise to turn her vision into reality, who could sort out the dead wood of the civil service and keep their power in check, who could disentangle the bureaucracy and ease government out of people's lives.

Each year that she had been in Opposition, there seemed some likelihood of an election, but none so acutely as in the autumn of 1978. In anticipation of this, Gordon Reece advised bringing in Saatchi & Saatchi, an advertising agency in the City known for its clever, creative television commercials, to promote the Conservative Party. Chairman of the company, Tim Bell, a hard working, pushy extrovert, took charge of the account himself, and Margaret was sold, as Denis Healey rather sniffily observed, 'as if she was a soap powder'. By August the country was strewn with eye-catching posters, such as the one depicting a long queue of people on the dole, with the slogan 'Labour Still Isn't Working'. Television exposure was stepped up, and Gordon Reece, still desperately keen that she should shed the aloof image, persuaded Margaret to speak closer to the microphone so that she would sound more intimate. One of the newspapers noted that this had given her voice a husky, even a sexy quality.

She was in Scotland when this report appeared, and didn't see it. But the story was that Jim Prior, her Employment spokesman, rang up and asked if she had a cold. No, she said, what had made him think that? He explained that he had seen a report in the papers that said her voice sounded sexy, and assumed it was because she had a bad throat. 'I've never been so insulted in my life,' she exclaimed with a laugh which was not altogether convincing.

She enjoys men finding her sexy, although she is far too entrenched in her Victorian morality ever to admit it. The men she likes are those that flirt with her. She likes extroverts, she likes people like Gordon Reece who look her straight in the eyes, laugh at her, and pat her on the hand. She enjoys the irreverence of someone like Ronnie Millar, who tells her she has the best cheek-bones in the business, but the lousiest hair-do. The flirtation is never overt – she would find that intolerable – and there is never any question of a pass, but it is the frisson that she enjoys. And when she feels this mutual attraction, she is warm, relaxed and even at times, quite witty. If the feeling is absent, she can be like an ice-box. ' She is like a matron telling you off for wetting the bed,' said one who knows.

While Gordon Reece and Tim Bell dealt with her public image, Margaret had already won a great reputation for herself in the Party. All good politicians, and party leaders in particular, make a habit of asking after their colleagues' families, in much the same way as they pat heads of babies when they are canvassing. It's all part of the game. Margaret asked too; the difference was, she remembered, and would ask again. She wrote hand-written notes to anyone in trouble, anyone who had lost a parent, or anyone whose wife had undergone an operation. One MP who sometimes wrote speeches, one day handed in a piece which was quite unusable. Margaret gave it to someone else to re-jig, 'But do it in a way that won't hurt his feelings,' she said. 'He's just separated from his wife.' And when she was told that another MP's young wife had been killed in a car crash, she was so shocked and upset that she had to retreat into a room by herself for half an hour.

But the Saatchi & Saatchi effort was a false alarm. In September, just as the Tory team had laid elaborate plans to hire an aeroplane to take Margaret on a fleeting tour of the country, accompanied by a band of reporters, Callaghan summoned his Cabinet to Number Ten, and the BBC announced that he had requested five minutes of air time the following evening. Everyone naturally assumed that he was going to give the date of the general election. 'I don't know what he's going to say,' said Margaret when asked for her reaction, 'but I don't imagine he is making a ministerial broadcast to say he isn't going to hold an election.'

For once her instincts were wrong. Jim Callaghan went on television to say precisely that. He 'would not be calling for a general election at this time,' because the problems of the country required a Government that would 'continue to carry out policies which are consistent, determined and do not chop and change'. He would carry on, he said, 'because we feel that is best for Britain'.

Margaret was furious. She had worked herself up to the pitch where she was ready to throw herself headlong into an election campaign. On top of which, she didn't much like being made a fool of. She also found Opposition horribly frustrating. 'Opposition can only question and exhort,' she said later, 'Government can talk and act. I like to get on with things.'

The next thing to get on with was the Party Conference, this year being held in Brighton, where her task was to give Party workers the fillip they needed to keep going. She delivered her speech on 13 October, her fifty-third birthday. Once again, she delivered a diatribe against Socialism and the Labour Party:

> Many of us remember the Labour Party as it used to be. In the old days it was at least a party of ideals. You didn't have to agree with Labour to understand its appeal and respect its concern for the underdog. Among those who lead the Labour movement something has gone seriously wrong. Socialism has gone sour. Object to merit and distinction, and you're setting your face against quality, independence, originality, genius, against all the richness and variety of life. When you hold back the successful, you penalize those who need help.'

The preparation that had gone into the speech had once again been a tortuous experience, but it was rapturously received, and Ronnie

Millar was sent his just deserts. In the early days this had taken the form of a book from Margaret in gratitude for his labours. Then she discovered that he had a penchant for cigars, and although she can't stand people smoking around her, she thereafter sent him a box of cigars. Once she gave him a box which had been specially made for Denis, who doesn't smoke cigars.

At the end of her Conference speech, while still on the platform, someone presented her with a large cake and a Paddington Bear. She was then whisked back to the Grand Hotel where she was staying, and despite the exhaustion of the week that was now over, she called together the policemen who had been guarding her for the last few days, and threw a party for them. She was then desperately worried about how she might get the bear and the cake back to London in time for a birthday party, which she happened to remember was being held for one of her aide's small children.

These were the sort of qualities which have made everyone who has worked for her so fiercely loyal. Her secretaries worked inhuman hours, which got only worse as the election came closer. They certainly never made a lot of money working for Mrs Thatcher, yet there is not one who is not utterly devoted to her. As one secretary explained:

> One of us would be there, until the House rose or until midnight, whichever was the earliest, and I would drive her home, so tired I could barely speak after a hell of a long day, and I'd have another four days like it ahead, but we always knew that she had to go home and start on her boxes. However hard any of her staff worked, she worked harder. She never had anyone on her staff who could have worked harder than she did, and it's very much easier to give your all to someone who you know is really giving their all too.

Jim Callaghan doubtless derived a great deal of pleasure from refusing to go to the country in October, when everyone thought he would, but he paid for it. Britain was plunged into one of its worst ever winters of strikes and industrial upheaval. By the New Year the press were likening it to the chaos in the General Strike of 1926. Hospitals and schools closed, Underground trains ceased to run, grave diggers refused to dig, and as refuse collectors came out too, rubbish and rats began to collect at each street corner. The Prime Minister, escaping from the gloom, the stench and the grips of a cold winter, had been away to a summit meeting in sunny Guadaloupe. And when greeted at the airport by reporters eager to know what he thought of the situation, he said, 'Crisis? What crisis?'

The final crunch came in March when, committed to its policy of devolution for Scotland and Wales, the Labour Government suffered so many defeats that it was forced into holding a referendum. The result of the referendum, while showing a definite 'No' in Wales, left room for doubt in Scotland. The clear forty per cent majority of those eligible to vote, which Parliament had insisted upon, was not forthcoming. In fact, thirty-five per cent of those eligible to vote had stayed at home. Before wiping the Act off the statute book, Callaghan said he wanted to give all the parties a chance to talk about the issues.

Margaret rose to her feet in reply and said that the people had given their decision in the referendum, and the Government was merely trying to buy time. With only three working months of Parliament left, discussions on devolution would inevitably be overshadowed, she said, by thoughts of the coming election. 'I don't think that's the way to consider matters as important as the government of Scotland and Wales and indeed the whole United Kingdom.' She therefore put down a motion of no confidence – her third in almost as many years.

This time, a nail-biting debate took place in the Chamber which lasted seven hours, with excellent speeches from both the Prime Minister, as to why the Government should remain in power, and from Mrs Thatcher, about why Parliament should seek a fresh mandate from the people. When the vote was cast at 10.00 p.m., the Chamber was filled to capacity, and both sides shouted so loudly that a voice vote was not good enough, and the Speaker had to call for a division. Those voting for the motion went into the right-hand lobby, those voting against into the left. Seventeen minutes later, the Government teller came into the Chamber and gave the Labour benches the thumbs up. A few seconds later, Spencer le Marchant, the Tory teller, appeared. The Conservatives had won by a single vote. The motion of no confidence was carried by 311 votes to 310.

Pent-up tension was released in a babble of expletives, as only MPs know how. Mr Callaghan immediately announced that he would be asking the Queen to dissolve Parliament as soon as essential business had been cleared up, after which Margaret Thatcher declared that the Opposition would do anything they could to facilitate dissolution at the earliest opportunity. There were loud cheers from the Conservative benches, front and back, and Willie Whitelaw put an arm around

Margaret and congratulated her warmly. It was the first time a prime minister had been forced out of office and into a general election since Ramsay MacDonald was defeated by Stanley Baldwin in 1924. Margaret went home to Denis in Flood Street that night, and said it had been an historic day. 'Exciting. A night like this comes once in a lifetime.'

Margaret's elation was not long-lived. Two days later, while she was opening a children's fête in Finchley, greeting well-wishers and talking excitedly about the campaign ahead, a bomb went off in the House of Commons car park, very seriously injuring Airey Neave.

Guinevere Tilney, Ronnie Millar and Chris Patten were all in Margaret's office at the time, just a few seconds before three o'clock, when there was the most ear-shattering blast. Chris said 'That was a bomb', and all three went to the window to look. Below them, on the ramp leading from the underground car park, they could make out a car with smoke pouring from it. In the confusion of everyone trying to discover what had happened, it was Guinevere who found out first. 'Oh my God, it's Airey,' she said. 'It's very serious, I think he's lost a leg, and they've taken him to Westminster Hospital.' She then left the others to try to contact Margaret, and went straight round to the Neaves' flat in Marsham Street to tell Diana, and to take her to the hospital.

Airey was still alive; although his injuries were very severe and he was in deep shock, the surgeons were fighting to save him. Tragically, he never survived the operation. Having lived through Colditz, and won the Military Cross, the DSO and an OBE for his bravery, plus decorations from France, America, Holland and Poland, he died at the hands of an INLA bomber who had sneaked into the car park and planted a remote-control explosive device to the underside of his car. His heart failed while he lay on the operating table, with his wife sitting anxiously waiting in the room next door. The surgeon came out and took Guinevere aside to tell her he was dead, and she then broke the news to Diana.

In the meantime the office had been having great difficulty in contacting Margaret since, as Leader of the Opposition, she had no telephone in her car. The first message, that a bomb had gone off in the House of Commons, had got through. Derek Howe, then her Press Secretary, had told her the news, but at that stage there were no details.

She said later that her immediate thought had been, 'Please God, don't let it be Airey,' and had got on with the job. It was not until she arrived at the BBC some time later in order to do a broadcast, that she learnt that it was indeed Airey. Shocked to the core, she drove straight back to the House of Commons, which had been entirely cordoned off, and went into her office. Ronnie Millar happened to be standing by the door when she walked in. 'Oh Ronnie,' she said, 'what a good thing when one wakes up in the morning, one doesn't know what one will have gone through before one goes to bed at night.'

She was utterly shattered, and yet composed. Airey had been the person who had made her Leader, he had become a great personal friend, and it was the job that she had given him of Shadow Secretary for Northern Ireland that had cost him his life. The shock was colossal; and yet, she was able to sit straight down at her desk and draft a tribute to give to the press.

Twenty minutes later she called in Ronnie. 'Well here's the rough,' she said, handing it to him. 'Do something with it; make it better.' It was almost perfect: he changed just one word. 'I wouldn't say "hero",' he said, 'I don't think any soldier would like to be called that.' Apart from that one word the tribute went out exactly as she had written it:

> The assassination of Airey Neave has left his friends and colleagues as stunned and grief-stricken as his family. He was one of freedom's warriors. Courageous, staunch, true, he lived for his beliefs and now he has died for them. A gentle, brave and unassuming man, he was a loyal and very dear friend. He had a wonderful family who supported him in everything he did. Now, there is a gap in our lives which cannot be filled.

Carol heard the news at 6.00 a.m. on the radio in Sydney, and immediately rang Flood Street, where it was now late evening. Alison Ward answered the phone, and told her that her mother had just arrived home, having come from Diana's flat. 'Oh Mum, I'm sorry,' said Carol, and for four or five minutes Margaret talked it out, described how she had heard, how worried she was about Diana, how ghastly the whole thing was. It helped to talk. Finally she said, 'We must win now, we'll win for Airey.'

Airey was buried a week later, and Margaret then persuaded Diana to come to join her, to work in the office and help with the election campaign. She thus gave her something positive to do with her time, to take her mind off Airey, while at the same time furthering the cause that had cost him his life. It was a thoughtful gesture, and entirely typical.

The campaign circus was underway. Election day was set for 3 May, and the intervening four weeks were a hectic round of trains, planes, helicopters, cars, coaches, speeches, rallies, walk-abouts, hand-shaking, child patting, television chatting, radio phone-ins, and press conferences. She out-walked, out-talked and out-lasted every member of her entourage. There was one night when they got to bed at the usual 2.00 or 3.00 a.m., having been up since 7.00 that morning, and having to be up again at 7.00 the next morning. Janet Young, vice chairman of the Party, who travelled everywhere with her, had been so exhausted she could barely stand up. She greeted Margaret at breakfast the next morning, and said she hoped she had managed to get some sleep. 'Oh I couldn't get to sleep for ages,' said Margaret, 'so I lay in bed and read Aristotle.'

Denis accompanied her most days, together with Carol, who had come home shortly after Airey Neave's death to give her mother some moral support. 'Your mother walks at fifteen miles per hour,' Carol was soon told. 'Keep up, don't get left behind.' Other members of the entourage were Gordon Reece, Margaret's Svengali, Alison Ward, Caroline Stephens, and maybe one or two other secretaries, some detectives, Richard Ryder, Ronnie Millar and another speech writer, David Howell from the *Daily Telegraph*, plus innumerable reporters and photographers. David Wolfson, a millionaire businessman whose father was co-founder of Great Universal Stores, provided a calming influence on the gang.

Much as Margaret Thatcher hated being sold as a personality, this turned out to be an election of personalities: 'Sunny Jim' versus the 'Iron Lady'. The Labour Party was out to propagate the myth that Margaret was a right-wing extremist. Her policies were divisive and reactionary, said Callaghan. 'The question you will have to consider,' he pronounced, 'is whether we risk tearing everything up by the roots? Whether we want to scrap programmes that assist firms on which a million jobs depend, slashing spending that is needed for families and hospitals and schools, having an upheaval in industry and with the unions? The answer must surely be no.'

The Tory Manifesto met the charge with a simple statement: 'This election is about the future of Britain – a great country which seems to have lost its way.' Meanwhile Margaret allowed herself to go through all sorts of indignities to woo the voters. She would be photographed setting off from Flood Street with a shopping basket over her arm, or popping into a butcher's shop in the middle of a walk-about in Moss Side to buy the Sunday joint. It was all designed to soften her image, to give her the appeal of a cosy housewife. At a farm in East Anglia she was snapped with a calf in her arms, something she had never held in her life before, and had in a vice-like grip about the throat. 'If you're not bloody careful,' hissed Denis, 'you're going to have a dead calf on your hands here.'

Saturdays were reserved for Finchley, where the pace was as fast and furious as ever. Denis would take one side of the street, she and Carol – making a rare appearance in the constituency – would take the other. Between them they could canvass a thousand houses in one and a half hours. Now that she was Party Leader and under police protection, she had to consider security precautions. She couldn't charge into someone's house unless it had been vetted first, and she was supposed to travel in the official car. Margaret declared that she wanted to go in chairman John Tiplady's car, just as she always had done in the past; and so, to everyone's horror, she did.

For four weeks she was on the go, leaving home at the crack of dawn. She packed her suitcases and bags herself – with each garment meticulously wrapped in tissue paper to prevent it from creasing. She did her own make-up, unless there was a television appearance, and her own hair, touching up between the weekly wash and set with heated rollers. There was never a dull moment in the day, as they whisked from one venue to another, with Margaret doing quick changes in between, while Denis would be furiously sticking the bits of her next speech together with Sellotape. It would often be two o'clock in the morning by the time they got back to Flood Street, where someone would have made a meal for them all. Margaret would immediately set to, laying the food out on the table, and fussing around making sure that everyone had a fork, a drink, or the salt and pepper.

She thrived on it all. While everyone around her sunk deeper into exhaustion and collapse, Margaret grew brighter, prettier and more charismatic every day. Vanished was the 'Duchess', the research chemist who had never known what to say to the men on the factory floor. She took people's hands in hers and talked to them with the concentration of a faith healer. Gone were the dull but detailed speeches of the spokesman on pensions, even the Minister for Education. She spoke with the urgency and zeal of a missionary. It was time, she

125

declared, for Britain to catch up with the free world, 'time we became a leader, not a straggler. Unless we change our ways and our direction,' she warned, 'our greatness as a nation will soon be a footnote in the history books, a distant memory of an offshore island, lost in the mists of time like Camelot, remembered kindly for its noble past.'

Labour had maintained the edge over the Conservatives in the opinion polls. Margaret, on the other hand, enjoyed the very considerable support of most newspapers, in particular the mass circulation tabloid, the *Sun*, whose editor Larry Lamb was one of those whom she had wooed so shrewdly during her years as Opposition Leader. There are many people who think his support was the decisive factor in the final results. But the outcome was uncertain right up to the end.

During the final week, the circus had been in Scotland. Margaret had just given a forty-minute, make-or-break speech to a meeting in Edinburgh. It had been a triumph, and they were all sitting down to dinner in the hotel, quite relaxed and pleased with the way the day had gone, when a telephone call came through from Peter Thorneycroft at Central Office. Margaret asked Janet Young to go to see what he wanted. Twenty minutes later she returned to the table, and Margaret gave Janet the go ahead to tell everyone what Thorneycroft had said. What happened next varies depending upon the teller. What most of the assembled company remember Janet then saying was that Peter Thorneycroft had suggested that Ted Heath might appear alongside Margaret at the Monday morning press conference. It would be a good demonstration of Party unity. What Margaret, Richard Ryder and David Howell apparently heard was the suggestion that Ted Heath should share the last party political television broadcast – the most important moment of the whole campaign, and quite a different proposition altogether.

Margaret hit the roof. She went white with fury, stood up from the table and stormed out of the room, leaving a group of astonished aides who couldn't understand why she should have found the suggestion so offensive. The next morning Denis said, 'I've never seen her so upset, never, ever.' It is an incident that she still refers to at the drop of a hat, to berate those who didn't see the harm in appearing with Ted. 'Even you,' she'll say, wagging her finger accusingly, 'even you.'

Back in Flood Street, with just a day to go before polling, the team was working on the final speeches, when Gordon Reece, who always got the polls from Fleet Street a few hours before they were published, arrived with the news that the *Daily Mail* carried a story that the National Opinion Polls were putting Labour one point ahead of the Conservatives. Margaret was out of the room, but would be appearing any moment to have some supper. They couldn't decide whether to break the bad news before she ate, or afterwards, or who should be the one to do it. David Wolfson was selected for the task. Margaret arrived, and no one said a thing, just helping themselves to some food. To break the awful silence, Carol started taking bets about the outcome. 'Mummy, what do you think your majority's going to be?' she asked, while everyone stared hard at their plates and tried to look hungry. 'Forty,' said Margaret optimistically, and assembled stomachs churned. Finally David told her that the latest poll had her one behind. There was a silence; then she said, 'I don't think I believe that.'

Election day was Thursday, 3 May, and the Thatcher family spent much of it in Finchley, visiting the polling booths and chatting to constituents. Such is the present Parliamentary system in Britain, that if the Leader of the Party fails to hold his own constituency, he will be out of the job and out of the House of Commons as swiftly as any novice, irrespective of how well the Party does nationally. So nursing the voters to the polls was no mere formality, although no great anxiety either, in view of the size of majority Margaret usually had in Finchley.

When there was no more to be done there, the family returned home to Flood Street, where the media were busy erecting stands outside the house. The agonizing hours between the time that the polls closed and the counting of votes were spent confined to the house. Margaret took advantage of the time to turn out the drawers of her desk, tearing up pieces of paper in a nervous compulsion to do something. She knew as well as anybody that if the Conservatives lost the election, the knives would be out and she would be replaced as Leader of the Party as fast as she could blink.

After something to eat, at 11.30 p.m. they drove back to Finchley, where Margaret's agent, Roy Langston, and Party officials and supporters were all feverishly gathered in a room with a television, so that they could watch the results as they came in. The early results were not very good: there was a recount in Peterborough, and another important seat was looking uncertain. Then a problem arose with Margaret's own count; a ballot box had gone missing and there was great confusion for a while. By the time it was found, and her result announced – a majority of 7,900 votes – Tory gains around the country were coming in thick and fast.

Meanwhile the rest of the team was ensconced at Central Office, eyes glued to television sets and the computer on which the early predictions were coming through. As early as ten o'clock, Gordon Reece, large cigar in hand as always, was standing in front of the computer saying they had a majority of sixty. Margaret and Denis arrived at three o'clock with Mark and Carol following in another car. As she arrived a great roar arose from the crowds in Smith Square, and everyone inside came into the corridor to greet her. She came up the stairs, lined with photographers, and stopped when she saw Ronnie Millar amongst the group.

'Oh do you think it's going to be all right?' she asked, uncertainly.

'I bloody know it's going to be all right,' replied Ronnie, 'You should have been here at ten.'

'I couldn't,' said Margaret, taking him quite literally, 'I had to be in Finchley.'

The results continued to come in throughout the night. Bottles of champagne were opened, but neither Margaret nor Denis drank much. Then at about four in the morning, Margaret turned to Ronnie Millar and said, 'Have you thought . . . if we win, have you thought of anything I could say at Downing Street?'

'Yes,' said Ronnie.

'Then let's go into another room,' said Margaret, 'Tell.' They found a room to themselves, and Ronnie Millar read the piece he had prepared from St Francis of Assisi: 'Where there is discord may we bring harmony, where there is error may we bring truth, where there is doubt may we bring faith, and where there is despair may we bring hope.'

For the first time that day Margaret showed emotion: her eyes filled with tears. They went and found Alison Ward to ask her to type the piece, and she too burst into tears all over the typewriter.

Margaret Thatcher was to be Prime Minister of Great Britain, and the Conservative Party was home and dry. It was not until the following morning, however, that they discovered they were home with a clear majority of forty-four seats in the House of Commons.

Elated beyond belief, the Thatcher household went home to Flood Street, arriving there at 5.00 a.m. to find the house surrounded by crowds of blue-ribboned, flag-waving well-wishers, singing, chanting and cheering until well past dawn. Margaret didn't go to bed at all that night. She sat up and made telephone calls, doubtless shedding the odd tear that one call couldn't be to her father in Grantham, who had made it all possible.

V

History in the Making

Election day had been a nerve-racking experience. The day after was simply awesome. Margaret Thatcher would not be Prime Minister until Jim Callaghan had been to tender his resignation to the Queen, Margaret had 'kissed hands' with the monarch and, in turn, been officially asked to form a Government. She would then, under the full glare of the world's press, take possession of the highest post in the land, and with it the occupancy of Number Ten Downing Street.

Lady Violet Bonham-Carter, daughter of Herbert Asquith, the Liberal Prime Minister, wrote of the house: 'If walls of brick and stone can hold, for all time, some intangible deposit of the great events which once took place within their span, no human dwelling should have a richer heritage than Number Ten Downing Street. It is the "house of history" in which the past is a living presence not to be put by.'

The family left Flood Street in mid-morning and drove once again to Smith Square where celebrations were already well underway. There was plenty of champagne and laughter, and a vast chocolate cake had been hastily made overnight in the shape of the door to Number Ten, with 'Margaret Thatcher's Success Story' across the top in sugar icing. Margaret, in very good spirits, thanked everyone for all their tremendously hard work; and then got down to business with Ronnie Millar, going over the final touches of what she was going to say when she stood outside the real door to Number Ten.

Gradually people began to drift away from the party, until just the family and a few others were left. Most of the office staff had already packed up their typewriters and equipment and gone to Downing Street. Caroline Stephens was still busy preparing for the move. Ronnie sensed it was time to let the family be alone, and made his excuses. 'No don't go,' said Margaret; and so they sent up to the canteen for some lunch. In due course it arrived: cold lamb, with an assortment of indeterminate and overcooked vegetables, for which no one could summon up much enthusiasm. After the meal, they continued to sit in the now rather barren office, silently contemplating history in the making, and awaiting the summons from Buckingham Palace. Denis had settled comfortably into an armchair and was quietly nodding off, Carol was beginning to feel the whole affair was a bit of an anti-climax, Mark stared aimlessly out of the window, and Margaret was sitting nervously upright on the edge of her chair, worrying about the logistics of getting to the Palace without meeting Callaghan on his way back to Transport House, scarcely three doors away from Tory Central Office.

'It would be too terrible if the cars were to cross,' she said.

'I honestly think that the Palace is quite used to this routine,' reassured Ronnie, 'I do think they know where the Labour Party Headquarters are. It'll be all right; you won't find yourself glaring at each other as you pass.'

The room returned to silence, broken only by the comings and goings of Caroline, and the soft snoring of Denis, asleep in his chair. Suddenly the telephone rang. Everyone tensed – would this be the call from the Palace? Caroline went into the outer office to answer it. Everyone strained their ears to hear what she was saying.

'Yes, yes, um . . . no.' She came back into the office.

'Wrong number,' she said. Silence fell, tension mounted. Five minutes later the phone rang again.

'This is it!' declared Caroline and went through to take the call. Again everyone strained to listen.

'Yes,' she was saying, 'Oh thank you; would you hold on.' She came into the room.

'Mr Heath would like to offer his congratulations,' she said. Margaret sat for a full thirty seconds, without moving. Then she replied.

'Would you thank him very much.' This wasn't the moment to talk to Ted Heath. Five minutes passed, and the telephone rang yet again.

'This is it!' declared Caroline for the second time, and leapt into the outer office to take the call.

'Yes, yes,' she said, 'just one moment.' She came back into the room.

'Sir Philip Moore [the Queen's Secretary],' she said. Margaret stood up from her chair, nudged Denis into consciousness, and went into the outer office.

'Good afternoon, Sir Philip,' she said, 'this is Margaret Thatcher speaking.' Then, just as all ears were finely tuned to hear and record the historic phone call for posterity, a foot came round the door from the outer office, and gently pulled it shut. Three minutes later she came back into the room.

'Right, we're off,' she said. Denis straightened his tie while Mark, bursting with pride, put his arm around his mother and said, 'Prime Minister.'

'Not yet,' corrected Margaret.

'The car may break down,' Denis suggested pessimistically.

'In that case,' she replied firmly, 'I shall walk.' And away they went.

Her audience with the Queen, which took place in the Queen's study on the first floor of Buckingham Palace, went remarkably well, lasting forty-five minutes. Both women had been very uncertain about how they would get on with the other, but with the Queen's diplomacy and Margaret's respect, the relationship got off to a good start and has worked very well over the years.

With the formality over, the new Prime Minister collected Denis, who had been waiting downstairs with some Palace aides, and they set off together for Downing Street. Mark and Carol had gone straight from Smith Square, and arrived ahead of them. The street was crammed with reporters, photographers, cameras and microphones, and crowds of enthusiastic supporters cheering, waving and singing 'For She's a Jolly Good Fellow', as her car made its way through and she was deposited outside the most famous door in the land.

Margaret stood on the steps of Number Ten, flanked by two uniformed policemen, and quoted St Francis of Assisi. Then she went on to say, 'To all the British people, howsoever they may have voted, may I say this: now that the election is over, may we get together and strive to serve and strengthen the country of which we are so proud to be a part. And, finally, one last thing: in the words of Airey Neave, whom we had hoped to bring here with us, "Now there is work to be done".'

With that she waved to the cheering people, turned and disappeared into the hallowed hall of Number Ten, to do precisely what she had said she would: get on with the job. As she entered the house she declared that she felt a sense of change and an aura of calm. But the calm was very quickly over, and the mammoth task of choosing a Cabinet and governing the country began.

During the campaign, one of the many interviews that she had given had been to Michael Cockerell, on the prestigious BBC television programme 'Panorama'. She was asked if she had any doubts about her ability to do the job. 'Of course you have doubts,' she had said, 'and you're tremendously aware of the responsibility. . . . I just hope that people will take me as I am for what I can do . . . . as a personality who

131

has an absolute passion for getting things right for Britain. I just can't bear Britain in decline.'

When asked in another interview, by Kenneth Harris of the *Observer* what sort of a Cabinet she would pick if she became Prime Minister, she had said:

> There are two ways of making a Cabinet. One way is to have in it people who represent all the different viewpoints within the Party. . . . The other way is to have in it only the people who want to go in the direction in which every instinct tells me we have to go; a Cabinet that works on something much more than pragmatism or consensus. It must be a conviction Government. . . . As Prime Minister I couldn't waste time having any internal arguments.

Nevertheless, Margaret couldn't fill her Cabinet entirely with her own supporters. As an untested Prime Minister with so very little Cabinet experience herself, it was imperative that those around her should have experience. The two people who fulfilled both criteria cited above were Keith Joseph and Willie Whitelaw, who had now entirely committed himself to her leadership and would defend her to the last. There were others, like Norman St John-Stevas, who were avid supporters, but had never held senior rank in the Cabinet. She was therefore compelled to bring in a large number of Heath men: Peter Walker, Ian Gilmour, Lord Carrington, James Prior, Francis Pym and Lord Soames, for example.

But Cabinet experience was not the sole reason for including the last group: all these men had strong lobbies of support in the Commons. If she had made a clean sweep and excluded the lot, the House would have become a very hostile place. Any mistake she and her Cabinet made, which they would be bound to do from time to time, would have had them baying for blood. However, Ted Heath himself was not invited. 'I couldn't have had him,' she later explained. 'He wouldn't have been interested in working with me. He'd only have been in there, elbowing, to get everyone else out of the nest.'

Most of those invited into the nest continued to cover the subject which they had shadowed in Opposition. Thus Willie Whitelaw, who had to some extent filled the gap in her life left by Airey Neave (to such an extent, in fact, that colleagues were saying he had become Margaret's 'major-domo'), became Home Secretary; Geoffrey Howe, Chancellor of the Exchequer; James Prior, Secretary for Employment; and Michael Heseltine, Environment Secretary. Lord Carrington became Foreign Secretary (the one post which could have gone to Ted Heath had she felt so inclined), with Ian Gilmour as his aide in the Commons as Lord Privy Seal. Lord Hailsham became Lord Chancellor for the second time in his career, and Keith Joseph took over the key portfolio of Industry, where so much of the work in reducing subsidies had to be done. Norman St John-Stevas became Chancellor of the Duchy of Lancaster, Leader of the House of Commons and Minister for the Arts. Lastly she brought one of the most dangerous Heathites of all, Peter Walker, off the back-benches, where he had been very influential, and into the Ministry of Agriculture.

All of these appointments required separate interviews, which Margaret conducted over the Bank Holiday weekend, and there was a host of others. She still found time, however, on that first Friday evening to write letters of thanks to the people who had helped her during the election campaign. Hand-written notes, posted that night, arrived first thing on Saturday morning. 'And that,' says Ronnie Millar emphatically, 'is what ties you to the woman.'

Thousands of letters poured into Downing Street, and most of them had personally signed replies. A few were overlooked, such as an old university contemporary with whom she had once had long and heated arguments over politics. 'I can't say I like your politics any more today than I did then,' she wrote, 'but congratulations; it's a tremendous achievement.' She received no reply. On the other hand, people like Diana Powell, her secretary from ten years previously, had a long, chatty, hand-written postscript to the formal typed letter of thanks. In this she talked about the avalanche of letters and how hard the girls in the office had worked to clear them; and how the summit season was upon her 'too much of it for my liking'.

Her arrival at Downing Street was viewed with mixed emotions by the band of employees who remain there while administrations of different complexions come and go. After the first couple of days more than a few were saying, 'I'm not going to be able to stand this for more than a week.' She swept through the place like a hurricane, exuding energy and demanding energy from everyone else. Everything had to be done now, not tomorrow or next week. Everything had to be neat and orderly, and anyone who hadn't grasped her drift by the second telling, felt the rough side of her tongue. Yet at the same time she was enormously kindly. She never made a mistake about the most menial person's name, never confused wives or ailments, and was always most meticulous about thanking people. A plate has scarcely ever been put in front of her at table without the waiter or waitress being thanked.

Number Ten Downing Street was once described by an official who served there as 'a gentleman's home in which a little government takes place from time to time'. Nowadays the house, with its famous door, the lion's head knocker and brass letter-box bearing the inscription 'First Lord of the Treasury' – the Prime Minister's official post – is nothing more than 'the office' for over one hundred and thirty people, who come in daily. The home part of it has been pushed up into what were the old attics, converted by Mrs Neville Chamberlain in the late 1930s. She decided that, being mixed up with the state rooms and the secretarial offices, the living quarters lacked privacy. She built a new staircase and raised the ceilings of the rooms, to make a totally separate section. 'These in our day,' wrote Violet Bonham-Carter after first seeing the conversion, 'were poky attic rooms reached only by back stairs. They have been transformed into the perfect bedrooms flooded with sunshine now used by the Prime Minister and Mrs Chamberlain. They open on a broad corridor with the atmosphere of a country house.'

Her description was somewhat poetic, but the flat does enjoy pleasant views, one way over St James's Park and the other over Horseguards Parade. Moreover, as well as being close to the job, it affords greater security than Flood Street. Margaret had long been unhappy about the house, with its front so exposed to the road, but ever since the financial problems at Burmah Oil, they had been unable to afford anything better. Not that the flat in Number Ten comes free. James Callaghan had initiated a system whereby prime ministers wanting to make use of the accommodation should pay rent for it, which was set at a flat rate of ten per cent of salary. In addition, the Prime Minister pays, as they have always done, all the running costs of the main part of the house; the wages and salaries of domestic staff and all the expenses of entertaining. The only bills that the Government foots are maintenance of the building which falls within the aegis of the Department of the Environment and the wages and salaries of the civil servants.

For the first few weeks of her premiership Margaret continued to live in Flood Street, while the flat and parts of the house itself were redecorated. In that time she worked on the contents of the Queen's Speech, to be delivered at the State Opening of Parliament twelve days after the election. It was a heartening start for those who had voted for the Party, encompassing most of the radical reforms promised in the Conservative Election Manifesto: stronger defence, more resources for law and order, lower taxation, more private enterprise and less Government control in people's daily lives. There would be legislation on picketing and the closed shop, a reduction in State ownership and the activites of the National Enterprise Board (set up by Labour to rescue troubled industries, and to speculate with Government money by investing in high-technology companies). Local authority and new town tenants would have the right to buy their own homes; education authorities would no longer be compelled to turn secondary schooling comprehensive. The new administration would introduce a Bill to promote wider use of private medical care; award a fourth television channel to the Independent Broadcasting Authority; amend the law on nationality, and produce stiffer controls on immigration.

Margaret had said in a well-publicized interview during the election campaign that she expected her reforms to take at least ten years. And no sooner was the Queen departed from Westminster than Callaghan was on his feet in the first debate of the session, scoffing at the great list he had just heard. Mrs Thatcher had promised the voters Utopia, he said, but now 'we hear that Utopia is going to have to be postponed for a day or two'.

It was indeed, although Margaret embarked upon the route to Utopia straightaway. The very next month, Geoffrey Howe produced his first Budget, which was so harsh that it shocked most of his own Cabinet, and rooted the Opposition in the Commons to their benches. 'Treason!' expostulated one back-bencher. Jim Callaghan was more restrained, 'a colossal gamble', unjust and inflationary, he said, while Denis Healey proclaimed it 'a she-wolf's budget in sheep's clothing . . . a classic recipe for roaring inflation, soaring unemployment, and industrial anarchy'. 'In ten minutes,' he said later, 'the Chancellor threw away the results of five years of hard, painstaking effort by the Labour Government in getting down inflation.'

The Chancellor had done what the Party had said they would do – quite an unusual step in itself. Income tax was cut; but the other side of the coin was that VAT went up to a flat fifteen per cent, and petrol, alcohol and cigarettes all became more expensive. Most dramatic of all, Government spending was to be cut by £4,000 million, and this would be removed from housing, energy, education, employment, foreign aid, transport and industrial subsidies. The only branches of Government that escaped the axe were the police and the armed forces.

Just the day before, the Government had announced that between 75,000 and 150,000 civil service jobs would disappear, while recruitment would be stopped for the next three months so that manpower could be reduced by £22,000. Not many days later, came the news that regional aid for industry would be cut by £233 million over three years; then, that the NEB would be run down, starting with the sale of £100 million of its assets. Expansion of the National Health Service would stop, parts of British Airways and British Petroleum would be sold off, British Shipbuilding, nationalized by Labour, would be given two years to stand on its own feet, and British Aerospace would be turned into a public company. The salvos came thick and fast; and the unions, not least of all, took a very dim view. The Government's popularity took a dive, and the normal honeymoon period, which new governments generally experience, lasted no time at all.

But then the bride had long given up flirting. She wanted change, she wanted to reverse the tide of Socialism. She had the opportunity, she had made her vision plain enough in the course of the previous three years, she had been voted into power on that vision, and she could see no possible reason for holding back. As she said angrily in the House of Commons, when challenged about her planned trade union reforms, 'We have an absolute mandate for these proposals. They are what the people want, and the events of last winter show that they were needed.'

It was not only the unions and the Opposition that provoked her anger. Margaret quite swiftly discovered that when it came to the crunch, some of her Cabinet were less brave about implementing those radical cuts in public spending to which they had agreed so happily in debate. Every minister was being told to come up with economies in their departments, just as they had been during Heath's first administration when she, at Education, had found hers in the provision of school milk. Those of her Cabinet that, as she saw it, lacked guts, she called 'the wets'. Over the coming years the distinction between 'the wets' and the brave, hard-line 'drys' became increasingly acute. They also became a recognized part of the language.

The reason that she and Geoffrey Howe were so adamant that the cuts had to be made was because domestic production had only grown by one per cent in the previous year, while consumer spending went up by five per cent and imports increased by thirteen per cent. The result was that inflation was rising, and in the first half of 1979 Britain's balance of payments had dropped well into the red. Increased oil prices had helped to plunge the world into recession. As the Chancellor explained at a conference in London in July, 'We do not have any real choice about the need to reduce the planned scale of public spending. A world recession may not seem the best background against which to put our house in order. The cure may in the short term make things more uncomfortable for us. But in truth we have no choice. The treatment may seem unpalatable. But without the treatment, our condition could easily become incurable.' He was convincing, and for the time being the Cabinet toed the line, although as time went by the wets grew increasingly troublesome and were not so easily suppressed.

Margaret had meantime begun the summit season, which she had written to Diana Powell about, and which as Prime Minister it was now her duty to attend. Tiresome and time-consuming though they could be, summits were an essential part in the game of international diplomacy, and Margaret made her debut in the ring at a meeting of Common Market heads of government in Strasbourg. Diplomacy was not Margaret's forte. In such matters she often displayed the finesse of a bull in a china shop, having always preferred people to call a spade a spade. This was the very characteristic which set her apart from the vast majority of politicians, and made her so popular with so many people. It was not, however, the sort of talk that went down well in delicate international negotiations, although, remarkably, she never upset as many apple carts as she might have done.

In Strasbourg she ploughed in, nervous though she was, with a demand that Britain's contributions to the EEC budget be cut. And while Lord Carrington, a diplomat par excellence, winced, she came away applauded, if not for her tact, then for her courage. In Tokyo, she had no occasion to be directly involved in any heated debate, and was a huge success, not least because of the colour of her hair which the Japanese found fascinating. Helmut Schmidt, the Chancellor of West Germany, was, however, more impressed by her 'knowledge of the subject, the authority and the sense of responsibility with which Mrs Thatcher took part in the deliberations'.

But in Australia, where she was combining a trip to Canberra with a chance to see Carol – who had since returned to the country – she made a gaffe. Rhodesia, which had long been a diplomat's nightmare, was in a particularly delicate condition. In 1965, when Rhodesia had made its unilateral declaration of independence, Britain had imposed economic sanctions against the 'illegal regime' of Ian Smith. In 1978, now calling itself Zimbabwe-Rhodesia, the country produced a new constitution introducing majority rule. After a general election, a black majority Government came into power under Bishop Muzorewa, but in which Ian Smith remained a minister without portfolio. Margaret had been in favour of recognizing the regime and lifting sanctions, but Lord Carrington had spent several hours of heated conversation seeking to convince her that the changes did not go far enough and sanctions should not be lifted. The young Winston Churchill's attitude was similar to Margaret's but, failing to be convinced as she was, he refused to vote as he was bid in the debate in the House of Commons, and was thus sacked from her Shadow Cabinet. Despite all this, at a press conference in Canberra, Margaret said words to the effect that she could not see Parliament renewing sanctions when they came to vote on it in the autumn.

The opportunity to redeem herself came a few weeks later at the Commonwealth Conference in Lusaka. She and Lord Carrington flew out together in an RAF VC10, to what promised to be a rough reception. They had been told to expect a violent and well-orchestrated anti-Thatcher campaign awaiting them on the tarmac; and Margaret sat throughout the flight nervously nursing a pair of sunglasses with particularly large lenses. As the plane came to a halt at Lusaka, out of the windows they could see a large group of chanting black faces, with banners and slogans. Margaret got up from her seat and strode purposefully down the steps into the intense African heat without her sunglasses. Carrington followed. 'What happened to the glasses?' he asked. 'I brought them because I was afraid they might throw acid in my face,' she said. 'But I changed my mind. I'm damned if I'm going to let them see I'm afraid.'

Just as Keith Joseph and Willie Whitelaw were supports in home affairs, so Peter Carrington was a vital crutch in those early days abroad. She relied very heavily on his guidance; and so guided, she made a great success of the Lusaka Conference. She called for a ceasefire in Zimbabwe-Rhodesia, a revised constitution, and new elections under British supervision – the terms of which would be worked out at a conference in London. 'A lot of people in Rhodesia, black and white,' she said, 'want to lead their lives in peace. That is the greatest prize. If we had not gone about trying to get that prize, we would have been very culpable.' But she admitted, 'I'm much too cautious to be starry-eyed about it. We've got to see how we get on.'

The outcome in Rhodesia was as highly successful as the conference, gaining Margaret and her Government a lot of admiration from people who were in other respects quite hostile to her administration. The proposed conference began at the Lancaster House Hotel in London in September. Three months later, Lord Carrington, Bishop Muzorewa, Robert Mugabe, leader of the Zimbabwe African National Union (ZANU) Party, and Joshua Nkomo, who led the rival Zimbabwe African People's Union (ZAPU), all signed an agreement for a ceasefire. Thus ended fourteen years of rebellion against the Crown, and the emergence of Zimbabwe as an independent state after ninety years of white rule. Parliament was dissolved, new elections were held under the supervision of Lord Soames acting as caretaker Governor during the transition, and in March 1980, Robert Mugabe, victorious in the elections, formed a coalition Government with Joshua Nkomo. Two weeks later Christopher Soames announced the end of martial law in the country, promised £7.5 million in British aid for post-war reconstruction, and returned to Heathrow Airport the hero of the hour, to a warm reception from Mrs Thatcher.

Not many months after Margaret became Prime Minister, Alison Ward, her much-loved, much-trusted secretary left Number Ten to go to work in industry. Her place was taken by Joy Robilliard, who had been Airey Neave's secretary, and who has been with Mrs Thatcher ever since. Alison had been in the job for eight years, and felt she needed a change. Now that Margaret was Prime Minister, a lot of the fun had gone out of the job. With Margaret once more a member of the Government, all the jobs that her secretary had previously done were taken over by civil servants. As Diana Powell had discovered many years before, Margaret's personal secretary was thus left mainly with work concerning the constituency, and buying the Sunday lunch.

As the Prime Minister's secretary, even that last job was superfluous much of the time. Margaret spent her weekends, as often as not, at Chequers, the Prime Minister's official country residence in Buckinghamshire, which is run by members of the armed forces. She would normally choose what she wanted for the meals for which she would be there, and all the buying, the cooking and general housekeeping would be taken care of.

Most prime ministers fall in love with Chequers. It combines the presence of a stately home with the friendliness of a country cottage, and Margaret was to prove no exception. She won friends there too. On the first Sunday that she invited members of her Cabinet to lunch at Chequers, the young Wren who was serving the roast lamb, carrying it from place to place so that guests might help themselves, lost her grip on the silver salver just as she was homing in on Sir Geoffrey Howe. The plate tipped, the lamb slid and rich brown gravy poured neatly into the Chancellor's lap. Margaret leapt to her feet, rushed to the scene of the disaster, put a comforting arm straight round the panic-stricken girl's shoulder and marched her out to the kitchen, saying there was nothing in the world to worry about, leaving Sir Geoffrey to mop up his suit himself.

Miss Thomas, the housekeeper at Chequers, is so fond of Margaret Thatcher that, when showing guests up the stairs, where the walls are lined with the portraits of previous prime ministers – like the staircase at Number Ten – many of whom she had kept house for, she is wont to say, 'I've told Mrs T that when hers goes up it will be three times the size of anyone else's.'

There is not, alas, much room at Number Ten. James Callaghan took the last place at the top of the stairs. Whenever Margaret is asked about it, she says that the others will just have to shove down a bit. Margaret brought quite a few changes to the house. She was appalled, for example, to discover at her first official dinner, given for Helmut Schmidt who had originally been invited by her predecessor, that Downing Street had no silver cutlery for entertaining heads of state. She didn't keep the secret to herself for long and, with the help of Marcus Kimball, MP for the Gainsborough division of Lincolnshire, managed to ferret out a good Lincolnshire Tory, in the person of Lord Brownlow, willing to lend the family silver for Prime Minister and country. A dawn raiding party duly sped up the A.1 to Belton House, just three miles from Grantham, and returned to Downing Street with a very valuable car load of treasure.

Number Ten was also rather thin on British heroes in the artistic department, and Margaret remedied this with the same alacrity. She wanted original portraits of Nelson and Wellington, instead of the copies that hung on the walls: and these were duly found. She wanted some British scientists about the place: and busts of Joseph Priestley (the discoverer of oxygen), Sir Humphrey Davy (the inventor of the miners' safety lamp), and Michael Faraday (the discoverer of electromagnetism) were in due course wheeled in. When Margaret discovered that the British Embassy in Paris had three Turners, while Downing Street had none, she immediately insisted upon borrowing three for herself. Her favourite, 'Men with Horses Crossing a River' hung thereafter in pride of place over the fireplace in one of the first-floor reception rooms. Margaret reorganized the furniture too, discarding rococo tables and replacing them with more solid English pieces which she extracted on loan from the Victoria & Albert Museum.

The flat upstairs came with furniture, but Margaret introduced a few of her own ornaments, paintings and lamps to make it more personal. Initially she and Denis moved in on their own. Carol had a nominal room which was given over to junk and storage, because she was away in Australia. Mark also had a room, which he used from time to time, but he began his mother's first term of office based in Flood Street. Later, however, with the gradual deterioration in the situation in Northern Ireland, it became known that Mark's name was high on the IRA death list, and Margaret thought it was easier and safer – and also less expensive for the taxpayer – to keep him with her at Number Ten.

'I feel if I have him under my roof,' she told a friend, 'a, he's safer, and b, it is only costing one lot of security.' She also recounted the horror of going round to Flood Street after Mark had been living there for several weeks with his friends. 'You know, I really felt I had to roll up my sleeves and start cleaning things,' she said.

Security is not something she worries obsessively about, but she is well aware that the 'it will never happen to me' school of thought is stupid, particularly after Airey Neave's murder. It could happen to her; but she worries far more about her children's safety than her own. 'You must vary your route,' she counsels, 'look under your car before you get into it, take heed of what the police say, it is serious, watch it.'

She herself is not going to be cowed by terrorism. She believes strongly in law and order and the freedom to walk the streets, and although she is inwardly extremely nervous on many occasions, she stubbornly refuses to show it. Northern Ireland has become considerably more bloodthirsty; and in August 1979, the Queen's cousin, seventy-nine-year-old Lord Mountbatten, 'Uncle Dickie' as he was affectionately known to the Royal Family, was blown up while out fishing on holiday in the Republic. His murder shocked and outraged the world, and cast a whole new complexion on the savagery of the IRA. The same day, eighteen British soldiers, including the Commander of the Queen's Own Highlanders, were killed in County Down by landmines detonated from across the border.

Angry Unionists began calling for the resignation of Humphrey Atkins, whom Margaret had appointed Secretary of State for Northern Ireland, and insisting upon economic sanctions on the Republic to force them to secure the border. In this hostile climate Margaret unexpectedly flew to Belfast and went out to visit the troops at Crossmaglen on the border. As a result of discussions with the Irish Premier, Jack Lynch, after Lord Mountbatten's funeral, the Republic did agree to cooperate with border security.

Margaret has had no full-time staff in the flat at Number Ten. The only help she could call upon was the service of two daily women: Mrs Moss, who has worked for her in Flood Street and comes in every morning at 8.00; and Edwina, who comes in for a few hours each week. Any food prepared in the flat she either makes herself, or with the help of her secretary, Joy Robilliard. Since Carol returned to the fold at the end of 1981, she has pitched in occasionally too, but Denis is no cook, while Mark's ability stops with a jumbo-sized sandwich, indiscriminately filled with the contents of the fridge.

It isn't often, however, that any of the family eat in the flat. If Margaret and Denis are not out together at a dinner, Denis frequently attends business dinners while Margaret might either eat in the House of Commons canteen – the first Prime Minister to do so regularly – or not eat at all. She is very well disciplined about her weight, and if she has had a spate of rich meals, she will simply skip one. Breakfast consists of a cup of coffee and a glass of orange juice, with a vitamin C tablet in the winter. The only time she eats anything for breakfast is at Chequers, where she can indulge in half a grapefruit and some toast and marmalade, prepared specially for her.

She does have a few weaknesses, of which chocolates are one. She has been known on more than one occasion to retreat after supper with a box of Elizabeth Shaw mints and eat the lot, while working on her prime ministerial 'red boxes'. Nowadays the minute a box of chocolates appears she will say, 'Don't open those because I'll eat them. Take them away.' She always used to like a chocolate biscuit with her coffee after a meal, a delicious vice she shared with her old secretary, Diana Powell. Eating was one of the high spots of their day at that time, and Margaret has an assignation with Diana Powell the minute she ceases to be Prime Minister, to eat macaroni cheese, which they used to have in the Commons canteen together, and apricot tart and custard, which they once enjoyed in a hotel. It was a pact made in fun long ago, and yet when Diana was invited to a retirement party for Margaret's agent, Roy Langston, at Downing Street last year, the Prime Minister remembered. 'I know,' she said, seeing Diana for the first time in years, 'we are going to have macaroni cheese and apricot tart and custard together.'

'Red boxes' are the battered and worn red leather brief cases, in which ministers carry the paperwork that has to be dealt with. Each full box represents about two hours' work, and most ministers will have on average one per night. A prime minister, however, can have two or three, and Margaret works away on her boxes until late into the night. 'Prime Minister, don't you want to get on and do the boxes?' weary colleagues will ask after a long session in her flat, really meaning, 'We would like to go to bed.' But she will reply, 'No, no,' kick off her shoes, fold her legs up under her body, and settle down with a whisky and soda for a good, invigorating debate. She has some of her best ideas late at night, when she is relaxed and surrounded by people she knows are friends. 'She is a night bird,' said one of them, 'although God knows she's a day bird too.'

Margaret's day as Prime Minister begins as it has done ever since she was a child, at about 6.30 in the morning. The early editions of *The Times*, the *Daily Telegraph*, the *Express* and the *Sun* are sent round to Downing Street late the previous night, for the press secretary to read and to point out any items she ought to see. She prefers to listen to the radio, to the current affairs 'Today' programme on Radio 4, and occasionally the programme that precedes it, 'Farming Today', while she bathes, dresses and cooks Denis's breakfast. The radio moreover is not mere background noise. Many a time an aide has been woken in his bed at home by a phone call from the Prime Minister. 'Are you listening to that interview with so-and-so?' she'll ask, as he tries hard to focus on his alarm clock. 'It's fascinating; you should be.'

Another colleague once came in to work one Saturday after an exceptionally busy week, with another busy day ahead, and described the lovely feeling she had at weekends: 'I always find, as I sit down to breakfast on a Saturday morning, there's five minutes,' she said, 'when I can relax and the weekend stretches ahead, before I realize how much I have to do. It's like getting a cheque at the end of the month and thinking you're rich for five minutes.' Margaret looked at her with total incomprehension. This was clearly a thought that had never crossed her mind. She would be hard put to find something to do with the prospect of a free weekend stretching ahead. Work is Margaret's life, as it always has been; politics are her only real interest.

Her official day begins at 8.30 in her study on the first floor of Number Ten, with an informal meeting to discuss the day ahead and the pitfalls she should beware of. This is attended by her press secretary, a handful of advisers, and Caroline Stephens, who became keeper, when

Margaret moved into Number Ten, of the diary which entirely rules her life. Even Carol had to ask Caroline if there was any chance of taking her mother to the theatre one evening, and usually was told 'there's not a hope in hell for the next three months'.

From then on the day is a round of meetings: committee meetings which she has to chair, and hates – she has a profound mistrust of committees; Cabinet meetings for two hours on Tuesday and Thursday mornings, which she would also happily do without; meetings with the Queen, with foreign statesmen, with heads of industry, occasionally with unions, and with her colleagues. She then has the gruelling business of Prime Minister's Question Time for fifteen minutes in the House every Tuesday and Thursday, when every face on the opposite side of the Despatch Box lights up at the chance of tripping her up. In addition, the day might involve speeches inside or outside the House, late night votes, banquets, broadcasts, visits to any part of the country; plus the normal daily mountain of paperwork, which Margaret Thatcher never skimps. There is a story that when presented with the Beveridge Report on social insurance, ninety pages of well-documented, finely argued, closely typed text, Churchill wrote across the top, 'Which page do I read?' and sent it back. Mrs Thatcher, on the other hand, was once given a four-page precis, and sent it back with the instruction: 'Show me the research on which this was based.'

One of the many bitter lessons she learnt in her years as a Junior Minister was never to accept advice without double checking it herself, especially the facts and the arguments that might be hurled in her face by the Opposition. Once the mud begins to fly, those civil servants who have been so enthusiastically advising a course of action can suddenly become rather hard to spot. Margaret no longer trusts advice or information from anyone without double checking herself. She becomes furious if anyone says something that is inaccurate, even in family conversations round the lunch table. When a speech writer once made a mistake with a set of figures in a speech she was taking to Northern Ireland, the year before the election, she castigated him roundly and threw the entire speech away.

When she was asked in an interview by Brian Connell in *The Times* how she took the strain, she said:

> I've no idea, it's just that I'm a round peg in a round hole. I don't feel any sign of physical strain at all. I've always led an onerous timetable but I like it. I have a tremendous amount of energy and

for the first time in my life it is fully used. I have always a little bit in reserve. In public life you must, because no matter how busy you are, there will be some time when you need a little bit extra. But when you are going flat out you never feel tired, it's when you've stopped.

This interview was written a year after Margaret became Prime Minister. *The Times* had been out of action when Margaret came to power, and the strike which had closed the paper for eleven months was not resolved until October. That strike was one for which her hard-line attitude was not responsible, but there were others for which it was. Her feelings about pay claims did not change with office:

> If you take too much, the goods will be too highly priced, consequently the order books will be empty and the whole firm will be forced to close down. If people take smaller wage increases or, alternatively, with bigger wage increases match every pound by increased productivity, we can sell on that basis. For a period we've got inflation rising and unemployment rising. We've got to get through that period. Government will do, is doing and will continue to do its part but, in the end, industry has got to respond to the stimulus. You've got to have leadership throughout industry. Government cannot do it alone any more than a general can win a battle on his own.

'We have taken all the necessary steps,' she declared confidently, 'and they will work through. It's like a patient; there is a time when you are still suffering from the disease and you take the medicine, and there is a time when you are suffering from both the disease and the medicine. That doesn't mean you stop the medicine, you know you have to take the medicine if you are to be cured of the disease.'

Margaret knew; she had a blinding vision of what was needed, but a great many of her Cabinet colleagues, who were, of course, still basically moderate Heath men, found the taste of the medicine unpalatable. And the longer she remained in office, the harsher the measures became, and the more rebellious grew the doubters. It was a very unhappy time, and there were moments towards the end of her second year as Premier when she began to despair.

Margaret had inherited various reports and recommendations on pay and comparability when she moved into Number Ten. These had been commissioned by the previous Government, and as a result of pressure from her Cabinet she went along with the first bout of increases, including a considerable rise for the civil service and for MPs (which had strong support on both sides of the House). This went thoroughly against the grain – she didn't think it right that MPs should be awarding themselves large pay rises when they were telling the rest of the country to tighten their belts – but she was advised that she must toe the line in these instances. Personally, however, she did practise what she preached, and took nearly £8,000 less than the salary she was entitled to as Prime Minister. The Lord Chancellor, Lord Hailsham, similarly took less than his award, both having chosen to take the same pay as their Cabinet colleagues.

When industry ran into trouble over pay, her instinct was that government should keep right out of it, as she had spelt out in her speeches in the past. She tried hard to remain true to that ideal, but pay and strikes dogged hers no less than her predecessors' governments.

1980 began with the first steel strike in fifty-four years, which dragged on for months. The steel-workers came out over planned plant closures and a pay offer of six per cent, which the unions had rejected. Action was precipitated by Keith Joseph's announcement that the Government would not intervene in the dispute. The workers were further angered when the Government revealed plans to replace Sir Charles Villiers, retiring chairman of the British Steel Corporation, by a Scottish-born, but in every other respect, American businessman, Ian MacGregor. His current employers, Lazard Freres of New York, were to be paid £675,000 for his temporary release. 'An insult to British management,' was one top businessman's opinion, voicing the outrage of many. But Keith Joseph stressed that MacGregor was the best of forty-five candidates for the job. 'What sort of country is it,' asked Margaret in a radio interview soon after the announcement, 'which says we can pay enormous sums to footballers, but not to get the best person here to Britain to get a steel industry, which is in trouble, thriving and flourishing again?'

Ian MacGregor was the cause of more and still fiercer controversy in 1983, when Margaret, by this time almost four years into her premiership, and very much her own woman, decided that he was the only man capable of taking on the mammoth task of the National Coal Board, which was losing money hand over fist. Once again there would have to be a payment to Lazard Freres to buy him out of his contract with the company. Quite apart from the fact that MacGregor had earned the reputation at BSC of being a hatchet man, there was long and sustained uproar about the cost of hiring him, and yet again his appointment an affront to British businessmen. Public opinion was stronger the second time around than the first, but Margaret was herself stronger too. By 1983 she was a changed woman: she had weathered many storms, scored many successes, and finally weeded those people she trusted least out of her Cabinet.

In August 1980, unemployment had risen above the two million mark for the first time since 1935. Imperial Chemical Industries Limited, one of Britain's largest companies, reported a loss for the first time in its history. British Airways announced its first-ever half-yearly loss; and British Leyland also lost hundreds of millions of pounds in the first half of the financial year, on top of implementing large-scale redundancies. The tough measures were beginning to be felt, and they continued to be so. The nightly news bulletin on television adopted a map of the country to record the number of jobs lost in a week. Small companies went out of business one by one, and the number of unemployed continued to rise ever higher and higher. In October 1980 the Confederation of British Industry's Quarterly Trend Survey called it the 'blackest ever issued'. In November, the Chancellor announced still more cuts in public spending to the tune of another £3,000 million, and by December unemployment had reached a post-war record of 2,133,000 – 836,000 more than the same month the previous year.

More and more of the Prime Minister's colleagues were thinking that the time had come to alter direction. The strict monetarist policies to which she and the Chancellor were adhering with such fervour were causing a great deal of misery in the country, and did not seem to be doing sufficient good to justify themselves. Inflation wasn't coming down; all that was happening was that businesses were collapsing, the dole queues were growing, and street violence was becoming prevalent. Those operations that were successful and potentially represented producers of wealth for the country, such as the North Sea Oil companies, were being bled dry by taxation.

By the end of 1980 two previous Tory prime ministers had spoken out publicly about their concern. In a television interview in October, Margaret's one-time hero, Harold Macmillan, said her policies were too hard and hitting the creators of national wealth. A month later Ted Heath intervened during an economic debate in the House to declare that official optimism was false; the recession was getting worse and would turn to disaster unless the Government changed course by lowering interest rates and the value of the pound. The unemployment brought about by high interest rates, he argued, was costing more than the anti-inflationary benefits.

Margaret retorted, not unpredictably, that the massive inflation that she had on her hands was the result of the woolly financial policy that Heath himself had exercised. To tell a family that was overspending its income to go on spending and borrowing, she said in a radio broadcast, was 'the morality of a man who has his hand in someone else's pocket. We have got to get it right this time, and we shall.'

Though she argued her pitch well, the feeling was growing nonetheless that Margaret was all the things her colleagues had feared; too hard, too right wing, and with not a twinge of compassion for those people who were being turned out of their jobs. Secrets began to leak from Cabinet meetings, appearing verbatim in the daily press. It became common knowledge that several of her team were criticizing her, and the media talked openly about the 'wets', the 'drys', and the general divisiveness of the Government.

Margaret will rant and rave at people in a way that has reduced grown men to tears, but she is remarkably soft when it comes to sacking them. The only grounds on which she feels able to do it is when they have been disloyal to her. This is the one failing she cannot forgive; and she has difficulty, like many a woman, in differentiating between criticism and disloyalty. First to go was Norman St John-Stevas who, as Leader of the House of Commons, had played a key role in rallying suppport. He was a witty man, a court jester of whom she had been very fond, and in the past he had been a good friend to her; but, as her distrust grew, she feared he might prove unreliable: too eager to be liked by everyone, too easily swayed by the current. She gave him his marching orders in January 1981; and thereafter he began to express his criticism quite openly with the wrath of one scorned.

He was not alone. Outside party politics, a group of 364 academic economists, including the President of the Royal Economic Society and several former chief economic advisers to governments, signed a memorial published in the newspapers:

> There is no basis in economic theory or supporting evidence for the Government's belief that by deflating demand they will bring inflation permanently under control and thereby induce an automatic recovery in output and employment. Present policies will deepen the depression, erode the industrial base of our

economy and threaten its social and political stability.

There are alternative policies, and the time has come to reject monetarist policies and consider urgently which alternative offers the best hope of sustained economic recovery.

Within the House Ted Heath continued his attack, but more worrying was a statement from a Tory MP, Robert Hicks, that if the Government continued with its present economic policies, then he and some twenty other back-benchers might seriously consider joining a centrist party. Even Edward du Cann, who had been behind Margaret for the leadership back in 1974, speaking in a Budget debate in March demanded a new programme for national recovery.

By now there was indeed a new centrist party for defectors to join: the Social Democratic Party, formed in January 1981 by Roy Jenkins, former President of the European Commission, and his 'gang of three' other ex-Labour Cabinet Ministers, Shirley Williams, David Owen and William Rodgers. It provided just the sort of middle ground between the extreme left, towards which the Labour Party was purposefully headed, and the extreme right, to which the Tory Party was moving; and a haven for all those in both of the established parties who disagreed with their leadership.

Soon after Norman St John-Stevas fell from grace, Angus Maude resigned, and Margaret swiftly brought in some solid, 'dry' citizens: John Nott, whom she appointed Secretary of State for Defence; John Biffen, who went to Trade; and Leon Brittan, who became Chief Secretary to the Treasury. She then pitched Jim Prior, who had always been a thorn in her side, out of Employment and across the waters to Northern Ireland, replacing him with Norman Tebbit. Ian Gilmour, who was more outspokenly wet, who had opposed her on every issue that came up in Cabinet, and who aroused her grave suspicions by, so her spies told her, having Roy Jenkins to dine in his house, was shown the door altogether. 'It does no harm to throw the occasional man overboard,' he said on his departure, 'but it does not do much good if you are steering full speed ahead for the rocks.'

Next to go were Lord Soames and Mark Carlisle, who pre-empted dismissal by handing in their resignations. Christopher Soames, the wonder boy of Zimbabwe, had undone all his good works by his handling of a civil service pay dispute which began in March, and had dragged on for five months at colossal cost to the country in both money and disruption. He had told Margaret in April that the strike could be ended by offering an extra half per cent on top of the seven per cent that was already on the table. In her eyes, giving in to the union by even half a per cent was tantamount to treason.

Christopher Soames, who has the reputation of being one of the rudest men in politics, who spares no one his tongue, came out of that meeting with Mrs Thatcher reeling. 'I have never, ever, been spoken to by anyone like that in my life,' he said. In the end, the civil service dispute was settled by a seven and a half per cent rise, the very amount that he had suggested four months earlier; and cost the country £300 million in lost revenue.

His place as Leader of the House of Lords was taken by Lady Young, providing a little female support in the Cabinet. Lord Thorneycroft, making a timely departure from the chairmanship of the Party Association on the pretext of age, was replaced by Cecil Parkinson, who had been Margaret's whip on the Finance Bill at the time she was running for the leadership. One of her closest admirers describes Cecil Parkinson as 'the son she wished she'd had' – strong, handsome and independent – and Norman Tebbit as 'the husband she wished she had had' – self-made, pushy, and hard-line. His approach was encapsulated at the Conservative Party Conference the next month, when he announced that his unemployed father in the 1930s had not joined demonstrations, but had 'got on his bike and looked for a job'.

Margaret could be vitriolic, not only in private, but also in front of others in Cabinet and committee meetings, or in briefings with her staff, and was not given to apologizing for her behaviour afterwards. If anyone did any mopping up it would be Ian Gow, her trusted Parliamentary Private Secretary, a thoroughly proper, totally loyal, somewhat infatuated, public-school Tory, who has proved invaluable in keeping Margaret in tune with the feeling of the House, and smoothing the way. He is one of her closest friends in politics.

Margaret demanded total loyalty from her friends, but by the same token she gave total loyalty in return. Fergus Montgomery, her old PPS from Education, and the man who sponsored her for the leadership, had found himself charged with stealing two books from a shop back in 1977, and a report appeared in the evening papers. Before eight o'clock the next morning Margaret was on the phone asking what he planned to do with his day. He would be going to court, he explained, then spending the rest of the day at home, not much wanting to have to see anyone. She persuaded him to go to the House. It was important, she said, to face people, to get straight back into the saddle. When he

The man in Margaret's private life: (*left*) Denis in his favourite stance, on the golf course; (*above*) The trials and tribulations of a Prime Minister's consort can be many. On a visit to India in 1981, Denis was obliged to don a turban to the delight of photographers, and ultimately of *Private Eye*; (*below*) Denis and Margaret emerging from a visit to 'Anyone for Denis', with their stage equivalents (John Wells and Angela Thorne) in the background

Margaret Thatcher may have had little experience in foreign affairs before she became Prime Minister, but she wasted little time in emerging as a dominant figure in Europe. In this photograph, she is showing who's in charge at a line-up of leaders from the EEC at a conference in Dublin Castle in November 1979. *From left to right, front row:* Jack Lynch, Prime Minister of Eire, Giscard d'Estaing, President of France, Dr Patrick Hillery, President of Eire, Margaret Thatcher, Francesco Cossiga, Prime Minister of Italy, and Roy Jenkins, President of the Commission

Margaret Thatcher has gained the admiration of many of her European colleagues, regardless of their politics: (*above left*) the British Prime Minister with President Mitterand of France; (*left*) Chancellor Schmidt of West Germany being welcomed by an uncharacteristically ruffled Mrs Thatcher as he arrived in May 1981 for talks at Chequers

During her premiership, Margaret Thatcher has travelled all over the world: (*above*) In Indian sari at a meeting with another female head of state, and fellow Somervillian, Mrs Gandhi, during her tour of India in April 1981; (*below*) Inspecting a guard of honour in China during her visit in September 1982; (*bottom*) Again in suitable dress, being received by Saudi Arabian princes on her arrival at Riyadh in April 1982

The two greatest crises facing Margaret Thatcher during her first term in office were the very private fear that she had lost her son Mark in the desert during the Paris to Dakar rally, and the very public fear that she might lose many men in the Falklands campaign

Above: Margaret with Mark in happy times, celebrating her victory at Finchley in the 1974 election. *Left:* One of the first pictures to come back of Mark and his co-driver, Charlotte Verney, after they had been found in the desert in Algeria – they had been missing for six days. *Below:* Margaret caught off guard by photographers – a mother beset with grief and worry

Left: Bowed down with anxiety and sorrow, Margaret Thatcher leaves Number Ten carrying the knowledge that members of the crew of HMS *Sheffield* were still missing, 6 May 1982. *Below:* The Prime Minister with Sir John Fieldhouse, Chief of Naval Staff, laying wreaths at the memorial to the Task Force dead at Blue Beach cemetery, near San Carlos Settlement in the Falkland Islands, January 1983

Peter Brookes' cartoon of Margaret
Thatcher as Snow White, with her Sev
Dwarfs, preparing for the general elect
of 9 June 1983. Michael Foot is inevita
cast in the role of the Wicked Witch, b
in the event his magic apple turned ou
pose little threat

Alison Ward, Margaret Thatcher's lon
serving secretary, was recalled to help
the 1983 election campaign. Here she i
shown (right) on the 'Thatcher bus' wi
left to right, Carol Thatcher, Roger Boa
and John Whittingdale, trying to repai
typewriter that had dived off the table w
the driver made an emergency stop

Margaret Thatcher's triumphant return to Number Ten Downing Street after her landslide victory on the evening of 9 June 1983. With this victory, she became the first Conservative Prime Minister since the Marquis of Salisbury to win a second consecutive term of office

Francis Pym's remarks about the perils of a landslide victory had made him a marked man in the Cabinet reshuffle following the election. Bluntly, he informed the press that he had been sacked, and his comments from the back-benches in the early debates of the new Parliamentary session established him as a thorn in Margaret Thatcher's flesh.
Cummings' cartoon in the *Daily Express*, 1 July 1983

Margaret Thatcher sits in the middle of her new Cabinet, following the election: one lady in an all-male establishment

Margaret Thatcher enjoying time off from the cares of government, at men's semi-finals at Wimbledon. She was lucky, for the match between Kevin Curren and Chris Lewis was one of the best of the tournament, and both players displayed energetic diligence and grim determination – both qualities that appeal to the Prime Minister

arrived, they had a talk in her office. 'Come on,' she suddenly said, 'we're going for a walk', and they spent much of the afternoon pacing the corridors and public rooms of the Palace of Westminster so that people would see them.

She did the same for Guinevere Tilney years later, when a story appeared in the gossip column of a Sunday newspaper to the effect that Lady Tilney had had a row with the Prime Minister and fallen from favour. Guinevere was deeply hurt, and when Margaret heard she was appalled. 'Right,' she said, 'you're going to come with me, and be seen in public so that everyone will know there is no rift between us whatsoever.' And for the next couple of weeks, Guinevere was by her side at every function she attended.

One day in March 1981, George Newell, Margaret's driver, had a sudden heart attack in Downing Street, and died. Her immediate thought was for his wife, May. She was deeply concerned about her: she didn't have a car, she couldn't drive, she didn't have anywhere in the world to go, and hadn't even been there when her husband died; and since they had had no children, who was going to take care of her? George's best friend, however, had been the other Number Ten driver, so Margaret called him in and gave him ten days' leave, with a car, so that he might go to see that May was all right and help with the funeral arrangements. She in the meantime was left with a temporary driver from the civil service pool. Then, despite a gruelling schedule, Margaret found time to drive out to George's funeral at Rochester Way Crematorium in South London. Six months later, quite out of the blue, she asked one of the girls in the office to ring May to see how she was; and again at Christmas time, she would make discreet enquiries to make sure May was not alone.

Margaret was always very anxious that people should have somewhere to go at Christmas time, and each year she has invited people to stay whom she knows would otherwise be alone. The year Keith Joseph's wife left him after thirty years of marriage, he spent Christmas at Chequers. When Gordon Reece's wife ran off with an out-of-work actor, taking their three youngest children with her, he too had a sudden telephone call asking him to Chequers. He has been a regular Christmas guest ever since, despite the fact that he left the fold and went to earn considerably more money (enabling him to contribute to the upkeep of his ex-wife, still out-of-work actor, and the three youngest children). With Armand Hammer as Vice President of Occidental Oil, Ronnie Millar is another regular. An ex-Cabinet colleague and his wife were also invited one year, after his wife had had an operation, so that she wouldn't be put through the strain of preparing Christmas at home. Margaret has even invited people who are not particular friends – such as a civil servant who was well known to be a strong Labour sympathizer; but his wife had just died, and Margaret felt sorry for him. During the course of the holiday other friends and supporters join the party. Last year, for instance, Margaret's doctor, Dr John Henderson and his wife, were at Chequers, together with an old friend, Daphne Scrivinger, and Laurens van der Post and his wife.

Christmas at Chequers is much the same for any prime minister because the house runs itself, but there is a tradition that on Boxing Night, when the staff have their Christmas dinner, they invite the Prime Minister to have a drink with them beforehand in the staff room. Mrs Thatcher put an end to that. She invites all the staff to come to the main part of the house to have a drink with her and her guests, which she serves. The staff then go and eat their dinner, which again she and her guests will serve, and at the end of it all she ropes in her hapless guests for the washing up. 'I'm not having these dirty dishes left for the staff,' she'll say, as she pulls on a pair of rubber gloves and gets to grips with the Fairy Liquid.

Margaret possesses an instinct for knowing how to make people feel better, and a direct and decisive way of dealing with problems. Unlike many a prime minister she is quite readily accessible to anyone who wants to see her; although once she has found time to fit them into an already hectic day, she doesn't want it wasted. ' Right,' she will ask, 'what's the problem?' Once that has come out, she will say 'And what's the answer?' Her colleague will do as best he can, Margaret will thereupon look him straight between the eyes and either say 'Yes, that's right', or she will launch into a diatribe, telling him precisely where he is wrong and why. He will then retreat, quivering with indignation and muttering 'the trouble is, that damn woman's right'.

Carol, so like her mother in many respects, admits she is hopeless at making decisions, and will often ring Margaret for advice. 'Mum'll say, look, these are your options, these are the plus and minus factors. For heaven's sake, stop hanging around, just make up your mind and get on and do it.'

Although Carol was based in Sydney during her mother's first term as Premier, mother and daughter kept in touch, mostly by telephone. Carol accompanied Margaret as mistress of the wardrobe and general helper on her trip to India and the Middle East in April 1982: to Delhi,

Bombay, and then on to Riyadh, Oman, Abu Dhabi and Dubai. In Riyadh they managed to fuse the entire lighting system in the palace in which they were staying, with Margaret's heated rollers. The Prime Minister was left in some state of alarm, with a meeting with Prince Fahad in half an hour and soaking wet hair. It was on this trip that Margaret was given the most dazzling pearl necklace, each pearl the size of a marble – a gift from King Khaled. They were exquisite, and, back in London, Margaret wore them with enormous pride. She also sported a somewhat gawdy gold watch set with diamonds and sapphires. But as with every gift of any worth she receives as Prime Minister, even those that are obviously personal, she has to hand them straight over to the Treasury. They will have them valued, and the moment that she leaves office, if she wants to keep anything (unlike members of the Royal Family, who can keep everything), she has to pay the valuation sum. A man from the Crown jewellers, Garrards, was at Number Ten within twenty-four hours of Margaret landing on British soil to value the gifts, which left, even her, shocked, and a little peeved. 'Don't you think she's stupid?' Denis asked of friends some time later. 'I'm sure I would have put something in my pocket.'

Margaret arrived home from the Middle East to learn that unemployment had topped the two and a half million mark for the first time since the 1930s. Not long afterwards there were three days of violent rioting in the Liverpool district of Toxteth in July, closely followed by riots in London. The Pope, John Paul II, had been shot and wounded in St Peter's Square in Rome in May, and in June a man with a gun fired blanks at the Queen during the Trooping the Colour. It was a turbulent summer all round, then came a touch of magic on 29 July, with the royal wedding of Prince Charles and Lady Diana Spencer, when the nation forgot its troubles, and sang and danced in the streets. The euphoria didn't last long, however, and Margaret was soon at Blackpool defending her pitch at the Conservative Party Conference. There she delivered a devastating speech which earned her a six-minute ovation. 'The lady's not for turning,' she declared, adapting the famous Christopher Fry play, *The Lady's Not For Burning*. 'I will not change just to court popularity. . . If ever a Conservative Government starts to do what it knows is wrong because it is afraid to do what is right, that is the time for Tories to cry "Stop". But you will never need to do that while I am Prime Minister.'

Although her speeches are now written for her, they still bear her stamp just as much as they did in the early days. She will have a preliminary meeting, usually in her study at Number Ten, about six weeks before the proposed speech has to be delivered. The first discussion will be about content, and will bear little relation to the resultant speech that eventually appears. The basic structure will then be worked out by a team: possibly Ronnie Millar, Peter Utley of the *Daily Telegraph*, or Alfred Sherman, head of the Centre for Policy Studies, with, formerly, Chris Patten or John Hoskins, and more recently, Ferdinand Mount, head of the policy unit. About forty-eight hours before D-Day they will all reconvene at night in Margaret's flat at Number Ten, often with Ian Gow present too, and again go through the content of the speech. Denis might drift in and out to refill glasses.

Both Thatchers are good hosts, constantly concerned that guests have enough to eat and drink. The only glass that often goes for the whole evening without a refill is Margaret's. She hates sherry, tolerates wine, and occasionally sips at champagne to be sociable, but the drink she enjoys is a whisky with soda, at lunchtime and in the evenings. She is nevertheless by no means a drinker, and one weak drink usually lasts several hours. On the other hand, her husband and children, her aides and colleagues are not so abstemious. Ian Gow drinks more than the odd White Lady, a devastating blend of gin and Cointreau. Gordon Reece sticks to champagne if he can get it. But Denis, who, it has to be said, does like the odd drink – gin and tonic for preference – and does say to chums, 'Just time for a tincture,' as the 'Dear Bill' letters suggest, is not an excessively heavy drinker. There was a time when Margaret first came into office that he found the going tough, and did drink rather more than was wise, given his extreme views on the 'bolshies' who run the unions, the 'pinkoes' in the BBC, and the 'incompetents that run the railways', – particularly when he had a tendency to express such views to the chairman of British Rail without realizing to whom he was talking. Nowadays he is far more circumspect, and makes quite sure he is among friends before he sounds off in a series of blunt Anglo-Saxon expletives on subjects that agitate. Margaret has long since given up trying to moderate his language.

Her own language, moreover, is not entirely colourless. Despite her prim image, more than thirty years of marriage to Denis has provided her with quite an extensive vocabulary. 'Stanley, you old bugger!' she exclaimed, when to her delight she spotted Stanley Booth, the man who had given her her first job at BX Plastics, lurking at the end of a queue at a reception in East Anglia not long ago. When told in the midst of the Finance Bill that someone was playing up, she would say, 'You tell so and so to go and get stuffed.' Or, when a particular group of civil servants were threatening to block her, she declared, 'I'm going to beat those bastards! They're not going to stop me this time.'

When she is holding an evening meeting in the flat at Number Ten, Margaret will usually cook everybody some supper: nothing elaborate – baked potatoes perhaps. There was one Sunday night when the potatoes emerged rock hard from the oven. No one liked to say anything, but quite suddenly she became aware. 'Don't eat them!' she said, 'Don't eat them! We'll meet again next Sunday and perhaps I'll get them right that time.' 'If you just leave them in, they might be done by then,' suggested someone bold.

Provided she is absolutely certain she can trust them, Margaret likes bold men around her: the slightly outrageous, witty, faintly flirtatious man that appeals to her feminine ego. She has even developed, if not a sense of humour, at least the ability to recognize wit, and to laugh. But she has to be certain she is among friends. People are divided into 'them' and 'us'. Denis refers to the 'us' lot as 'the Home Team', and Margaret is very careful to include wives in the team, and make them feel that they are all part of one big happy family. She is particularly good at receptions, which she gives frequently, in Downing Street, and large lunch parties at Chequers, where she is an excellent hostess, gliding round the room, putting an affectionate arm round people, and moving on. She moves on because she does not, in fact, have any small talk. Not many politicians do, but she at least makes an effort. Ted Heath, by contrast, would go to dinner with a colleague at his home and not address one single word to the man's wife throughout the entire course of the evening. Margaret does have a tendency to assume that wives will know about shopping and children and very little else, and has made some serious blunders in her time, but those who are not political do appreciate that she tries.

Margaret has been through some very harrowing experiences during her first period in office. By the autumn of 1981, her battle with the wets in her Cabinet almost plunged her into despair. 'There are times,' confided Denis to a friend, 'when she feels like jacking it in. You just can't have a situation when every time the Cabinet meets there are people in it who are prepared to leak everything to newspapers. Her authority is being eroded; she just doesn't know whom to trust. Nothing like this has ever happened to a prime minister before. But you know Margaret, she'll keep on fighting.'

No experience was more harrowing, however, than learning that Mark, taking part in the Paris to Dakar rally, had been lost in the Sahara Desert. The drama began with a telephone call from the *Daily Express* to the flat at Number Ten one evening in January 1982, wanting to know whether a report, that had just come in on the telex that Mark and his female co-driver had missed a checkpoint in the race, was true. Carol, home from Australia just a month earlier, happened to answer the phone and, not having a clue about the race, went to ask her parents. Denis was quite cross. 'All you're doing is worrying your mother unnecessarily,' he said, and so she apologized and no more was said. The newspapers ran the story, and over the next couple of days the family made phone calls to some of Mark's friends and the race organizers, to see if they could find out what was going on.

Then the news came through that Mark had turned up, that he and his glamorous French companion, Charlotte Verney, had been rescued by a helicopter, and the panic was over. Two days later Derek Howe, from Margaret's political office in Downing Street, came into the sitting room in the flat and said, 'There's very bad news. Mark is still missing.' He and Denis then went straight down to tell Margaret in her study below, and her nightmare began. Gone was the thick-skinned, hard-line politician, totally in command of every situation, with the solution for every problem at her fingertips. Suddenly she was nothing more than a mother sick with worry, terrified that the worst had happened, and quite unable, despite her position, to do anything about it. The newspapers were filled with stories about Mark, all written chillingly in the past tense, about people who had been killed in the six-thousand-mile race, and about the extremes of weather that reduced terribly man's chances of survival in the desert.

Margaret tried to carry on as normal. She held a Cabinet meeting as usual and, although not as forthright as most days, did manage to get through the business. The only time she cracked and publicly burst into tears, was when a reporter caught her off guard as she was arriving to address a lunchtime meeting at the Imperial Hotel in Bloomsbury. 'I'm sorry, there is no news,' she said, tears welling up in her eyes. 'Naturally, I'm very concerned.' The tears then began to roll uncontrollably down her cheeks and she sobbed quite desperately for a moment, before pulling herself together sufficiently to go into the lunch, and to speak for twenty-five minutes.

In private she cried more freely; but she also worked. She would sit down with her red boxes, then stop all of a sudden, look up and ask, 'I wonder if there's any news?' What news there was was confused and conflicting. One group would say 'We know the area, don't worry, he can't be far', while others would declare 'We know the area, he hasn't got a hope'. There was nothing she could do but rely on other people to do what they said they would do. She felt guilty that two days had been lost, between the time when it was thought that he had been found and the confirmation that he was still missing; two days in which she had carried on with her life.

Denis was very calm and controlled about the whole affair, providing great strength. Finally, he took up Sir Hector Laing, Chairman of United Biscuits, on the offer of his little Beechcraft private plane, and flew out to the Sahara to find out what on earth was going on. Margaret later recounted the ordeal to a friend, quite naively touched by the offers of help. 'You know, when you're in difficulty you see who your real friends are. Before the morning was out, when Denis had decided to go out, we had offers of three planes.'

Carol was living in Downing Street at the time, while the house in Flood Street was being repainted. She was devastated to see the pain that her mother was going through as they waited for news. Margaret didn't like to be alone, and rang up some of her closest friends. She wanted to talk, to go over the details of the sequence of events, and to talk through all the possibilities that were passing through her head. When an unconfirmed report arrived that he had been found, she refused to believe it, having experienced the earlier false alarm. She wouldn't trust anyone until she heard from Denis.

Letters and messages poured in from friends and from the public. One newspaper wrote saying, 'We'd like to be able to lead tomorrow's paper with the story that your son has been found.' There were notes from mothers who said, 'We know how worried you are, our thoughts are with you.' Her face would light up; quite genuinely grateful for each kind sentiment.

Eventually the call did come through from Denis, although they had first heard that Mark was safe in an interview on the one o'clock news: Mark was fine, Denis had seen him, everything was all right, and they were coming home. Margaret was back to normal instantly. She didn't collapse with relief. She snapped straight back to normal; she was the Leader, in command again, sure of herself, and of her ability to cope.

Mark appeared quite puzzled by the fuss when he finally reached civilization. 'I am absolutely staggered. I have seen less journalists at a

Conservative Party Conference,' he quipped. 'All I need is a beer and a sandwich, a bath and a shave.' When he arrived in England he was wheeled smartly down to Chequers for a reunion and a short sharp lecture on taking pretty girls into the desert, and throwing two entire countries – Algeria, whose troops were out in force, and Britain – into a state of alert.

Nothing had ever proved as personally traumatic to Margaret Thatcher as those six days when Mark was missing. But taking the country to war over the Falkland Islands came a very close second. The Falklands – two big, and two hundred tiny, barren wind-blown South Atlantic islands, largely populated by sheep, eight thousand miles from Britain – had been British territory for the past one hundred and fifty years. For those one hundred and fifty years Argentina, just three hundred miles away, had disputed Britain's claim to the Malvinas, as they called them. Successive British governments had found the islands a headache: they were too far away to be able to protect adequately; they were no great source of wealth and, although the sea around them was thought to be rich in oil and minerals, it was uneconomic to utilize. More than one administration had unofficially toyed with the idea of giving them back to Argentina; but there was always one major problem – the will of the people. They numbered just eighteen hundred, almost all of British origin and English speaking, with no desire to become a part of a foreign culture.

In the past twenty years, retaking the Malvinas had become something of a national crusade in Argentina. A new military regime, headed by General Leopoldo Galtieri, decided to court the popularity of his people – with whom he was in other respects extremely unpopular because of his blood-thirsty fascist regime – by launching an attack that appeared to take British intelligence by surprise.

The first news to reach Britain was that some 'scrap metal merchants' had landed on the isolated island of South Georgia, and had erected an Argentinian flag. The Royal Navy ice-patrol ship *Endurance* – mercifully still in the Falkland capital of Port Stanley although, thanks to defence cuts, shortly due to be sent home – was dispatched to investigate.

Then, at seven o'clock on the evening of Wednesday, 31 March, Margaret was sent news in her office in the House of Commons that it looked as though the Argentine fleet was on its way to the Falklands.

The Foreign Secretary, Lord Carrington, was in Israel, the Chief of the Defence Staff was in New Zealand. Margaret had to cope alone. She called a meeting with the Foreign Office and the Ministry of Defence, and through the night they thrashed out the possibilities and the alternatives in the event of an Argentine invasion. The expert opinion from the First Sea Lord, Sir Henry Leach, was that it would be feasible, if necessary, to mobilize a task force which could be ready to leave for the Falklands on Monday, 5 April. Although there would be difficulties inherent in fighting a war eight thousand miles away, it would be possible to defend the islands.

This was all the essential information Margaret needed. The rest was a matter of principle. She quickly wrote to President Reagan, whom she had met on a visit to Washington the previous February soon after his inauguration as President of the United States, and to his Defence Secretary, Al Haig, to see if they might bring some influence to bear on Galtieri. Both were flabbergasted by the news. She then contacted Galtieri and asked him what was going on. The next day the Prime Minnister chaired her usual Thursday Cabinet meeting in which she spelt out contingency plans, then prepared herself for a rough ride in that afternoon's Question Time. 'Do you know,' she told George Gale of the *Daily Express*, when the war was all over, 'that Thursday afternoon, the day before the invasion, in spite of everything people have said since, there was not one question to me in Prime Minister's Question Time.'

The next day Argentine troops took Port Stanley, and Governor Rex Hunt surrendered. London received a thinly disguised message breaking the news from the local Cable and Wireless office:

LDN   HELLO THERE WHAT ARE ALL THESE RUMOURS WE HEAR THIS IS LDN
FK   WE HAVE LOTS OF NEW FRIENDS
LDN   WHAT ABOUT INVASION RUMOURS?
FK   THOSE ARE THE FRIENDS I WAS MEANING
LDN   HAVE THEY LANDED?
FK   ABSOLUTELY
LDN   ARE YOU OPEN FOR TRAFFIC IE NORMAL TELEX SERVICE?
FK   NO ORDERS ON THAT YET ONE MUST OBEY ORDERS
LDN   WHOSE ORDERS?
FK   THE NEW GOVERNORS

LDN   ARGENTINA?
FK   YES
LDN   ARE THE ARGENTINIANS IN CONTROL?
FK   YES YOU CANT ARGUE WITH THOUSANDS OF
TROOPS PLUS ENORMOUS NAVY SUPPORT WHEN YOU
ARE ONLY 1800 STRONG
STAND BY PSE

Margaret called an emergency debate to make a statement about the Falklands on the Saturday morning, 2 April. It was the first time that Parliament had been convened on a Saturday in twenty-five years; the most humiliating day a government had ever suffered. She addressed a very hostile House and, some say, made the worst speech of her career that morning. But she nevertheless spelt out her convictions. 'They are few in number,' she said of the islanders, 'but they have the right to live in peace, to choose their own way of life and to determine their own allegiance.' More important still, Argentina had taken the islands by force. The fact that, all other things being equal, they were welcome to them, did not count. There was a vital point of principle at stake, and it was over this that Margaret Thatcher led her country to war. She did, it is true, have little opotion if she wanted to keep her job: her whole election platform, after all, had been based on the principle of standing up to the aggressor. This was the philosophy of the Iron Lady; and she knew better than anyone that if she lay down and let Argentina walk all over her, she too would have enjoyed the attentions of the scrap merchants, and would have been disposed of faster than she could walk to the door. Yet to her that was not the overriding factor. She was brought up in an age when the map of the world was predominantly pink, showing the vast spread of the British Empire, and that Britain was indeed great. But over the years she had seen the pink recede further and further, until even parts of England were no longer so very pink. Britain was a country to be proud of, a nation with dignity. Nobody could snatch what rightfully belonged to her without getting their teeth kicked firmly down their throats. God was an Englishman (just as He had been for Oliver Cromwell, William Pitt and Winston Churchill), and He would surely smile on her action.

Carol watched her mother from the gallery and followed on to Number Ten afterwards. She found an atmosphere of gloom and despair in the normally hushed corridors of power, as everyone busied themselves preparing obituaries of Margaret and the Government.

When she went in to see her mother she was somewhat lost for words. 'I'm sorry,' she said, 'I thought you were very good in the House.' Margaret didn't allow herself to show a moment of fear, not even to her daughter. She was as solid as a rock. 'There's no point in anyone panicking or falling apart,' she said. 'This is what's happened, this is what we're going to do; and we fight back.'

The first ships of the fleet thus set sail from Portsmouth on the morning tide of 5 April, leaving scenes of emotion on the quayside that Britain had not witnessed since the two World Wars. The two aircraft carriers, HMS *Invincible* and the somewhat elderly *Hermes*, due to have been sold to the Australian navy, were the first to go. Thereafter ships of every shape and size were recalled and requisitioned from all over the world, refitted as troop carriers and ships of war, and sent off with men and troops provisioned for a long stay at sea.

The very day the first boat sailed, Lord Carrington handed in his resignation. Margaret had spent the weekend trying to persuade him to change his mind, largely because she relied very heavily upon him and, although he was rather arrogant at times, she trusted him. But she had enough instinct to know that someone's head had to roll if the Government was going to survive, and as the man in charge of the Foreign Office, he was the obvious man. She was subsequently to miss him greatly, and was desperately sorry to see him go.

Other heads rolled too: Humphrey Atkins, Lord Privy Seal, and Richard Luce, Minister in the Foreign and Commonwealth Office. John Nott, Secretary of State for Defence, tendered his resignation, but was asked to stay. 'The Ministry of Defence,' she wrote, 'is not the department responsible for policy towards the Falkland Islands. I wish you to remain at your post.'

Britain immediately declared a two-hundred-mile total exclusion zone around the Falklands to keep out foreign air and sea vessels. There followed several agonizing weeks while the Task Force continued south, and the two protagonists negotiated. Margaret would have happily come to an agreement without firing a single shot, but as the Argentines proved more and more indecisive, she became impatient. Winter was drawing on in the South Atlantic, and if it came to a fight, the conditions would become worse the longer they waited. Galtieri had boxed himself into the position where he could settle for nothing less than sovereignty – his whole position in the junta depended upon it. Thousands of people thronged outside the Casa Rosada, the presidential palace in Buenos Aires, in a fever of patriotic excitement, chanting for the return of islands that were rightfully theirs, and that had been snatched by the British aggressor all those years before. Margaret was likewise trapped and could concede almost anything except sovereignty.

Talks were begun. Al Haig volunteered his services as mediator, and for the first few weeks commuted almost daily between Buenos Aires and London, but as one of his assistants said later, 'We started out quite hopeful. Surely to God nobody was going to war over a bog. But the deeper we got, the more we saw the problem was intellectually insoluble.' The talking eventually broke down, and London sent orders for the Task Force to land and to restore the British flag to the Falklands. The first operation, the retaking of South Georgia, went well despite appalling weather conditions, frozen seas, blizzards and fierce gales, in which two helicopters crashed. The Argentine force on the island surrendered, and the British were lulled into a false sense of security.

A week later, on 2 May, the realities of war struck home. The *General Belgrano*, an Argentine cruiser in convoy with two destroyers, came dangerously close to *Invincible* and *Hermes*. The trio had been tailed for a day by a British nuclear submarine *Conqueror* as it zig-zagged in and out of the total exclusion zone, and shortly before dusk, the War Cabinet★ in London gave orders for the *Conqueror* to fire. Two torpedoes ripped into the port side of the *Belgrano*, sinking her and claiming the lives of 368 men. The survivors took to the sea in dinghies, but in the rough weather that blew up in the night, many of the injured died of exposure.

The incident shocked the British just as much as the Argentines. Two days later the latter retaliated. The *Sheffield*, guarding the two aircraft carriers thirty miles to their west, was hit amidships by a French Exocet missile, fired from an Argentine fighter. *Sheffield*'s captain, John Salt, later described what happened: 'It was fifteen to twenty seconds before the whole of the working area of the ship was filled with black, acrid pungent smoke. . . . On the upper deck you could feel the heat of the deck through your feet with your shoes on. The superstructure was steaming. The paint on the ship's side was coming off. Around the initial area where the missile penetrated the hull was glowing red, it was white hot.' Miraculously only twenty men died. The rest of the crew, many seriously hurt, were flown onto *Hermes*.

★ The War Cabinet consisted of Margaret Thatcher, Cecil Parkinson, Francis Pym, John Nott and the chiefs of staff.

Margaret had to give a speech to the Women's Conference at the Royal Albert Hall the day that she heard the news. She knew the ship had been hit, but didn't yet know the number of casualties, and was obviously in a highly emotional state. She arrived dressed entirely in black, put aside her prepared speech, and with the strain showing on her face, spoke about the horrors of war, the uncertainty, and yet the absolute necessity of standing up to an aggressor. At the end, instead of her normal gesture of holding out her hands for applause, she simply bowed, with an instinctive feel for the change in mood, her hands limp by her side. The audience cheered and roared.

Efforts were still being made to put an end to the hostilities. Perez de Cuellar, Secretary General to the United Nations, attempted to mediate, as Al Haig had done before him. Arguments raged in the House of Commons, where Michael Foot led the condemnation of Mrs Thatcher's action. Protestors with banners and placards took to the streets, and there were rumblings of discontent among some of the troops. 'Dying for Queen and country is one thing,' a marine officer was heard to remark. 'Dying for Mrs Thatcher is quite another.' Someone else potentially dying for Mrs Thatcher – a fact that weighed heavy on her mind as she drew closer to hostilities – was the Queen's son, Prince Andrew, a helicopter pilot with the aircraft carrier *Invincible*.

Finally on 18 May, Perez de Cuellar's attempts to find a solution collapsed. In London, the War Cabinet brooded on the implications for twenty-four hours, then gave the command to 'go'. From that moment on, it was total commitment. By dawn the next day, 2,400 marines and paras had landed around San Carlos Waters, and there was no turning back. As Margaret said to her fellow Members in the House of Commons, she had seen half a dozen peace plans, Al Haig and Perez de Cuellar had both flown back and forth across the Atlantic innumerable times to no avail. Someone had to make a decision and, as the bleeding hearts were busy looking for compromises, winter in the South Atlantic was setting in and the chances of winning any encounter grew ever more difficult.

For the next month Margaret's entire mind was eight thousand miles away. She had taken the decision to fight because of a gut instinct that it was right, but as the casualty figures became part of the daily briefing, an awesome weight fell on her shoulders, which in the early days she found hard to bear without showing her emotions. As ships went down, as harriers and helicopters plunged into the icy seas, and soldiers on the ground ran into land mines or ambushes, she couldn't help seeing each name on the list as a mother's son, a wife's husband or a child's father.

She spoke at twice her normal pace. 'What are we going to do?' she would say, 'what can we do for these people? Oh dear, oh dear, oh dear, I do hope they're all right . . . do you think they're all right?' It was Willie Whitelaw, who had lived through a war and commanded men, who took her gently aside and explained the need for strength. It was vital, he told her, that generals must respect their leaders at all costs and never be allowed to see a trace of doubt. Because, if they once become aware that casualties were going to cause anguish at the top, they were liable to pull their punches, hold back, and very possibly lose more men, and the battle into the bargain, than might have been achieved by fierce combat.

From that moment on Margaret was utterly steadfast. She grew through the Falklands crisis, to a leader of great stature, and displayed quite remarkable courage. Whatever advice may come from colleagues, whatever support there may be in Cabinet, in the media and from the country, there is no fact more stark in politics than when things go wrong, and the going gets tough, the buck finally stops at Number Ten Downing Street. The Falklands war could have gone disastrously wrong. It was a gamble that she took, and ultimately she would pay for, very possibly with twenty-seven thousand British lives. This was the reality she lived with for nearly three months.

She dressed in dark colours throughout, she showed concern, she showed shock, she showed revulsion, but she never allowed herself to show the feelings that were buried deep. She later told George Gale of the *Daily Express*:

> The worrying times one lived with were when we lost our ships. Of course, we knew it would be difficult to fight a battle with a navy bobbing about on the ocean against a shore-based fascist regime. Yes, one would have bad luck, yes, the odd thing would get through. And of course we did have extremely bad luck when the *Sheffield* went down. I wondered how they were all coping and I realized that these things happen in war.
>
> I knew the invasion, the retaking, was going to happen. That Friday I was in my constituency all day with an extremely busy programme. I knew that the invasion was underway and that I couldn't cancel anything. I had to carry on and I knew that I couldn't get home until the invasion was complete. That day and

night is etched on my mind; and when we got back home, the action was complete. That was marvellous; and we did not lose any ships then. But later, when they came to bomb, bomb, bomb, that's when we also had a very depressing time.

For the first time politics were allowed to encroach upon the Thatcher family. Margaret was unable to turn off. 'In a way,' she told George Gale, 'the Falklands became my life, it became my bloodstream.' Because of the time difference, bombing raids used to begin late at night by British time, and the news wouldn't start coming through until after midnight. Margaret would sit up waiting for the phone to ring, often with Denis, Carol and occasionally Mark too, waiting and wondering what was going on, what the weather was like, who had the upper hand, how it was all going. The weather played a significant part in the success or failure of a mission. One sunny day she was sitting out of doors at Chequers – a brief respite from meetings with chiefs of staff and the War Cabinet – and she said, 'Oh it's a lovely day here, I just wonder what they're going through down there.' Over breakfast, she would suddenly look up from her newspaper and say, 'It's clear down there', or 'the weather's terrible', or 'there's cloud cover'.

Once again letters poured into Downing Street, both kind and critical, and she took great comfort from the former. One day she had a single rose that she had put into a small vase of water in the flat. It had been sent by a boy, not yet eighteen. 'Don't worry,' he wrote in the note that accompanied the flower, 'when I'm old enough I'll sign up and go and fight.' She was very touched.

The losses were terrific. Fourteen ships were either hit and damaged or sunk in the process. Miraculously, no more than two hundred and fifty men died. One of the most memorable and remarkable episodes of the war was the battle for Goose Green, in which 2 Para succeeded in overcoming a crack Argentinian force which far outnumbered their own, and which posed a serious threat to the British bridgehead at San Carlos. Their colleagues at Bluff Cove were less successful. In one afternoon two supply ships, *Sir Galahad* and *Sir Tristram*, were hit, killing fifty-three men aboard, and injuring forty-six. And so the weeks went on, with good news followed by bad, and with the agony of not knowing the outcome of an offensive she had sanctioned until late into the night.

Finally triumph came: after a dawn raid on Monday, 14 June, 2 Para were on Wireless Ridge, a high point with a good view. 'Suddenly we saw all these specks running off Sapper Hill,' one officer recalled. 'Then we saw them coming off Longdon. All running, running back to Stanley.' Half an hour later, the Gurkhas' second-in-command, Major Bill Dawson, at their headquarters on Two Sisters, came off the radio and said, 'Gentlemen, a white flag has been seen flying over Port Stanley.' At 9.00 p.m. local time the next day, the Argentine commander, General Mario Menendez, formally surrendered to Major-General Jeremy Moore, and the fighting was over. 'The Falkland Islands are once more under the government desired by their inhabitants,' declared Major-General Moore. 'God Save the Queen.'

When Margaret heard the news in London, she simply said, 'Rejoice.' The single word spoke volumes. 'I felt colossal release,' she later told George Gale. 'It was the most marvellous release I have ever had when the news came in. It was a day I dreamed of and lived for. And when the surrender was confirmed . . . then I knew that whatever the problems and troubles I would have in the rest of my period in office, they were as nothing then and now.'

It had, nevertheless been a close run thing. At one point there was only enough food left for two days, and after Goose Green, medical provisions were down to three days' supply. Ninety per cent of the troops had trench-foot, and dysentry was epidemic. The skill and the courage of the men was unmatched. Even so, the Argentines had the odds stacked in their favour; had they not been so inept in the air, so green on the ground, and so generally demoralized, the outcome could have been very different. Had *Hermes* been hit, for example, or a troop carrier such as the *Canberra*, Margaret's fortunes would have sunk with the wreckage.

Instead she gave the British a national pride, which, apart from a brief period the previous summer during the royal wedding, had scarcely been felt since the Second World War. Men who previously would have brought an entire industry out on strike rather than work half an hour over their shift, pulled together and laboured round the clock to get the ships ready and seaworthy, to get supplies to the docks, to step up production of the necessary equipment, and to volunteer their services. 'We reflect upon the absurdity of it all,' one reporter with the Task Force later wrote. 'We have come eight thousand miles, crossed half the world, to liberate a place that looks like western Scotland, where the people speak with Devon accents and give their children names like Heather, Jenny, Tony, Keith and Ken.' But it appealed to the British instinct. Poetic names of places like Goose Green, Tumbledown and

Pebble Island were soon as well known as Trafalgar Square, and words like 'yomping' – marine slang for a long march under heavy kit – became common parlance. The common fear for men's safety brought people together – the ultimate equalizer – and winning made every expense worthwhile. As the ships made their way back throughout the summer months, each one came home to a hero's welcome.

It wasn't long, however, before Margaret's opponents started blaming the Government for ever having allowed the Argentines to invade in the first place. A 'Tory loyalist', Mrs Madge Nichols, suddenly sprung into the limelight waving a letter signed by Mrs Thatcher, just two months before the invasion, reassuring her that the islands were satisfactorily protected. Mrs Nichols had written following the decision to withdraw the ice patrol ship, HMS *Endurance* from duty in the South Atlantic, a decision taken by John Nott as part of the Ministry of Defence spending cuts. Mrs Thatcher said in her letter: 'Our judgment is that the presence of the Royal Marines garrison which – unlike HMS *Endurance* – is permanently stationed in the Falklands is sufficient deterrent against any possible aggression.' 'Mrs Thatcher herself,' declared Stanley Clinton-Davis, Labour spokesman on Foreign Affairs, 'must now accept responsibility directly for misleading the country about the threat of an invasion by Argentina.'

In July an independent six-man committee was set up to investigate the events which led to the invasion. Chaired by Lord Franks, it included two former Conservative and two former Labour Cabinet Ministers, and when it reported six months later, Mrs Thatcher was entirely exonerated. 'The machinery of government,' it found, 'could have been better used' at times, but there was 'no reasonable basis' for suggesting the Government could in any way have prevented the Argentine invasion.

This was a tremendous blow to the Opposition who had hoped that the Government would take the blame fairly and squarely on its shoulders. As Frank Johnson, writing in *The Times*, observed:

> Labour had two choices: either to suggest that, if read *in toto*, the report was a serious indictment of Mrs Thatcher. The other was to suggest that of course the report did not blame Mrs Thatcher because it was an Establishment cover-up. The Party compromised by suggesting both.
>
> . . . After a while we got to Mr Foot's next point. This turned out to be: what about paragraph 115? . . . But the paragraph

contained no denunciation of Mrs Thatcher. So Mr Foot accepted it – rambling at some length about 'what this illustrates is a collapse of Cabinet government in this country,' which would have been news to Lord Franks.

Margaret knew the Franks Report inside out and upside down when she gave her statement on its findings to the House. She could quote chapter and verse, and proved beyond doubt that she had grown, not only into a great Prime Minister, with a good feel of the British public, but also an effective Leader in the House of Commons.

The Falklands had lasted well into the autumn. Each returning ship was given a rapturous welcome, and the media scarcely let a day pass without some heart-rending interview with a war widow, whose soldier husband she knew had died doing what he wanted, fighting for a cause he believed in. Margaret Thatcher's popularity was at a peak unparalleled by any prime minister since Churchill. She was on a high: confident and exhilarated as she had never been before.

At the Conservative Party Conference in Brighton in October, she gave one of her best speeches ever. 'Jokes. . .' she had said dubiously, when discussing the content with Ronnie Millar and the rest of the speech-writing team. 'This is the most important political year of my life. I have a feeling that perhaps this year I should be stirring rather than entertaining.' She was also aware that everyone would be expecting her to 'milk' the Falklands. When she stood up on the rostrum of the new conference centre on Brighton's seafront, she began: 'This is not going to be a speech about the Falklands campaign, although I would be proud to make one.' She hit the perfect pitch, and at the end the packed hall gave her a six-minute standing ovation.

Her delivery was helped by the fact that she didn't once look down at her prepared speech. She employed the same reflective device with which Ronald Reagan had so astounded the British earlier in the year during his visit to England, when he spoke, apparently off the cuff, without a single hiccup. Denis was dubious about using it for the first time at Brighton without a trial run. 'I don't think it's very wise,' he told Ronnie Millar. 'Shouldn't she be starting this thing on a less important speech?' But Margaret's confidence was at such a peak that nothing could have thrown her.

There was another change for the Party Conference: Margaret's hairstyle. In the past she had appeared on important occasions, such as the Lord Mayor's Banquet and the day of her speech at the Conference, with an extravagant bee-hive, as Ronnie Millar says, 'which really looked as though a swan could nest in it'. He finally summoned the courage to say something to her about it. 'All I can tell you,' he said, choosing his moment carefully, 'is you've got the best cheek-bones in the business, a beautiful face, a good figure, you put on the simplest clothes, because you want people to look at the person not the clothes, and what you don't want is that elaboration on your head.'

'But it's the man who does my hair,' she said. 'He does it that way. You don't think it's a good idea?'

'No,' replied Ronnie. 'You never do it privately, it's not you at all.'

If she resisted the temptation to 'milk' the Falklands at the Conference, Margaret certainly played them to their full advantage for the next few months. General Galtieri and most of the junta departed in ignominy, but the Argentine Government has never officially conceded British victory, nor given up its claim to the islands. Having liberated them, Margaret is therefore morally committed to maintaining a garrison there for the foreseeable future. It was this issue, with the tremendous cost involved, that has thus kept the Falklands an indefinite talking point, and inspiration for many a back-bencher to star in Prime Minister's Question Time. Margaret will not brook any sort of bargain with Argentina so long as the islanders themselves wish to remain British, the more so after a surprise visit to the Falklands in January 1983, which provocatively coincided with the islands' one hundred and fiftieth anniversary in British possession.

Dressed immaculately as ever, she and Denis made the gruelling twenty-three-hour flight to the South Atlantic: ten hours to Ascension Island, changing planes and on for a further thirteen hours to Port Stanley. The last lap was aboard a very basic Hercules transport plane – not only an uncomfortable, but a risky flight too, which involved refuelling twice in mid-air. The Hercules was refuelled by a Victor tanker, whose stalling speed was about the same as the maximum speed of the transport plane. The two would couple then, to overcome the problem of stalling, dive from twenty thousand to ten thousand feet to increase air speed, a terrifying sensation known to the regular pilots as 'tobogganing'.

Margaret showed no apprehension at all, nor fatigue. She was overcome, if anything, by emotion. She had taken the islanders by surprise – for security reasons it had been totally secret – so the welcome was spontaneous, and for that the more touching. Margaret Thatcher was their hero, their saviour, the one person they knew they could trust.

169

So long as she remained Prime Minister of Great Britain, no Argentinian aggressor would set foot on the Falklands again. She drove along the bombed and pot-holed streets of Port Stanley, incongruously in Governor Rex Hunt's maroon London taxi. She went to look at the sites at which the major battles had been fought, visited the War Graves Commission cemetery, where she was almost reduced to tears. Her hair blew out of place in the wind, and for the first time since Mark was missing in the desert, the façade was gone and she looked as though the emotions she felt were one hundred per cent genuine. She talked to the four-thousand strong garrison stationed on the islands, and, still dressed more appropriately for the streets of London than the rough moors of the Falklands, walked about, breathing it all in. A few days after she left for home, the army major who had briefed Margaret on mine disposal, Stephen Hambrook, stepped on an anti-personnel mine at Fox Bay and had a foot blown off.

Her visit, of course, was not without its critics. Miners' leader, Arthur Scargill, called it 'obscene'. There were questions in the House about how much it had cost, and how much was it to take Denis along for the ride? The answer was £200,000, which produced a great deal of excitement from the Opposition, for it was normal practice for the costs of spouses accompanying prime ministers on official trips to be met.

Denis has accompanied Margaret in general considerably more frequently than spouses of prime ministers have in the past. This is not out of any great desire to be up there among the top lot, but because he is fiercely protective and likes to be there, to give 'the Boss', as he calls her, some moral support. He does support her – he is far and away her greatest fan – and she relies upon him quite heavily. He is like an old overcoat of which she has become inordinately fond: rather dull but very kind and comfortable. He is also the nearest person Margaret has to a confidant; and she frequently announces in Cabinet meetings that she has asked Denis's advice about this or that, and these were his feelings.

Her opinions do come from a wide assortment of random encounters and conversations, however. She met an old friend who was doing work for the British Council some time ago, who said in the course of catching up on old times, that in her opinion the Council did a good job. A few months later the friend was at a British Council lunch at which the Director General made a speech. They were very lucky, he said, to have been given some more money by the Government. Although Mrs Thatcher disliked the British Council when she first became Prime Minister, she now, for some reason, seemed to like it.

Far from cashing in on Margaret's fame, Denis would actually rather be retired to the country, drifting into the odd board meeting, and playing golf. He has never much liked politicians. He finds the pace at which his wife works exhausting, wishes she, and therefore he, could take more holidays, and was not looking forward to a second term in office one bit. 'Do you know,' he grumbled to friends some time back, 'she's now talking about a second term.'

Margaret has grown to hate holidays. After four days she is bored stiff and desperate to get back to work. Since she became Prime Minister she has taken seven weeks' holiday in all. In 1979 she and Denis had a week on the island of Islay, on the west coast of Scotland. The next summer they spent one week in Switzerland with the late Sir Douglas and Lady Glover, who owned a secluded castle set in fifteen hundred acres of parkland near Zurich. This was followed by five days at Scotney. In 1981 they went to stay with David Wolfson, her Chief of Staff, in his large, luxurious bungalow in north Cornwall. But shortly after Margaret became Prime Minister Denis was overheard to say 'We're off to Portugal for a holiday.' A paper had the scoop, 'Maggie's Secret Trip,' ran the headline. There were more than a few red faces when this turned out to be Denis's one luxury in life, an annual golfing holiday with Bill Deedes in the Algarve.

Part of Margaret's holiday in 1982, despite the exhausting year, was spent in the Fitzroy Nuffield Hospital in London, having her varicose veins stripped. She went in on the morning of 23 August, underwent a general anaesthetic, an hour-long operation, and walked out of the hospital that very evening. Her sole concession to human frailty was a pair of pinstripe trousers – a very rare departure, and certainly the first time she had ever worn trousers in public. Her decision not to stay in overnight was partly a dislike of hospitals, but mostly because she didn't want to be seen to be a weak woman. As her general practitioner, Dr John Henderson, said: 'I can't say how overwhelmed I am with the way this woman has recovered. She is really behaving as though nothing had happened. She simply won't allow herself to be ill.'

She didn't even allow herself the luxury of collapsing once she got home. The very next day she was off to have her teeth capped at the dentist. Both operations were largely cosmetic, with a medical excuse. Her legs were not improving with all the standing she did, and her teeth were causing minor problems, but the prime reason for both was a concern about the way she looked.

She has become obsessed in many ways about her appearance, and has grown increasingly aware of the tricks of the trade, particularly with television. If she is to be interviewed in a studio, preparations beforehand are meticulous. Margaret's press officer will go along to the studio, meet the production team, and work out every detail right down to the shape and colour of the chair she will be given to sit in. On one occasion a chair had to be specially flown in from Sweden for a Thames Television programme, because she approved of the design, but didn't like the colour of the chair they had chosen.

On another occasion, when she was being filmed inside Downing Street, answering schoolchildren's questions, her own first question to the television crew was whether she needed extra make-up. No one liked to answer one way or another. She thereupon asked to see herself on the video monitor, which her press officer, Bernard Ingham, had specifically requested be brought with the equipment so that she might know how she was going to look on screen. Next, she asked to see a shot of the girl interviewing her that day, a young, glamorous blonde who had just been abroad and was very tanned. Margaret immediately said she would like to be made to look like that, and called a halt to everything while she went away and was made up.

The questions soon got underway, with Bernard Ingham recording everything that happened as an insurance, no doubt, against biased editing. Half an hour later the television time came to an end: the director called 'cut', and the floor manager thanked Mrs Thatcher for her cooperation. But Mrs Thatcher was not ready to be 'cut'. She asked the children which of them had not yet asked a question. About half the children in the room put up their hands. Then they should carry on until they had all had a turn, she said, and 'Thames Television will, I am sure, continue to record.' There followed another half hour, producing some of the best exchanges. When it was over, Margaret took the children on a guided tour of Number Ten, taking particular care to point out a small model depicting a group of paras running up the Union Jack on the Falklands. Then it was orange juice and sticky buns for the children, and back to the business of government for the Prime Minister.

For someone who was not especially good with her own children, Margaret gets on very well with children now. On more than one occasion she has found a group of them standing, craning over the railings at the entrance to Downing Street, as she has driven through in her official car. She has thereupon climbed out of the car to talk to them, or led them, like the Pied Piper of Hamelin, down the street to point out the houses and their history.

The only time in four years that Margaret has shown fatigue – and then for a fleeting moment – was in September 1982, less than a month after the operation on her legs. She undertook a two-week tour of the Far East, which reduced most of her aides, and almost all of the accompanying journalists, to a state of total exhaustion. She began in Japan, where she stepped off the plane after an eighteen-hour flight, looking as fresh as she had boarded it in London. One hour later, she was briskly inspecting the guard at the Akasaka Palace, setting the pace for the entire two weeks.

From Japan she flew to China, where she made history as the first British prime minister ever to visit the country. It was there, too, that she stumbled and fell on all fours while walking down a long flight of steps outside the Great Hall of the People in the centre of Peking. She leapt to her feet immediately, insisting she was quite all right. A little later, her voice gave way in the midst of a statement she was reading to the world's press, and she was reduced to a croak, but she carried on. And later still, she was to be seen leading her hosts around the gardens of the Summer Palace, while they had virtually to break into a trot to keep up. She was constantly eager to be looking at one thing and pressing on to the next.

From Peking she flew to Hong Kong, for talks on the delicate subject of Britain's lease of the territory, which expires in 1997. No opportunity was missed to see people. She took the long route home to London via Delhi, where they arrived at two in the morning, in time for breakfast with Mrs Gandhi at 8.00. An hour and a half later she was back on the plane and, when it stopped to refuel at Bahrain, she was out again for a fifty-eight-minute talk with the Trade Minister, who had come to the airport to meet her. Back in London, the very next morning, she plunged straight into a lengthy Cabinet meeting.

As we have seen so clearly, Margaret drives herself obsessively. No previous prime minister has worked at the pace she sets for herself, nor has there been another with such a limited field of interest. She works far harder than she need: prime ministers do not have to exist on seven to ten days' holiday a year in order to do the job. There is a strong argument, indeed, against working at that pace, for taking time off to reflect on the wider picture. But she sees that as a waste of time. When someone working in the Foreign Office told her that he was taking a year's sabbatical in America to reassess the picture, and get a broader outlook on the work he was doing in England, she rather curtly said that that was the sort of thing one ought to get over and done with during one's student days.

There is nothing frivolous in Margaret at all. She claims to read John le Carré spy novels and enjoy the Two Ronnies on television. But the occasions on which she does either are very rare. Her basic reading is philosophy, history and politics, which she will read late at night, often in bed; and the television that she watches is almost exclusively current affairs and news. She might wander in to have a break from her work at about half past ten or eleven o'clock on a Saturday night at Chequers and, finding Denis watching television, pour herself a whisky and join him for a while. But an evening spent in front of the television is virtually unheard of.

What she hates most of all is to look at herself on television. Carol considers it a great triumph that she has just once persuaded her mother to watch herself. It was a lengthy interview on 'Panorama' during the Falkland crisis, which Carol had recorded.

'No, I don't want to watch it,' said Margaret firmly.

'You did actually look very nice,' said Carol, 'and if I didn't turn the sound up, you could just see how nice you looked, because that suit worked very well.'

Margaret fell for the bait and, once she had seen herself mute, became intrigued to know how she sounded, and then immediately wanted to know how the answer to this or that specific question sounded, and so they would press the fast forward button. But many is the time, to the fury of her family, when Margaret has suddenly looked at her watch in the middle of an evening and said 'Phew! I've just finished being on the telly.' Or, when Denis has gone to dinner with friends, he's been asked, 'Did you see your wife on the box last night?' and he had no idea that she was going to be on.

This is just one of the many unexpected traits that make Margaret Thatcher such an extraordinary blend of self-conscious vulnerability and certainty in her own destiny.

VI

Living with the Job

While five thousand delegates were standing on their feet, clapping, roaring and cheering their applause for six whole minutes at the end of Margaret's speech to the Party Conference at Brighton in 1982, Margaret was busy worrying about how Carol was going to get back to London.

'Stop fussing Mum, for God's sake,' said Carol, who was twenty-nine years old, had travelled the world, and was quite up to coping with the thirty miles between Brighton and London unaided. 'You've got a standing ovation going on here,' she pointed out, 'get on and acknowledge it.' 'Yes, yes,' replied Margaret, smiling broadly at the floor and holding her hands in the air in thanks, then slyly turning to a helper said, 'You will take Carol to the station, won't you?'

Her family are a very central part of Margaret's life, and a great prop to her confidence. She likes to have them around her and, even with her hectic schedule, if she doesn't hear from Carol for a few weeks, she will ring and say, 'Hello, why haven't I seen you – have you been busy?' 'No,' Carol is likely to reply, 'but you were.' Family life has inevitably suffered considerably over the years, and more acutely since she became Prime Minister, but Margaret still likes to keep tabs on her children, and spend any free time she may have with them. Her choice of a night out on her fifty-seventh birthday last year was to take the family to see *Cats*, the hugely popular Andrew Lloyd Webber musical still running in London. It was the first family outing in a long time, accompanied as usual, of course, by two detectives who go everywhere with her. In the interval people began to queue up in the aisle to ask for Margaret's autograph. She began scribbling away, which she enjoyed, while across the auditorium one of the characters in the musical, playing the cat called Deuteronomy, was also busily signing autographs. The two waved to each other.

One occasion when she spent many an hour signing autographs she didn't find such fun. This took place in March 1979, virtually her last venture on a train. She was travelling to Knutsford, just outside Manchester, for a by-election where 'Jock' Bruce-Gardyne was the candidate, and where she was due to join the local Party in time for dinner. Margaret, Derek Howe and a detective were due to leave Euston Station on the 5.30 p.m. train and, thanks to secretarial foresight, all arrived at the station with mini-hampers to sustain them for the journey lest there be no restaurant car. But at Euston there was no train, let alone a restaurant car. The next one running appeared to be 7.30, and a long queue was already stretched across the platform ready to board it. Margaret was offered the comparative luxury of the station manager's office, where it was discovered that there was a train running at 6.15. No one appeared to have told the queue that had settled down for a two-hour wait on the station platform, but Mrs Thatcher and her entourage boarded the 6.15 without a hitch. There was no restaurant car, nor buffet, so they were glad of their hampers; particularly as the train sped approximately twenty miles up the track towards Manchester, and stopped dead for two hours. As passengers became restive with the wait, they began to walk the length of the train, and very soon word got round that Mrs Thatcher was on board. By the time the train pulled into Piccadilly Station in Manchester at 1.30 in the morning, she had signed her name more than two hundred times; and had long since finished all the work she had brought to occupy herself with during the journey. She had also made a silent vow to herself never to travel by train again.

Denis doesn't have any protection, and is quite frequently to be seen humming merrily as he walks by himself in the streets of London, or driving down to the country in his green Ford Cortina estate, as often as not with his golf clubs in the back.

Carol has no bodyguard either, and has always resisted any attempt to give her one. She lives her life like any ordinary single girl in London. She has a small Ford Fiesta for driving out to the country. In London she tends to take public transport or to walk, and it is rare that anyone recognizes her. 'You don't know that bloody woman?' a taxi driver will say as he drops her outside the house in Flood Street. 'Yes I know her rather well, actually,' says Carol, 'she's my mother.' Carol left LBC after Christmas 1982, mostly because a three-hour show in the middle of Saturday night was killing her, and it was becoming increasingly difficult to persuade personalities to join her at that hour. She then began working full time for the women's page of the *Daily Telegraph*.

None of the family has been exempt from the odd snipe. Carol has had the least publicity and least criticism of them all, although her appointment at LBC caused a great union outcry. Denis has weathered a fair share of storms. First came when his family chemical company, Chipman's, was found to be selling 'Agent Orange', 245T, the defoliant that was used to devastating effect in Vietnam. The company was in trouble again at the beginning of 1983 with the Saudi Arabian authorities for employing people in the country who didn't have work permits. He was then at the centre of a huge row when, acting as consultant for a property company called IDC Ltd, he wrote to the Secretary of State for Wales, Nicholas Edwards, on Number Ten notepaper, asking him to speed up the appeal hearing for a planning application, involving a £3 million scheme lodged by the company, which the Welsh Office had turned down. Copies of his letter, which had begun 'Dear Nick', thereby, so his critics claimed, blatantly abusing his position, filled the newspapers for weeks. He was in trouble yet again with another company, Quinton Hazell, the spare parts firm of which he had remained a director after retiring from Burmah. The company was accused of paying workers in South Africa a wage below the level recommended by Britain and the EEC. But neither Denis nor Carol combined have attracted the flak that Mark has suffered in the four years that Margaret has been Prime Minister.

Whatever lucky star Margaret was born under, Mark was not similarly blessed. He first ran into trouble when, having failed to pass his accountancy exams, he described himself as a chartered accountant in a motor-racing press release, when he was not technically qualified to do so. He was, moreover, never very successful as a racing driver. He crashed at Mallory Park in Leicestershire in 1979 and had to be pulled from the blazing wreckage. A year later he lost control on an S-bend at 80 m.p.h., and crashed into the barriers. Two months later he escaped from another wrecked car during the practice run for the Super V race at Hockenheim in West Germany. He was lost in the desert in the Paris to Dakar rally and then ten months later, broke down in the Mexican desert in the one-thousand-mile Baja rally, which he described as 'the most frightening experience of my life'.

Sponsors in Britain were thus not falling over themselves in the rush to sign up Mark Thatcher. He has been quoted as saying he was 'shown the door' by several companies that he tried, and was eventually forced to look elsewhere. Just a year after Margaret's election, the news broke that he had signed himself up with a Japanese clothing firm, Kanebo, to model mock suede jackets in return for £10,000 to cover the cost of a motor-racing trip to the Far East, on a Japan Airlines flight paid for by the Japanese car manufacturing company, Toyota.

When the storm broke about his ears, Mark seemed genuinely flummoxed that what he saw as a perfectly straightforward business deal should have caused so much fuss. Other racing drivers found sponsors abroad, after all, and he had tried to find a British firm first. Besides, he was acting quite independently of his mother. Margaret herself was evidently quite unaware of the deal her son had struck. Paul Raymond, the king of Soho's club and theatreland, came to the rescue by offering to better the Japanese deal by £15,000. This was greeted with almost the same indignation as the Japanese contract: to think that the Prime Minister's son should contemplate racing on ill-gotten gains from strip clubs! In the end a British team at Brands Hatch came up with a sponsorship deal, which solved everyone's problems.

But Mark's troubles didn't end there. He became involved in a second contract to model on Japanese television, albeit selling Cutty Sark Scotch whisky. He gave an interview to *Honey* magazine in which he said that the trouble with the British was they ought to get off their 'arses' and do a day's work. More serious still, *Private Eye* discovered that he had been tenuously involved in a company engaged in an arms deal with Argentinians during the year of the Falklands crisis. What he actually does for a living is a little woolly. He owns a company called Monteagle Marketing (London) Limited, a small management consultancy based in Surrey, but he has always been very loath to talk about it. Racing is nothing more than a hobby; but between business and pleasure, he has travelled the world quite extensively, taking his bodyguards with him. This has been a further cause for complaint, that the taxpayer should be funding one and sometimes two men to travel abroad with Mark Thatcher, who always gave the impression of being something of a playboy.

On one occasion he flew to New York on Concorde, at a cost of £1124 one way. The bodyguard, it seemed at first, had travelled by Jumbo jet. This was so: but it transpired that a second bodyguard had flown on Concorde with Mark, at taxpayers' expense. Back in London, he drives a turbo-charged, Lotus Esprit sports car, which is too small for his bodyguards to travel with him, so they follow behind in an unmarked Rover. Even senior-ranking members of the Cabinet have secretly expressed fears that Mark could pose a serious threat to Margaret, and wish he would stop jetting around the world and get himself a proper job.

Margaret is well aware of the problem, but she won't hear a word against Mark. She blames herself for any inadequacies, and like many a working mother thinks that she may have contributed to the problem because she didn't spend enough time with him when he was a child, curiously echoing the abusive letters she received when she was first elected to Parliament in 1959 that accused her of neglecting her children. Friends try to point out that she spent precisely the same time with Carol as she did with Mark, and Carol turned out all right. But to little avail.

For all his blunders, his inability to know when he is being exploited for his name, and his apparent preference for fast cars and women over work, Mark would never wittingly betray Margaret in any way. He adores his mother: if she is likely to be free at any time over a weekend, he will choose to go and spend it with her – even now at the age of twenty-nine. He is fiercely protective about her. When out walking with lunch guests at Chequers one day, a man suddenly appeared around a corner, and Mark, who had fallen behind his mother's group, was by her side within seconds. The man, in fact, turned out to be a security officer, so all was well, but Mark is constantly on his guard.

While she still has a particularly soft spot for Mark, Margaret is enormously proud of Carol's independence and her career. At the time of the Party Conference in Brighton Carol was still doing her LBC show, and Margaret was always very keen to know who she had had on the show, and how it had gone. Occasionally she would help. One week, for example, Carol's show coincided with the tenth anniversary of Britain's entry into the Common Market, and she had been planning to do her research for the programme from the Saturday morning's newspapers, which she thought were bound to saturate the event. They didn't; it was a Bank Holiday and there were no papers that day at all. Carol panicked, but her mother happened to walk into the room. 'Don't worry, I can tell you all about the Common Market,' she said, and thereupon delivered a small lecture on the subject. She then acted out the show, with Carol throwing the sort of questions at her which she might have to answer from listeners, like 'Why don't we get out?' and 'Why is our food so expensive in the EEC?', all of which Margaret answered so simply that Carol suggested she go and do the show in her place.

There was another occasion when Carol was speaking in a debate at the Cambridge Union with Elspeth Howe against the motion that the Equal Opportunities Commission should be abolished. She was terrified, and when it was all over, Margaret asked how it had gone. 'It was all right,' said Carol, 'until I got lost and I looked at my notes and couldn't find where I was and started to panic.' 'You should have asked me,' said Margaret. 'You have to leave big gaps between sentences,' and went on to explain exactly how to lay out notes for a speech.

Carol is genuinely amazed that her mother should take the time when she has so many important things on her mind: just as colleagues are amazed to find Margaret piling up the dirty dishes after a working supper, or fussing over whether guests have had enough to eat, or the proper implements with which to eat. But distractions of this kind are obviously therapeutic, and submerged in the depths of Margaret Thatcher's psyche is the need to play mother.

Margaret has also felt isolated from the real world, shut away in her eyrie at Number Ten. The house itself has the hush of a silent order of monks, and after office hours and over the weekends, the place is deserted. Even when it's full, Margaret is at one remove from reality. She is, like any prime minister, perforce surrounded by obsequious civil servants who call her 'Prime Minister' in every second sentence, and tell her what she wants to hear. She can't go shopping any more, she can't walk down the King's Road, as she sometimes used to, she can't go out to a restaurant without elaborate security arrangements. She lives in a totally artificial world, and it is contact with the mundane, like baked potatoes and dirty dishes, which keeps her sane.

When the family are together it is rare that they talk about politics. They respect Margaret's need for a sanctuary. She once exploded when one of them was attacking her over some issue, and she said, 'My God, to think that I have to come home and argue politics with my own family.' Since then they have tended to steer clear of contentious issues. They are also wary of her moods, and pick their moment to tell Margaret news, to ask her favours, or to seek advice. She has a very cutting tongue if interrupted at the wrong moment, and is no more tolerant of her family than of anyone else who says something stupid or inaccurate. 'Nonsense Denis, you've forgotten,' she will frequently say in company.

Denis is put in his place quite regularly, yet he maintains a dignity of his own, and is much loved. Friends have a habit of referring to him as 'Dear old Denis', or 'Poor old Denis' and do feel that he has had a very rough deal, being thrown into a role he would much rather not play. He is a very easy-going character, and quite happily recognizes

Margaret is the one-who-must-be-obeyed. She bosses him around, marshalls him into dinner if he's lingering for too long over the cocktails, and takes more than a passing interest in the clothes he wears. When asked what she thought of Michael Foot turning up at the Cenotaph for Remembrance Sunday looking his usual dishevelled self, she simply expressed surprise that his wife had let him go out like that. At a dinner party with friends quite recently, Denis arose with the women at the end of the meal and went upstairs, and Margaret, locked in conversation, stayed at the table with the men.

But time for friends and even for family has been scarce during Margaret Thatcher's period in office. Chequers is the Prime Minister's official country residence, it is not a place for mates, and so the weekends tend to be taken up with official entertaining. For example, she will give lunch parties for important Conservative supporters, heads of industry, national newspaper editors, and big names in the arts. She sometimes invites members of the Government, with their wives or occasionally Finchley Party workers. During the Falklands campaign, she invited a handful to come for a drink one evening, the day the *Sir Galahad* was sunk, when she was feeling particularly low and in need of friends. Ian Gow and his wife, Jane, spend the weekend there periodically. On one occasion Margaret invited them down because she thought Ian was tired and in need of an early night. They reflected on this as all three climbed the stairs to bed at three o'clock on Sunday morning.

The family always try to get her off down to Chequers at the weekends, because they reckon that if she's going to insist upon working all weekend wherever she is, the change of scene will do her some good. She can also be persuaded to put her nose out of doors for a quick sprint around the rose garden; and there is no cooking to worry about if she is there. But she seldom gets much rest. On Saturday nights Carol used sometimes to drive down to Chequers after her LBC show, not arriving until half past two in the morning, yet Margaret would come bouncing out of her study to say hello, with a red box in one hand and a pile of papers in the other, wide awake and ready to sit and chatter.

The opportunity to chat is otherwise strictly limited. Carol will look into Downing Street to collect her mail at about seven o'clock in the morning most days, and may pop up to the flat to see her mother. Or, she might look in on her way home from Fleet Street in the evenings, just in time to find the dress and the shoes into which Margaret is hastily changing. The nearest Margaret gets to panic is when she is running late: she might start to flap if she can't find the right shoes or the right bag, or if the hair spray runs out half a circuit around her head, and she's lost her speech. If she is nervous about the speech, then it is more likely to aggravate. She couldn't find her earrings once before her speech at the Party Conference in Brighton. 'Here, take mine,' said Carol, pulling her own off her ears, and Margaret did. They quite often lend one another clothes and jewellery. Carol will borrow her mother's long black cape if she's going to a formal dinner, for example. On her trip to Hong Kong last year, Margaret brought home for Carol a dress like the one that she herself had bought on a previous visit.

Margaret has always been very generous about presents. On her first trip to America – the occasion on which her passport was found to have expired – her secretary, Diana Powell, as a parting shot asked her to bring back something for her charm bracelet. 'I want stars and stripes,' she had said. 'Oh, I shall be far too busy,' said Margaret; but a week later, sure enough, she returned with a silver charm for Diana's bracelet.

Nowadays, if she wants to give someone a present, she has to decide what she wants in advance and then ask someone else to go out and buy it for her. She misses the occasional shopping expedition, and she often says, 'You are lucky, I wish I could go shopping too.' Everything comes to her. Since becoming Prime Minister most of her clothes are specially made, although she does still occasionally buy the odd garment from Marks & Spencer's, which has always been a favourite store. But she is a tough customer: she knows almost as much about cloth and cut, tucks and bias, as a professional, and is not a bit hesitant about saying so.

The job of prime minister is a desperately lonely position. Margaret is basically a loner anyway: although she likes to be surrounded by friends, she has never needed them emotionally. She has never given much of herself away to anyone. But the schedule and the security problems have made her even more inaccessible.

When she went to have Sunday night supper with some old friends not long ago, the Special Branch had to go round to the house three days earlier to check it out. On the Sunday night, Margaret and Denis arrived with two detectives in tow for what had been planned as a relaxed, informal get-together. Spontaneous invitations have sadly become a thing of the past; and a number of friends have inevitably kept their distance, feeling that she is too busy or too important to want to spend time with them. Yet often it is quite the reverse. After innumerable notes, hand-written on the bottom of letters and Christmas cards imploring her to phone when she was next in London, Margaret Wickstead did telephone one day last year, to say she was coming south, and gave Margaret's secretary, Caroline Stephens, a couple of possible dates. Margaret chose the first, scarcely a week away, a Sunday night, and Margaret and her husband Arthur were invited to drinks. Fully expecting a formal reception, they arrived at Number Ten appropriately attired and were amazed to find Margaret greet them at the door herself, quite casually dressed, having just driven back from Chequers. She and Denis were on their own, and Margaret first gave her friends a guided tour of the house, and then the four sat down in the flat and talked about every subject under the sun, for nearly two hours. But such respites are rare.

VII

A Second Term

Speculation about when the Prime Minister would call a general election was a subject which dominated the newspapers with increasing intensity in the early spring of 1983.

Three possible options emerged: June, October, or May of the following year. If she went to the country in October, and was returned to poweer, many political observers considered that she would have a fresh mandate before the winter, with which she would be better equipped to counter the inevitable round of union wrangles. Others thought that, with the value of the pound sliding, she would have to go for June. A few felt she would wait until the spring of 1984, which she would have been well within her rights to do, but by which time her success in the Falklands, which had boosted her popularity enormously, would no longer be so fresh in people's minds.

Election fever reached such a pitch that in the end it was this factor that forced Margaret into opting for June. As she told Carol, certain international investments weren't being made in Britain because the perpetual state of election jitters was scaring off prospective investors, which was bad for the country, the economy and the pound. If she had hung on any longer, the intervening time in office would have developed into 'non-stop electioneering', which would have been a very unhealthy as well as an undesirable state of affairs. Denis from his 'pitch and put' patch at Chequers, explained more succinctly: 'I became a Juner after the horses had bolted with the carriages.'

Michael Foot, rather predictably, accused Mrs Thatcher of 'cutting and running' by going for a June election. But as she herself pointed out, had she failed to go to the country in June, he would have accused her of hanging on to office and not daring to face the electorate.

She made the announcement on 9 May, though the Conservative election campaign did not get underway until the 20th, almost a full week later than the launching of the Labour and SDP/Liberal Alliance Manifestos. For all the parties it was to prove a unique campaign from the start, manipulated by the media, dominated by opinion polls, and focused, not upon policies, but to an unprecedented extent upon personalities.

The Labour Party, nominally led by Michael Foot, was in disarray. It was split by internal power play between the extreme left wing and the moderates, who had compromised to such an extent that their Manifesto, entitled 'The New Hope for Britain' was the most extreme yet. It promised a public spending programme of £11.5 billion and a reduction in unemployment to below one million within five years. It provided commitments to take Britain out of the Common Market and to unilateral nuclear disarmament. It also contained provisions for extensive nationalization, re-nationalization, and more power to trade unions. 'This party,' declared *The Times*, 'promises the moon; but it would have to borrow the moon. Somebody else, as always, would have to pay. There is no "new hope for Britain" in this document. There is no hope.'

The Tory Manifesto promised nothing new, but a continuation of the policies with which Margaret Thatcher and her ministers had been governing for the last four years. *The Times* called it a 'cautious manifesto, carefully worded to see that it threatens nobody with a radical cutting edge, while asserting in moderate language the underlying principles which have inspired this Government's effort to change direction.'

Margaret's first speech, in a hectic and gruelling three-week campaign, took place in her own constituency of Finchley and Friern Barnet. There she took the bull by the horns and pre-empted the very criticism upon which she knew her opponents' attack would be based – unemployment:

> Now, let's look at Labour's record. Let them try and find a single Labour government since the war which has left office with unemployment lower than when they came in. There isn't one. When Labour's present Leader was Secretary of State for Employment, in two short years unemployment doubled from 618,000 to 1,284,000. He did not have a magic formula then and he has not got one now. Mr Chairman, every Labour government has promised to reduce unemployment, and every Labour government has in fact increased it. And if ever there were to be another Labour government, the same thing would happen again.

She listed her own Government's achievements in the last four years:

> We have brought down the rate of inflation to less than five per cent and going down, the lowest rate for fifteen years. We have brought down interest rates. The strikes which gave British industry such a dismal reputation are far fewer and mostly confined to the public sector. We have brought down tax rates for managers and workers alike. We have slashed the National Insurance Surcharge – Labour's tax on jobs – giving £2,000 million back to industry.

She canvassed high and low, on the hustings, in the streets, and over the air, in a punishing schedule. Most mornings began with a press conference at Central Office, before which she would be briefed by Party Chairman, Cecil Parkinson, and the newly appointed Press and Publicity Manager, Anthony Shrimsley, former editor of *Now!* magazine. The remainder of the day would be spent travelling the length and breadth of the British Isles to factories, shopping centres, receptions, walk-abouts, local radio and television stations and rallies. Sometimes the entourage travelled in a specially furnished election bus, nicknamed 'Thatcher Tours', which was equipped with desks, telephones and electronic typewriters. At other times they transferred to an assortment of helicopters, planes and cars. Denis and Carol accompanied Margaret throughout the campaign, but Mark was fortuitously in the United States during the latter part of the campaign, returning only in time for polling day.

Her secretary, Caroline Stephens (otherwise known as Mrs Richard Ryder), was out of action for the campaign as she was expecting a baby. In addition, her husband was standing as prospective parliamentary candidate for Mid-Norfolk and she had canvassing of her own to do. Margaret had therefore appealed to the better nature of her previous secretary, Alison Ward, who was by that time working for Tory Party Treasurer, Alistair MacAlpine. Alison thus returned to the fold and, with the help of Tessa Gaisman, a secretary from the political office at Number Ten, spent three weeks typing, amending and re-typing speeches from early in the morning until early the next, and reliving the exhausting pattern of February 1979.

Speech-writing sessions began at night in the flat at Number Ten, with principal writers, Ferdie Mount and Ronnie Millar. But Margaret would go on making alterations and insisting on rewrites until minutes before the address was delivered.

Outwardly, Margaret exuded the charisma of a Prime Minister who was confident that she would be returned to power. Four years' fielding Prime Minister's Question Time in the House had improved her performance immeasurably, particularly in aggressive television interviews and radio phone-ins. And when Carol, who had been trying to buy a flat so that she could move out of Flood Street, said, 'I hope I get my flat in case you need Flood Street back,' her mother replied, 'I have no intention of needing Flood Street back.'

Inwardly, however, she never allowed herself the luxury of believing the lead that she was given in the opinion polls. 'We don't count our chickens until they hatch' was a cliché often on her tongue. Early on in the campaign the polls showed a Conservative landslide which, to her irritation, Foreign Secretary Francis Pym had declared would be a bad thing. She quickly put her own feelings about the matter, (and tacitly about those members of her Cabinet who say such things) on record. 'We were a small party in Opposition after 1945,' she stressed. 'We were very effective.'

She canvassed with the energy and urgency of a new girl, snapping nervously at her helpers when events took her by surprise, such as suddenly discovering that she would be expected to speak when she had not been forewarned, when the 'circus' was running behind schedule, or when she was anticipating a stiff television interview.

The services of Saatchi & Saatchi were secured once again; and the Labour Party, far from sneering at this as they had in the last election, now took a leaf out of the Tories' book and employed an advertising agency too. Gordon Reece returned from California, ostensibly to help again with Margaret's television appearances, much to the resentment of some people inside Number Ten, jealous of the trust with which she imbues him. Other vital cogs in the campaign wheel, both on and off the road, were Campaign Manager, Roger Boaden; her PPS, Ian Gow; Deputy Chairman of the Tory Party, Michael Spicer; Derek Howe from her Political Office, who handled the press on tour; David Wolfson, her Chief of Staff (and chief calmer of tempo); and a young and controversial newcomer, twenty-three-year-old John Whittingdale, known to his friends as 'Mole' or 'Bat' – a one-man think-tank, who insisted upon travelling everywhere with two leaden suitcases filled with facts and figures essential to the political aide who would go far.

For all her caution Margaret did, however, have sufficient confidence in her chances of returning to Downing Street to leave the election trail for the weekend of 28 and 29 May to attend an economic summit, hosted by President Reagan in Williamsburg. She returned, after a shattering two days spent on trans-Atlantic flights, and in multi-lingual discussions and press conferences, with an important feather in her cap. Five other world leaders were there: President Mitterand of France; Chancellor Kohl of West Germany; Prime Minister Fanfani of Italy; Pierre Trudeau, Prime Minister of Canada; and Yasuhiro Nakasone, Prime Minister of Japan. They concluded that Britain was on the way to recovery, and backed her economic policies; they confirmed that there was no quick cure for unemployment; and declared that Polaris and the French nuclear deterrent should not be put into arms control talks with the Russians.

Margaret also returned to find that both the Labour Party and the SDP Liberal Alliance were in even greater states of disarray than when she left. Both had undergone a change of face, with their actual leaders relegated to the second division in the election campaign. Thus Denis Healey replaced Michael Foot as media front man for the Labour Party, and David Steel, Leader of the Liberals, was brought forward in place of Roy Jenkins, SDP Leader.

By the end of the second week of the campaign, the Falklands, an issue which Margaret had determined to keep out of her electioneering, came dramatically to the forefront. In an off-the-cuff speech in Selly Oak, Birmingham, Denis Healey, Deputy Leader of the Labour Party, had accused the Prime Minister of 'glorying in slaughter'. 'She is wrapping herself in a Union Jack and exploiting the services of our soldiers, sailors and airmen and hoping to get away with it,' he said. It was a speech which shocked and outraged people right across the political spectrum. Dr David Owen, Deputy Leader of the SDP, observed, 'To talk of Mrs Thatcher glorying in Falklands slaughter is to move from the politics of the gutter to the politics of the abattoir.' Although Mr Healey made a partial retraction the following day, many felt that he had done irreparable damage not only to himself, but to the Labour Party campaign as a whole.

Margaret was horrified by his outburst, and somewhat bitter about the subsequent Labour demand for an investigation into the sinking of the Argentinian cruiser, *General Belgrano*. 'They have the luxury of knowing we came through all right,' she told Carol. 'I had the anxiety of protecting our people on *Hermes* and *Invincible*, and the people on the vessels going down there.'

Yet, despite wide condemnation of Mr Healey's remarks, they were not to be the last of their kind, and the latter stages of the campaign degenerated into a rather base mud-slinging exercise. There was another attack from Welsh MP, Neil Kinnock, Shadow Minister for Education, who declared that it was a pity Mrs Thatcher had had to show her own guts by leaving the guts of British servicemen strewn on Goose Green. He too retracted, but again the damage was done.

Labour insisted that the Conservatives had a 'secret manifesto', and spoke of leaked documents which indicated they would dismantle the Welfare State, reform the National Health Service, and reduce Government spending if they were returned on 9 June. But, if they were scratching for dirt, they were provided with ample ammunition on the last Sunday before polling day. On that day a Youth Rally was held at Wembley, much more in the style of an American presidential jamboree than anything the British Conservative Party might have dreamed up. It was an electric occasion with much cheering and singing. The audience wore jeans and T-shirts, and had gathered from all over the country to watch and listen to a star-studded cast of entertainers and sportsmen and women who had come to add support to the Party and to play the part of 'pot-boiler' before the Prime Minister's speech in the afternoon. Disc jockey Kenny Everett, who has built his reputation on making tasteless and outrageous jokes, came on to the stage waving outsize hands fisted to the 'thumbs up' sign, and screamed to an already excited and hyped-up audience of thousands, 'Let's bomb Russia. Let's kick Michael Foot's stick away.'

Margaret's own reception was rapturous. She had been nervous beforehand, afraid of being outshone by so many showbusiness personalities. But, once on stage, her nerves evaporated and she fell very comfortably into a quite uncharacteristic performance. 'Could Labour have managed a rally like this?' she asked. 'No,' more than two thousand voices roared back.

But the next day it was the Labour Party that roared: gales of protest at Kenny Everett's remarks, which it fell upon Margaret to defend. She scraped by on the assertion that with the exception of her speech, everything that had happened at Wembley that day was meant as entertainment, and should have been taken as such.

It had become obvious from quite early on in the campaign that the Labour Party did not pose a serious threat to the Tories. The unknown quantity was the Alliance, which had made considerable by-election gains and was looking well supported in the opinion polls. There was little serious risk that they would poll high enough to obtain a majority themselves, but they posed the danger of taking enough votes from the Conservatives to give Labour an unwarranted advantage.

The Alliance Manifesto was also something of an unknown quantity – a combination of left and right, designed to appeal to anyone in favour of a centre line, who wanted to defect from either Labour or Tory to something less extreme. The only clear issue was a commitment to electoral reform, and the introduction of proportional representation in place of the current first-past-the-post system. In the end, although the Tories countered the threat of the Alliance quite well, the Alliance secured twenty-five per cent of the vote, and just twenty-three seats in Parliament to show for it.

Margaret Thatcher was returned to power on 9 June with a substantial majority. Four years earlier she had been the first woman Prime Minister. When she returned home victorious at five o'clock on the morning of 10 June, and walked through the door of Number Ten, she became the first Conservative Prime Minister in this century to return to Downing Street for a second term without a break.

Carol, who had been writing a diary of the election, congratulated her mother as she prepared for bed. 'It's history,' she enthused.

'But history,' said Margaret thoughtfully, 'when you're making it, doesn't seem like history. They expect you to jump up and down but you're always thinking of the next job in hand.

'I wonder if there is world news,' she asked, picking up the transistor radio that sits by her bed.

'I think you'll find you're it,' said Carol.

The weekend following the election was spent dealing with the next job in hand – selecting her new Cabinet. At last Margaret felt free to bring in the people she wanted and to throw out those she didn't. The most noticeable in the latter category was Francis Pym, who was replaced as Foreign Secretary by Geoffrey Howe. Nigel Lawson took Howe's place as Chancellor, Leon Brittan was appointed Home Secretary in place of Willie Whitelaw, who was made an hereditary peer, and Cecil Parkinson was appointed Secretary of Trade and Industry. The remainder was reshuffled.

While Margaret was juggling with her Cabinet, the two other major parties were sorting out their houses in the aftermath of defeat. Michael Foot swiftly announced his resignation as Leader of the Labour Party. Tony Benn, at one time potential successor, had lost his seat in the election, leaving three possible contenders: Shadow Chancellor, Peter Shore; Shadow Home Secretary, Roy Hattersley; and Neil Kinnock, Shadow Minister for Education. In the SDP, now minus two from the 'Gang of Four' – Shirley Williams and William Rodgers had both lost their seats – Roy Jenkins handed over leadership to David Owen.

It had been a remarkable and memorable election. At one time it would have seemed inconceivable that a Government who had allowed unemployment to soar over three million would be returned to power, let alone with a landslide majority. Yet Margaret Thatcher did it. She convinced people that the medicine had to be taken and that stopping the treatment halfway through because it was unpleasant would be a waste of all that had been swallowed so far. She proved that her instinct, her gut feeling was right, and that a vast number of the British public shared the same values. As she said in the final party political broadcast of the campaign: 'May I suggest to every citizen of our country, every man and every woman of whatever political persuasion, that on Thursday you pause and ask yourself one question – who would best defend our freedom, our way of life, and the much-loved land in which we live? Britain is on the right track. Don't turn back.'

VIII

Her Style of Leadership

The hallmark of Margaret Thatcher's leadership is her strong and fundamental belief in the Christian ethic. Some say that she has been the first fully committed Christian Prime Minister since Lord Salisbury, who died in 1903. She has certainly taken a far greater hand in episcopal matters than any First Lord of the Treasury has been wont in recent times; and her policies can all be seen to follow the very basic tenets of right and wrong that were learned without question in the Methodist church in Finkin Street. The importance she attaches to her marriage and to the family are also part of the same pattern, as is her belief that people should be allowed to develop according to their own talents, and be permitted the freedom of choice that the Christian faith holds so dear.

She once said:

> Our religion teaches us that every human being is unique and must play his part in working out his own salvation. So, whereas Socialists begin with society, and how people can be fitted in, we start with man, whose social and economic relationships are just part of his wider existence.
>
> The religious tradition values economic activity – how we earn our living, create wealth – but warns against obsession with it; warns against putting it above all else. Money is not an end in itself, but a means to an end.
>
> The increased involvement of government with economic life has coincided with a marked worsening of economic performance. It has heightened tensions between different groups of workers, some struggling to keep differentials, others trying to over-ride them; between producers and consumers, landlords and tenants, public services and the public.
>
> To observe these things is not to deny a role to government in economic life; it is not to preach *laissez faire*. That was preached two centuries back when industry and commerce were fighting to

192

free themselves from state monopoly and interference which were holding back their development. There is much that the state should do, and do much better than it is doing. But there are also proper limits which have long since been passed in this country.

To understand why and how these limits can be adduced, we must come back to the nature of man. This is a matter where our understanding and our case, based on religion and commonsense, is so much sounder than that of the Socialist doctrine. Yet the Socialist travesty has succeeded in gaining wide acceptance by default, even among our own people. I refer to the question of self-interest as against the common good. Socialists have been able to persuade themselves and many others that a free economy based on profit embodies and encourages self-interest, which they see as selfish and bad, whereas they claim Socialism is based on, and nurtures, altruism and selflessness.

This is baseless nonsense in theory and in practice. . . . For man is a social creature, born into family, clan, community, nation, brought up in mutual dependence. The founders of our religion made this a cornerstone of morality. The admonitions 'love thy neighbour as thyself' and 'do as you would be done by' express this. They do not denigrate self, or elevate love of others above it. On the contrary, they see concern for self and responsibility for self as something to be expected, and ask only that this be extended to others. This embodies the great truth that self-regard is the root of regard for one's fellows. The child learns to understand others through its own feeling initially towards its immediate family. In course of time the circle grows.

This belief is the very essence of the woman, and the explanation for the crusading zeal with which she fought to roll back the frontiers of the state during her first four years in office. The codes of right and wrong lie at the bottom of every decision she takes. They account for the inflexibility, the black-and-white approach to life, and for the lack of imagination, or real interest in debate.

A colleague observed that the worst mistake Margaret made before she announced the date of the General Election in May 1983, was the speech in which she said: 'Maggie may, Maggie may not.' 'Maggie has never been indecisive about anything in her life,' said the colleague vehemently, 'Maggie knows perfectly well: it's either yes, no or she's still thinking about it. But she knows.' This is Margaret Thatcher through and through, and in many ways she has been her own Government's harshest critic. She had a very clear idea of what she wanted, and suffered the agonizing frustration of not being able to get it done fast enough. The machinery of government grinds exceedingly slow, and she was impatient. She would have liked to have been able to transform the country overnight, in the way that she has transformed dozens of tired and grubby rooms by stripping off the old wallpaper and hanging something better in its place.

One of Margaret's constant cries is 'Bring me some new ideas. Don't give me the arguments for not doing something. Think hard about it. What can we do to make it different? Bring me new ideas.'

Yet, although she has sought change, she is not an innovator. Someone who worked as a close adviser for several years sums her up as 'the most conservative radical'. She has lacked the imagination to go outside the existing framework. She has been all in favour of new technology in industry, of computer literacy in schools, and heightened efficiency outside government, but ideas which have been put before her by political advisers for improvements inside the machinery of government, for making the whole of government operation more effective, have fallen on deaf ears. To some observers the essential problems that need tackling are what effective government means, how citizens communicate with it and know that it's good, and how it relates to Parliament. But these are vast and complicated problems, and Margaret, no less than any other politician, is afraid of moving into areas outside her knowledge, or of trusting others to show the way. Part of the problem is that there are no professional managers in government at all: there is no training to speak of for either civil servants or Members of Parliament in the United Kingdom. Thus Britain is run to a very large degree by amateurs. But paradoxically, although Margaret has undergone two formal trainings herself, first as a chemist and then as a barrister, and has insisted upon Carol and Mark both undergoing formal trainings, she has been opposed to any fundamental change in the system. To the dismay of her advisers, for all her bold talk, she has fallen into the classic prime minister's trap of being flattered by her civil servants, to the extent that she has now become, they say, 'an apparatchik of the machine'.

Although outwardly she is regarded as infinitely more radical, in many ways her policies have been very similar to those outlined by Ted Heath in the 'Selsdon Man' policy statement before he came into office in February 1970. Where he wavered, lost courage and effected U-turns, however, she has carried on. With a mixture of feminine intuition and luck – which Napoleon said was the first requirement for his marshals – she has articulated what a lot of people in the country feel but have not expressed.

She once said, 'The women of this country have never had a prime minister who knew the things they know, and the things we know are very different from what men know. . . . Any woman who understands the problems of running a home will be nearer to understanding the problems of running the country.' She has repeated these kind of sentiments time and again and, simplistic though they be, they do echo her fundamental good-housekeeping philosophy, with which the vast majority of people, who are not really interested in politics, can identify. She has shifted the whole balance of support for the Conservative Party: losing five per cent of the A, B and C1 vote, yet gaining eight per cent of the C2 vote, that of the skilled working class, which has never previously voted Tory.

What these people have admired above all else is the fact that she speaks plainly, gives what appear to be straight answers, and does what she says she's going to do. Margaret's ideas and ideals over the first four years that she has been in power, have varied not at all. The change has come in the personal style of her leadership. In the early days, while never allowing herself to be seen to be needing help, she did take advice, and relied quite heavily on trusted experts. Today, with the success of experience, she is more likely to trust her own judgments than anyone else's. Her instincts have been proved right time and time again; so that she has grown more confident in every area of her life, and more impatient with time-wasters and with people with whose views she disagrees.

Her style in Cabinet has been quite unlike that of any of her recent predecessors. Margaret 'leads with her chin', putting all her cards on the table very early on in any discussion. This means that if the rest of the table goes against her, she is in the awkward position of either having to back down, or fight. Other prime ministers would have held back until they had seen what everyone else had to say on the subject first. But subtlety has never been one of Margaret's talents. She gets irritable with people who go on speaking too long. She cuts them short in mid-sentence if she disagrees with their line of argument. She has no patience, no tact, and can frequently be downright rude. She is cutting, tart and totally unreasonable from time to time. One Cabinet colleague described it as 'a lack of self-control. She can't resist taking a quick hack at people's ideas as they go by without waiting until they've finished, when sometimes it is stronger to say nothing'. She has a certain smile reserved for people who don't agree with her, which is not a friendly smile. Even good, loyal supporters have been known to have their egos decimated; and she has never noticeably apologized. An invitation to lunch may be proffered some time later, which could be seen as an olive branch, but no apology as such.

Margaret is not good at handing out praises either. She expects hard work and competence from eveyone around here, and fails to see the need to compliment people when they do what she expects of them. She is no more laudatory of colleagues who appear on television; never saying thank you, never enthusing about their performance, never, in fact, making any comment at all.

Back in her Ministry of Education days, Margaret had suddenly rung her old friend Margaret Wickstead out of the blue. It was before 8.30 in the morning, and Margaret wanted her namesake to do a job for her, to sit on the BBC Schools Broadcasting Council as Ministry of Education representative. 'But I don't know a thing about TV,' said Margaret Wickstead, whose husband was a local Director of Education in Lincolnshire. 'There's radio as well you know,' rejoined Margaret testily, implying that if she didn't know, then she could jolly well find out. Thus reproved, Margaret took the job, and became extremely involved, travelling all over the country visiting schools and talking to teachers, although she was always a little embarrassed at meetings when her name appeared on the agenda as representing the Ministry of Education, lest anyone ask how she came to get the job. At a subsequent meeting, she told Margaret how much she was enjoying the Council, but mentioned in passing that it was quite hard work. 'I should think so,' said Margaret curtly. 'I don't ask people to do things that aren't hard work.'

In the early days in Cabinet, Margaret was particularly aggressive. For five and a half years she had more Heathites around her than she had supporters of her own, and she knew, given the opportunity, that they would outvote her. She was therefore more hectoring, desperate to dominate proceedings from the start, to intimidate the Cabinet and to impose her will on it.

Now that her supporters are in the majority in Cabinet, she can be more relaxed. She still argues like hell; Margaret loves argument, and particularly loves winning, but latterly she has known that she could let the argument rage, secure in the knowledge that she will win in the end.

If she looks like losing, the subject will be adjourned to another day.

Margaret hasn't won many friends by her behaviour in Cabinet, and her treatment of her colleagues, but she has earned their respect. One very senior Minister said, with a great deal of reluctance, 'I find her irritating, rude – all the things – but I have to tell you she's usually right. Her judgment is very good, and she is just the best there is.' They also acknowledge that she is very loyal to them. She might be critical of them to friends from time to time, but if they are in trouble they know that she will stick with them.

They also know that, for all her inflexibility, Margaret can be persuaded to change her mind. It takes a determined man to do it, with some very convincing points, and some well-prepared, well-documented arguments, but it can be done. She had been totally opposed to Jim Prior's initiative in Northern Ireland in 1981, for example, which went against her conviction that while there were still people in the province who wanted to remain British, their wish should be sacrosanct. But she realized that the majority in Cabinet were in favour of setting up an inter-governmental council with the Republic's Prime Minister, Dr Garret FitzGerald, and so she went along with it. She also changed her mind about taxation in the North Sea, which had threatened to send the oil companies elsewhere; and rethought about the cutting of student grants to foreigners, which she finally accepted was counter-productive.

On other contentious issues she is less flexible: most glaringly in her economic policy – fundamental to her style of government – which has led the number of unemployed to exceed over three million during her first period in office. She stuck rigidly to a strict monetarist policy, aided and abetted by Professor Alan Walters, whom she brought on secondment from the United States at a fee of £50,000 a year, half of which was paid for by the Government, the remainder by the Centre for Policy Studies. Her policy has been criticized by highly respected economists and politicians alike, but Margaret is utterly convinced that she is right, and that if she has enough time, she will bring the country to prosperity again. She feels that if there is an alternative, no one has yet produced it, and what the others are offering is no answer.

She once said that the one thing that could set the country back was if the Government lost its nerve. 'I will not change,' she told a Party Conference, 'just to court popularity. . . . If ever a Conservative government starts to do what it knows is wrong because it is afraid to do what is right, that is the time for Tories to cry "Stop". But you will never need to do that while I am Prime Minister.'

As for her concern about the unemployed, friends feel that there is an element in Margaret's attitude that they in some way brought it upon themselves: that the organization they worked for was at fault, and they may have contributed to its collapse. She does, however, feel desperately sorry for the unemployed on a personal level, but is so convinced that the only way the problems are going to be solved is by being hard to be kind, by continuing with the medicine she once spoke about, that she refuses to let sentiment get in the way. She also feels that the people who shed the biggest crocodile tears are not necessarily the most concerned; that weeping with the unemployed is a rather feeble way of helping, and that what she is doing economically offers them the best prospects for the future.

Another adviser that Margaret brought into Number Ten soon after the Falklands crisis, causing a few feathers to be ruffled, was Sir Anthony Parsons, former British Ambassador to the United Nations. His appointment as Special Adviser on Foreign Affairs was seen as an affront to the Foreign Office, which she thereafter rather noticeably by-passed. Foreign affairs have never interested her particularly, but having begun as a complete novice, relying upon Lord Carrington at every turn, she has now developed into one of the most influential leaders in the Western world, and one of the senior statesmen of the international scene.

Foreigners are, by and large, fascinated by Margaret Thatcher, no less in America where women are no longer strangers to high office, than in countries like China and Russia, where they still are. In the West, the man-in-the-street's reaction to her is coloured by political outlook, in much the same way as it is in Britain. Conservatives say, 'If only we had someone who would stand up for us like Mrs Thatcher'; Socialists scarcely have the vocabulary to describe her. In Russia, where newspapers are state-controlled, she is seen as the enemy to the Russian way of life.

Relations with the United States have seldom been warmer than during Mrs Thatcher's first premiership. President Reagan regards her as 'a sheet anchor of stability in the West', and as 'a leader whose policies and leadership have been vindicated'. Former President Richard Nixon, who has met most of the post-Second World War leaders over the last thirty-five years, rates her 'among the best'.

'Some women leaders I have known acted like men but wanted to be treated like women,' he explained. 'To her credit Mrs Thatcher acts like a man and expects to be treated like a man. She asks no quarter and gives none simply because she happens to be a woman. . . . Her leadership has been tough, forthright, consistent, and inspiring. She has attracted the attention and earned the respect of people all over the world.'

In Australia she is held in high regard by both sides of the political spectrum. Labour Prime Minister, Bob Hawke, has little time for what he calls the 'anachronistic ties' with Britain, but admits that Margaret is a force to be reckoned with. 'Mrs Thatcher is a tough lady,' he says. 'Like her or like her not, she knows what she wants and she knows how to get it.'

Alois Mock, leader of the Conservative Austrian People's Party, says, 'She is one of the great politicians of our time, and I admire her greatly.' Curiously in Socialist France under François Mitterand, she has scored more popularity points than she ever did with Giscard d'Estaing's administration. One female adviser to the French Government has said, 'I think Mrs Thatcher has made the economic recovery of Britain a reality. She has a high reputation in France as Premier of Britain; and she has earned high praise within the Common Market community as a negotiator even when she has won advantages for Britain to the disadvantage of France.'

Shortly before the June election in 1983, the title on the influential French magazine *Paris Match*'s editorial column read, 'If only Margaret Thatcher was French.' The article went on: 'Margaret Thatcher got herself elected on two issues: her country's moral rearmament and a return to a respect for certain of the financial and economic rules that had made Great Britain's fortune.' It was a plea that France's Socialist Government should take a lesson from Mrs Thatcher. 'The present Opposition in France has but a single chance to save itself and to save the country,' the writer continued. 'And that is to learn the English Lesson. For what the Opposition should say, and what it should do, it has only to borrow from Margaret Thatcher, the Western World's Mother Courage.'

Ex-Prime Minister of South Africa, John Vorster, said of Mrs Thatcher after she had visited his country shortly before she became Prime Minister: 'She has all the femininity of an attractive woman; but she has the mind and the courage of a strong man.' Current opinion among politicians is that she 'is courageous, stands for her principles, is not scared of taking a chance and is willing to fight for what she believes in'. Many are said to stop at nothing short of 'adoration' for her.

In Zimbabwe, where she brought about independence, she is generally respected, and quite fondly referred to as 'Margret'. They haven't forgotten that her initial inclination had been to support Bishop Muzorewa, but appreciate that she did change her mind, and that since the settlement she has given the country substantial backing, keeping to promises of aid, whatever her personal feelings may have been. They were further impressed that she took the time, in the midst of the Falklands crisis, to see Mr Mugabe on his visit to Britain in 1982.

Margaret Thatcher will go down in history as a remarkable woman. On the minus side, her most obvious disadvantage is lack of a sense of humour. She has never been good on television, although her performance during the 1983 election campaign was a vast improvement on previous appearances. She never comes across as a real person, but has always spoken as though she is addressing the deaf or, as Keith Waterhouse, columnist on the *Daily Mirror*, once so perfectly described it, as though she were telling someone that their pet cat was dead.

She also lacks the callousness required of a truly great leader: she is flattered by loyalty, although there are few prime ministers who have been any different. Her most fundamental failing, however, is a crippling lack of personal confidence: an inability to drop the pose and the affectation, and be real – to swear, curse, laugh, cry and show some warmth and emotion. If she could do that, she would take many more of the electorate with her.

On the plus side, Margaret has stuck to her guns, she does what she says, and is never apparently afraid to say what she believes because it might make her unpopular. In that respect she is a most remarkable politician, for which she has her father, Alf Roberts, and her tough childhood in Grantham to thank. If she has made mistakes it isn't for lack of good intentions. She has a crusading flame in her head, which has never so much as flickered. She believes that leading Britain away from the darkness of Socialism and into the light of freedom and Christianity is her destiny. Her intention is to lead it to greatness.

Whether Margaret Thatcher goes down in history as a great leader remains to be seen. Indeed, whether her convictions turn out to have been right also remains to be seen. But as former President Nixon observed:

> Those commonly acclaimed as 'great' leaders are not necessarily good men. Russia's Peter the Great was a cruel despot. Julius

Caesar, Alexander the Great, and Napoleon are remembered not for their statesmanship but for their conquests. When we speak of the great leaders of history, only occasionally do we refer to those who raised statecraft to a higher moral plane. Rather, we are talking about those who so effectively wielded power on such a grand scale that they significantly changed the course of history for their nations and for the world. Churchill and Stalin were both, in their different ways, great leaders. But without Churchill, Western Europe might have been enslaved; without Stalin, Eastern Europe might have been free.

Only time will tell what posterity will write of Mrs Thatcher.

Books Consulted

The Conservative Opportunity, edited by Lord Blake and John Patten, Macmillan, 1976

Let Our Children Grow Tall, Centre for Policy Studies, 1977

Number 10, Terence Feely, Sidgwick and Jackson, 1982

Margaret Thatcher, George Gardiner, William Kimber, 1975

Britain Can Work, Ian Gilmour, Martin Robertson Limited, 1983

Out of Order, Frank Johnson, Robson Books, 1982

Margaret Thatcher, Russel Lewis, Routledge and Kegan Paul, 1975

Madam Prime Minister, Allan J. Mayer, Newsweek Books, 1979

Margaret Thatcher, Patricia Murray, W.H. Allen, 1980

Leaders, Richard Nixon, Sidgwick and Jackson, 1982

War in the Falklands, The Sunday Express Magazine Team, Weidenfeld and Nicolson, 1982

Diary of an Election, Carol Thatcher, Sidgwick and Jackson, 1983

Index

unemployment; rises in,
147, 153, 197; election
comments on, 185;
Margaret's concern for,
198
USA; Margaret's visit to,
114; relations with, 198-
9
Usher, Vic, 55
Utley, Peter, 154

Vacani, Betty, 49
vacation work, 19
Value Added Tax, 77
Van der Post, Laurens, 152
Vassall, William, 53
Vaughan, Dame Janet, 18
Verney, Charlotte, 156
Victoria & Albert Museum;
furniture from, 141
Villiers, Sir Charles, 146
Vorster, John, 199-200

Walker, Peter, 132, 133
Wallace, Mary, 20
Watkins, Alan, 98
Walton Street, No 18,
Oxford; digs at, 19
Waltus, Professor Alan,
197
Wales; rejecting devolution,
121
War Cabinet, 163
Ward, Alison, 78, 100;
becomes secretary to
Margaret, 74-5; working
with Denis's secretary,
103-4; on election tour,
124; leaves Margaret,
139; returns for 1983
election, 186
Warrender, Sir Victor, 12-
13
Waterhouse, Keith, 200
Waterhouse, Victor, 14
Wembley Youth Rally,
189
Westminster Gardens,
Marsham Street; flat in,
58, 67
'wets', 136, 137
Whitelaw, William, 93, 98,
138; candidate for
leadership, 81, 92, 94;
becomes Deputy Leader,
97; in Margaret's
Cabinet, 132; advises

Margaret during
Falkland War, 164; made
Peer, 190
Whittingdale, John, 187
Wickstead, Arthur, 183
Wickstead, Margaret (née
Goodrich), 102; at
Oxford, 15, 16-17;
friendship with, 19, 20,
183; recalls Margaret's
political ambitions, 25-6;
on BBC Schools
Broadcasting Council,
196
Williams, Miss Gladys, 13
Williams, Elizabeth;
becomes Margaret's
secretary, 68
Williams, Shirley, 18, 149,
191
Wilson, Harold, 18;
becomes leader of Labour
Party, 54; Prime
Minister, 54, 77, 80;
fighting 1966 general
election, 59-60; prices
and incomes policy, 62-3;
attempts to curb power
of unions, 65; smear on
Heath, 66; plans for
unions, 75; promises to
unions, 77; Margaret's
reaction to, in House,
109; resigns, 110-11;
agreements with unions,
111-12
Winning, Norman, KC,
14
Wolfson, David, 114, 124,
127, 171, 187
Wolverhampton; riot in,
116
women; at Bar, 37;
Margaret's views on, 69,
195; speech for women's
rights, 32
Women's Conference;
Margaret's speech at,
162-3
Women's National
Commission, 102
Wood, Richard, 52
Woolfson, Michael, 23
Woollcott, Mrs (landlady),
31
World in Action (Granada
TV), 116-17

World War II, 13-14; war
work, 19
Worth, George, 25

Young, Reverend David,
117
Young, Janet Mary,
Baroness, 98, 124, 126,
180
Youth Rally, Wembley,
189

Zimbabwe; situation in,
137-9; independence,
139; views of Margaret,
200
Zurich Economic Society,
115